C000002201

ON THE SUBJECT OF DRAMA

Although much has been written on how the drama elements of the English curriculum might be taught in schools, there is less guidance available for teachers who regard drama not as an adjunct of English but as an arts subject in its own right.

In this volume, David Hornbrook and a team of experienced drama specialists show how the subject of drama may be defined and taught. Drawing on literature, visual art, music and dance as well as the rich and varied traditions of drama itself, they map out an eclectic subject curriculum for students of all ages. Opening up the field in new and exciting ways, the book embraces the widest possible range of dramatic knowledge and skills, from the Nātyaśhāstra of ancient India to contemporary classroom improvisation.

The book is divided into three sections:

- **The teaching and learning of drama**: ideas about interculturalism, creativity and craft – key concepts informing the drama curriculum – are interrogated and re-theorised for the classroom.
- **Making and performing drama in school**: the fundamental processes of reading and writing plays for performance are explored, along with the potential of dance to enhance and extend students' experience of dramatic performance.
- **Watching and understanding drama**: ensuring the curriculum is appropriately balanced between the production and reception of drama, this last section emphasises the role of students as audience – for both live and electronic performances – and the development of a dramatic vocabulary.

David Hornbrook was Staff Inspector for Drama for the Inner London Education Authority until its abolition in 1990. He is now based in the London Borough of Camden and inspects schools and colleges throughout England. A former teacher, actor and theatre director, Dr Hornbrook is an Associate Fellow of the Central School of Speech and Drama and an influential author in the field of drama education. His publications include *Education and Dramatic Art* (second edition, Routledge 1998) and *Education in Drama* (1991).

ON THE SUBJECT OF DRAMA

Edited by
David Hornbrook

London and New York

First published 1998 by Routledge
2 Park Square, Milton Park, Abingdon, Oxon, OX14 4RN

Simultaneously published in the USA and Canada
by Routledge
270 Madison Ave, New York NY 10016

Transferred to Digital Printing 2005

British Library Cataloguing in Publication Data
A catalogue record for this book is available from the British Library

Library of Congress Cataloguing in Publication Data
On the Subject of Drama/edited by David Hornbrook
Includes bibliographical references and index.
1. Drama–study and teaching (Primary)–Great Britain. 2. Drama–Study and
teaching (Secondary)–Great Britain. 3. Theater–Study and teaching
(Primary)–Great Britain. 4. Theater–Study and teaching (Secondary)–
Great Britain. I. Hornbrook, David.
PN1701.048 1998
809.2'0071'241–dc21   97–44628

ISBN 0–415–16882–1 (hbk)
0–415–16883–X (pbk)

CONTENTS

CONTENTS

NOTES ON CONTRIBUTORS

Sharon Bailin is Professor of Drama Education in the Faculty of Education, Simon Fraser University, Vancouver, Canada. Her research has focused on creativity, critical thinking, and the nature of justification of drama education. She is the author of *Achieving Extraordinary Ends: An Essay on Creativity* (1994) which was awarded the Canadian Association for the Foundations of Education book award.

Sita Brahmachari is a freelance arts education consultant working in schools, colleges, community groups and theatres in London. She is a visiting lecturer and director at the Central School of Speech and Drama and has contributed to a number of journals including *Viewpoint* and *Black Theatre in Britain*.

Stephen Daldry is Artistic Director and Chief Executive of the Royal Court Theatre, London. The Royal Court has an international reputation for new writing and has received innumerable awards both for productions and for overall artistic achievement. Stephen Daldry won Olivier awards for best director for his productions of *An Inspector Calls* (1992) and *Machinal* (1994).

Jane M. Gangi is an Assistant Professor of Education at Sacred Heart University, Fairfield, CT, USA. She holds an MA in Theatre from Northwestern University, and a PhD from New York University. An area of interest is the role of the arts – drama in particular – in teacher education.

David Hornbrook is Arts Inspector for the London Borough of Camden and an Associate Fellow of the Central School of Speech and Drama. A former teacher, actor and theatre director, he is the author of *Education and Dramatic Art* (1989 [1998]) and *Education in Drama: Casting the Dramatic Curriculum* (1991) and was editor of the Arts Council of Great Britain's guidance on drama education, *Drama in Schools* (1992).

Andy Kempe leads the Postgraduate Certificate Course in secondary drama education at the University of Reading, UK. He has published hand-books for teachers, curriculum guides and articles on a wide range of drama education topics. His books include *The GCSE Drama Coursebook* (1990), *Drama Education and Special Needs* (1996) and *Starting with Scripts* (with L. Warner) (1997).

Helen Nicholson was formerly Head of Arts at Brislington School, Bristol, UK. She is now a Senior Lecturer in Drama at Homerton College, University of Cambridge, where she teaches undergraduate and postgraduate students. She has published widely in journals and contributed to books on the arts and education including *Drama and Theatre in Education* (1996) and *Voices Off* (1996).

Christopher McCullough is Head of the Drama Department at the University of Exeter, UK. He has published on the dissemination of Elizabethan and Jacobean drama on the contemporary stage and early twentieth-century European political theatre. His book *Theatre and Europe* was published in 1996.

Ruth Taylor is Head of Dance and Drama at Brislington School, Bristol, UK, where she has taught for seven years. She completed her degree in dance in 1990, and is currently working towards a Masters degree at the University of the West of England.

Dan Urian is Senior Lecturer in the Theatre Department of Tel Aviv University and Head of the Curriculum Committee in Theatre of the Israeli Ministry of Education. His books include *Drama and Theatre* (1988) and *The Arab in Israeli Drama and Theatre* (1997).

FOREWORD

Stephen Daldry

The future of the theatre lies with young people. This glaring cliché surfaces whenever the relation between drama and education is discussed. Yet the gap between theory and reality is vast. There are shining exceptions, but the general trend in the work of both theatres and schools in this country suggests that the future of drama is a low priority. I welcome this book as a call to arms for those in education and the theatre who do care about that future, and wish to work together in bringing it about.

The subject of drama is undeniably neglected in British schools. Some of this is the fault of politicians and bureaucrats. Drama has been denied the status of music or the visual arts in the curriculum and its practice is often spread chaotically between English and drama departments and between compulsory and extra-curricular activity. Effective work demands resources of time and space which are regularly denied. Yet, in a paradox of which David Hornbrook has consistently reminded us, the practice of drama teaching can itself sometimes fail to engage creatively with one of the most important and influential art forms experienced by young people – theatre.

Since the Royal Court Theatre started work with schools thirty years ago, there has been a revolution in the content of drama lessons. Homelessness, bullying, child abuse – an alphabet of social concern is spelled out in the drama studio, often in more detail than anywhere else in the school. What we see more rarely, however, is an exploration of theatre forms. Unsurprisingly, in view of young people's exposure to the electronic media, the dominant mode of expression is an imitation of poor television – a semi-improvised naturalism. As the contributors to this book point out, left unquestioned this leaves young people shackled to a monocultural and constrained form of expression, disadvantaged both as creators of drama and as audience members.

Responsibility for this does not lie solely with the education system. Theatres too share the blame for the abandonment of the future. There are theatres all over Britain which never have children in the audience from one Christmas pantomime to the next. There are even venues which prefer not to have young people coming in at all rather than upset their regular clientele. I am sympathetic – what artistic director would not be – to theatres' pleas of financial stress and I am the first to admit that the history of the Royal Court Theatre, too, is far from perfect. We are, however, proud to present on our stages more theatre created by young people as writers and performers than any other national company. When George Devine founded the English Stage Company at the Court in the 1950s, it was with the hope of educating a whole new audience, just as Shaw and Granville Barker had done in their brief tenure of the theatre half a century before. 'I am deeply and entirely convinced', he wrote, 'that the solution lies in the schools and a radical appraisal of the teaching of drama'.

As it is, too much drama work with young people privileges content over form and sentiment over passion. We have to remember our priorities: to entertain and inspire, to excite and provoke, to unsettle as well as celebrate. The pervasiveness of mediocre drama in all our lives makes bad soap actors of us all. This rather debased performance language is a convenient medium for glib generalisation – witness the self-dramatisation of the talk show – but its effectiveness as a tool to understand complex issues is more debatable. A central error made by the missionary wing of the theatre-in-education movement has been to assume that the aims of education and art are the same. They may complement each other, but they are just as likely to clash. Why should drama improvisation be useful in combating AIDS, for example? Is it any more effective than music or visual art in knocking up health or social propaganda? Drama is an exploration of emotion, reason and imagination in a complex web of time and space. It has its uses, but cannot be defined backwards from them. Of course drama can be used as a tool, but that is rather like watching a magnificent mask being used to carry cups of coffee.

Plays are a blueprint for performance, and those whom we teach about drama deserve an insight into dramatic form and convention. Certainly, plays are not the only form drama can take, but a rejection of them is a barrier to understanding the *culture* of drama, not only in Britain but across the world. If drama is a serious subject in its own right, let us ground it in the practice of making theatre. Innovation depends on a secure foundation of knowledge and skills, which should not simply be the accidental property of a lucky élite. It is thrilling to work with a group of young people on the processes which have gone into writing and producing a 'difficult' new play and then see their rapt concentration during a performance. Their discussion afterwards invariably shows sensitivity and insight, demonstrating a growing understanding of the skills involved in making theatre. This is the future which George Devine was convinced 'lies in the schools'.

For gifted young writers, the most helpful thing a theatre can do is to put on their plays. Play development which does not seriously intend to become play production is a waste of everyone's resources. Successive artistic directors have recognised the centrality of the Royal Court's work with young people. We see no contradiction in one of Europe's leading theatres welcoming the work of an eleven-year-old playwright onto its stage. Nor is it unusual for our leading playwrights to spend time working with young people. Edward Bond, Caryl Churchill and others contributed to the early work of our Writers' Group, and our current Playwriting in Schools project links professional playwrights with schools across London. The workshop programme devised by Elyse Dodgson has engaged many hundreds of young people in playwriting for the first time. Of course, we acknowledge that not every young person with whom we work will write great drama; some may write good plays and then go on to do other things. At a time when most young people do not have any voluntary involvement in arts activity at all, one strand of our policy must be to create in everyone we encounter the potential to join that inspired and engaged new audience.

There is certainly plenty of bad playwriting for young people – scripts which claim to address teenage issues but instead patronise the dramatic imaginations of those they seek to inspire. For me, the best new writing for young people is simply the best new writing – full stop. A play which cannot say something to someone under twenty is unlikely to communicate to anyone. Few of the many plays from the Royal Court repertoire that have gone on to become resources for drama in schools would have survived an initial reductive assessment of their so-called 'relevance' to young people. We learn from our contact with young people how to communicate with everyone else. At the same time, the voices of the new generation are only going to be heard here if we go out and listen for them very carefully.

Economic, educational and cultural changes over the last eighteen years have almost silenced a generation. One-third of British children live below the poverty line. Their brothers and sisters are destitute in St Petersburg's tenement attics, slave labouring in Faizabad's glass factories, tortured by electric shock in Istanbul prisons, sold for a few dollars on Sri Lankan beaches. Among them, there are writers of potential genius – the heirs of Brendan Behan, Arnold Wesker, Joe Orton, Andrea Dunbar – whose voices are not being heard. We have to ensure that the theatre of the twenty-first century will resound with their cries. Some of what we hear will challenge and unsettle us – it will only be worth doing if it does.

It may seem easy for a theatre director to exhort beleaguered teachers that risk and danger are all part of the practice of theatre. But the theatre industry is part of the educational equation. We are partners in the same project. The Royal Court in its work with young people has always recognised and encouraged this, not least in its partnership with David Hornbrook at the Holborn Centre for the Performing Arts in the 1990s. His ideas, and those of his fellow contributors, enlighten our collective practice, and it is a pleasure to welcome this provocative and inspiring book.

Stephen Daldry
Royal Court Theatre, London
January 1998

Part I

THE TEACHING AND LEARNING OF DRAMA

INTRODUCTION

Even if we never visit a theatre, the subject of drama impinges upon our lives, every day of our lives, leaping out at us from newspapers, loud-speakers, film screens and television sets, informing the way we think and the way we feel. Drama is simply part of the discourse of life.

This book is an attempt to break loose from the conversations which have characterised half a century of drama education and to articulate an alternative programme for drama in schools, rigorous and coherent enough for a world quite different to that into which the subject was born. Drama has had a strenuous climb to educational legitimacy, and historic, bourgeois suspicions of the theatre, coupled with a sentimental view of childhood, lured many pioneers to some peculiar diversions. Consigning these manoeuvres to the past, this collection lays the foundations for the development of drama as a fully-fledged subject on the school curriculum. It brings together voices in the field which, while not afraid to be critical of what has gone before, are united in their commitment to the subject and to its future. Acknowledging the quality of teaching and learning in many drama classes, contributors are not themselves concerned to unravel teaching methods or learning theory. If the protective embrace of post-war educational enthusiasms shielded many drama teachers in England from the rigours of curriculum planning and assessment, it did allow them to develop a sophisticated form of pedagogy. In placing the emphasis on the *what* rather than the *how*, the book tries to redress the balance rather than simply add to the stock of methodological wisdom.

The opening chapter offers a glimpse of drama's heterogeneous place in world cultures and suggests that what we know as *drama-in-education*, with its generalised aims and tenuous links with the theatre, may be better understood as a vagary of history rather than (as was once thought) an educational metamorphosis. For years, the aims and outcomes of drama lessons were either developmental, the general well-being of the student being seen as a sufficient end, or moral and social, with students being invited to act out imaginary dilemmas. But times changed, and with them the educational environment. By the 1990s, concerns in Britain were growing that the extreme open-endedness of many drama classes was not giving students a systematic education in the subject, and although it was accepted that teaching methods in drama had been developed to a high degree of refinement, what was going on in classes too often seemed random and directionless. In proposing that the subject of drama must embrace concepts like dramatic literacy and cultural induction if it is to counter accusations of aimlessness, the chapter signals some of the arguments which follow.

All the contributors to this book want to give drama a strong foundation in the modern curriculum by establishing its roots in culture; at the very centre of this enterprise is an acknowledgement that drama is a world phenomenon. Sita Brahmachari challenges the parochialism of a drama education based on television-fed naturalism and proposes an alternative curriculum in which a diversity of forms from world cultures may be represented. Using Indian drama as an example, she shows how the richness and complexity of traditional practices, such as those contained in the ancient Nāṭyaśhāstra, can be interwoven into contemporary drama practice in a way which both enfranchises students whose cultural backgrounds already resonate with those forms and liberates those whose horizons have been limited to popular Western conventions.

It is sometimes claimed that induction of this kind inhibits students' natural creativity by forcing them into predetermined ways of thinking. In a challenge to the assumptions that have shored up theories of arts education since Rousseau, Sharon Bailin exposes many of the most cherished shibboleths of creativity and shows that established dictums resting upon a belief that creativity is a kind of human faculty – that individuals can be creative even if they never actually create anything – remain either unproven or internally contradictory. True creativity, she argues, is not a kind of inspired innocence, but is crucially dependent upon the possession of rules, skills and knowledge. Without a grasp of tradition and the conventions which constitute it, students have no basis from which to work, no tools with which to build and transform. Creativity can only be understood in context and judged in relation to ideas of quality production.

In some quarters of drama education there has been considerable resistance to the idea that students should acquire specific theatre skills. Yet throughout the world, arts teachers are accustomed to teaching the skills that make art possible. The young painter will need to know something about how to paint, the dancer to dance, the musician to play – and the actor to act. Aptitude in the arts does not come naturally but, as any musician knows, through explanation, imitation and practice. In my chapter on the craft of drama, I argue that it is naïve to think that young people can make a successful drama with no learned aptitude in acting, play writing or directing. Craft is as essential to the subject of drama as it is to art or music. If we cannot expect students to be creative in a vacuum then we must teach

4

them the grammar of drama, together with a framework for appreciating and understanding its manifestations and some of the craft skills they will need to realise their ideas. By proposing a simple model for the subject of drama and a portfolio of drama-specific skills, knowledge and understanding, the chapter finally closes the gap between classroom drama and the theatre.

1

DRAMA AND EDUCATION

David Hornbrook

to study an art form is to explore a sensibility ... such a sensibility is essentially a collective formation, and ... the foundations of such a formation are as wide as social existence and as deep. ... A theory of art is thus at the same time a theory of culture.

Clifford Geertz[1]

The subject of drama

For as far back into history as we can know, human beings have stepped out before others in a prescribed space to portray aspects of an imagined reality. Ghosts, spirits, kings, citizens and fools have been made substantial as performers and audience connive in that profoundly satisfying act of the pretence we recognise as drama.

Language is not a precise art, and drama, like many other categories of experience, has suffered from attempts at crude and limiting definitions. The exact point at which a dance becomes a drama, for example, or to what extent we are justified in calling dramas those aspects of ordinary life, such as trials or carnivals, which seem to have dramatic features, will doubtless continue to be a matter of debate.[2] The boundaries of any subject will be healthily fluid and it is not the concern of this book to enter into territorial disputes.

We can be sure, however, that any attempt to catalogue even the undisputed manifestations of drama in the world would consume much computer megabytage; the merest dip into such a database would be sufficient to establish the prodigality of drama as a form of human expression. A casual enquirer venturing no further than the first alphabetical entry point might come across the highly stylised dream-seeking mime of the Australian Aranda people, for example, or the dramatic narratives of the Arctic, where Inuit male actors and a chorus of women portray the liberation of the forces of light at the end of the long polar winter. Entries for Aeschylus, Aristophanes and Aristotle indicate the birth of a sophisticated European dramatic tradition, which itself will contain references to forms as varied as those of Artaud, Appia, Anouilh and the Aldwych farces. Clicking on 'African theatre' uncovers the Zauli dancers of the Ivory Coast and the Kaukouran fertility mimes of Senegal; 'Asian drama' the Wayang Kulit shadow plays of Java, the classical Cambodian Lakon Kbach Boran female dance-drama or the many interpretations of the Ramlila plays of north India. What binds these variegated categories of activity together, allows us to describe them and thousands of others as *dramas*, is that they all involve the enactment of stories. Drama, in Martin Esslin's words, is 'narrative made visible, a picture given the power to move in time'.[3]

At the centre of this moving picture, of course, is the actor. Elaborately masked and costumed in Chinese Ching Hsi opera or clad in the rough shifts of Jerzy Grotowski's Teatr-Laboratorium, the actor is the primary agent of make-believe. It is the actor who is the focus of our attention, whose speech and action drive the dramatic narrative forward. But, however skilled he or she may be, the actor cannot alone create drama; we should not forget that make-believe is also the territory of the child and the lunatic.[4] It is the contract with an audience that distinguishes drama from the explorative fantasies of the child and the psychotic delusions of the mental patient. 'Let us agree', says the tacit understanding between a performance and its spectators, 'that for a brief period we actually *are* that which we represent'.[5] While for the vast majority of dramas, the audience is a tangible presence – in a theatre, possibly, or gathered around a village square – there will be some cases where the audience is assumed. Rehearsal is the most obvious example of the existence of implicit spectators, while in some forms of spontaneous dramatic improvisation, such as those developed for use in education or for therapeutic purposes, members of the group are simultaneously actors *and* audience.[6]

The agreement on the part of the audience to suspend disbelief, however, is not open-ended. Dramatic performances are temporally and spatially *framed*. There is an understanding about when the performance begins and ends and of its physical boundaries. The actors cannot travel home with you on the bus still playing their parts. In Western theatres, plays commonly begin with curtains going up or lights going down and end with curtain calls. A Bengali Jatra theatre performance signals its beginning with a climactic event, such as the firing of a gun or the entry of a demon. Most dramas are performed on stages, and these delineate the territory of the make-believe. Actors may be hidden behind a curtain or in the wings of a theatre before making an entrance. Alternatively, they may remain in full view, sitting on benches at either side of the stage. Whatever the conventions employed, as members of an audience we know that it is only when the actors move from 'offstage' into the agreed playing area that our contract with them begins. Likewise, placing them within that same playing area transforms and aggrandises simple objects, as Chorus from Shakespeare's *The Life of Henry the Fifth* reminds the audience.

And so our scene must to the battle fly;
Where (O for pity!) we shall much disgrace,
With four or five most ragged foils,
Right ill-disposed in brawl ridiculous,
The name of Agincourt. Yet sit and see,
Minding true things by what their mock'ries be.[7]

Actors, audiences, depicted narratives, an agreement to enter into make-believe; the characterising features of the subject of drama begin to take shape. The significance for education of this emerging picture is the matter of this book.

Teaching drama

We might reasonably expect of those professing to be proficient in a field that they know something about its history and conventions, that they are accomplished in at least some of its characterising practices and that they understand the field's particular contribution to the sum of human experience. Knowledge, aptitude and understanding, in other words, indicate conversance.

Of course, it is quite possible to become accomplished in only one aspect of a field. Drama is no exception. It is not unusual for universities to offer academic qualifications in drama in which knowledge of the subject is regarded as paramount and may be tested by written examination. A student may study Balinese theatre to doctoral level, for example, but would not be expected to have the skills necessary to perform the Barong dance. Conversely, and historically more commonly, respected and highly trained performers may find it unnecessary to have specialist knowledge of practices beyond their own. The first acting school, established in China during the T'ang period between the seventh and ninth centuries, had no other purpose than to prepare performers for the court theatre. In fourteenth-century Japan, the acting schools founded by Ze'ami Motokiyo for the teaching of Noh theatre had a slightly wider curriculum, not only training young actors in the tightly structured conventions of Noh, but also inducting them in the literary and cultural heritage of Japanese theatre. In Europe, for centuries, acting was a matter of apprenticeship and, in some cases, birth. It was not unusual for seventeenth-century Italian Commedia dell'arte performers to be born into a company and to grow up with a 'mask' by which they became completely identified, even to the extent of forsaking a baptismal name for that of the adopted character.[8]

While universities, apprenticeships and academies all contribute to specialist induction in important elements of the field of drama, when the spotlight is turned onto mainstream education, which is, after all, the focus of this book, we shall not want to see a concentration on single aspects of the field to the exclusion of others, but rather an eclectic approach in which knowledge, aptitude and understanding are equally prominent. In this sense, the school subject of drama embraces the whole field of drama, allowing students to sample and engage with its diverse forms in ways which establish an appropriate balance between a knowledge of drama and the mastery of its practices.

The acceptance of drama as a legitimate part of a general education is by no means universal. The arts may seem of peripheral importance to the educational project in countries where few can read or write, however prolific what we know as artistic activity may be there. In the European Community, drama is rarely identified as a separate subject within the compulsory curriculum, although most countries do include it within a broader concept of the arts.[9] In the English-speaking world, drama is certainly no stranger to schools and performances of plays by school children can be traced back at least to the first half of the sixteenth century. The famous Boys' Companies of the late 1500s were a great public success,[10] and at the height of their popularity these 'little eyases, that cry out on the top of question, and are most tyrannically clapped for't'[11] could command the talents of playwrights like John Lyly, George Chapman and Ben Jonson. While the Boys' Companies did not last to outlive Shakespeare, the tradition of performances in schools from which they grew survived and flourishes still. For educationalist David Hargreaves, arguing that the expressive arts should have a place in a compulsory core curriculum for all students, the school play continues to make 'a unique contribution to the dignity and community solidarity' of a school.

> Pupils and their parents know the deep impact of public performances
> of the arts. . . . It is not at all uncommon for parents to report to
> staff how the play has engendered a new pleasure, interest and
> commitment – and sometimes a new willingness to come to school.
> Pupils tend to remember these events longer than almost anything
> else about school.[12]

Drama is an increasingly popular educational activity. In England and Wales, four hundred years after the Paul's Boys ceased performing, it was estimated that it was a significant presence in over two-thirds of secondary schools.[13] But as anyone familiar with drama education in schools will know, it is not only to the school play – that 'exemplar of differentiated team-work'[14] – that we should turn to understand this growing enthusiasm. While performances of one kind or another continue to feature in the annual cycle of most schools, it is drama's place *within* the curriculum that has allowed the subject to gain legitimacy in the eyes of students and their parents. Nearly 80,000 students were entered for General Certificate of Secondary Education (GCSE) examinations in drama in 1996 – twice as many as were for music, despite the latter's prescribed status in the National Curriculum.[15] This would hardly have been possible had drama remained only a performance activity.

Despite this impressive achievement, the drama curriculum of English schools does not yet provide the degree of breadth or eclecticism offered by other arts subjects. This deficiency is partly explained by dissimilar histories. After centuries on the stages of school halls, drama made its entrance into British classrooms as part of the revolution in educational thinking which followed the Second World War, a revolution which profoundly altered ideas about teaching, learning and how education should be organised, and which had at its core the idea that the aim of education was to cultivate happy, balanced individuals.[16] This powerful emphasis on personal development led to the displacement of theatrical performance by a more therapeutic, developmental approach, based in the classroom itself. For pioneers like Peter Slade, the school play was an irrelevance; what mattered was what happened in lessons where, he believed, drama would help children discover 'life and self'.[17] Forty years earlier, the headmistress of a Sussex village school, Harriet Finlay-Johnson, had expressed similar sentiments about the dramas made by her young students. 'However crude the action or dialogue from the adult's point of view, it would fitly express the stage of development arrived at by the child's mind and would, therefore, be valuable *to him* as a vehicle of expression and assimilation ... rather than a finished product'.[18] Drama, thus finds its way onto the curriculum less like a subject than a way of promoting social and mental health.

At the time, it has to be said, drama was not alone in its advocacy of the arts as vehicles for the spontaneous expression of students' feelings about life. In 1943, Herbert Read had argued that 'art should be the basis of education',[19] and dance was transformed after the Second World War by the ideas of Rudolf von Laban who saw dance, as Slade saw drama, as an expression of 'the life of feeling'. By emphasising spontaneity over the acquisition of knowledge and skills, accounts of this kind turn the arts into psychological processes, so that *what* is produced becomes of marginal importance compared with the simple act of production. The outcomes of students' creativity are thus removed from the public realm and, at the same time, from public adjudication – one would no more want to make judgements about a student's art acts than one would about a patient's dreams. An essentialism of form in the arts – that is, a belief that certain artworks have intrinsic worth – is replaced by an essentialism of process, and, in a highly influential inversion, education *in* the arts becomes education *through* the arts. Thus, half a century of drama in the curriculum of English schools has been characterised not by what the great theatre teachers of the past might recognise as an education *in* drama, but instead by the pressing of a small number of dramatic forms (improvisation, role-play, and so on) into the service of students' general development – drama *in* education.

Songs of innocence and of experience

It has to be said that this self-regarding account of drama and the other arts represents a curiously Western way of looking at things. The preoccupation with the private and the personal suggests common cause with the pinched individualism of our narcississtic society rather than with the vibrant, culture-affirming dramas of, say, the Yahgan fishermen of Tierra del Fuego whose elaborate funeral enactments flamboyantly celebrate the collective responsibility of the community to the individual. Yet it must also be acknowledged that the post-war revolution in education was inspired by a wide belief in the possibility of human betterment. Born of the Enlightenment and coming of age in Britain with the great reforms of the late nineteenth century, the so-called 'Whig' view of history tells us that, give or take the odd setback, things on the whole continue to get better; we make progress in that we become more *liberal*, more *humane*.[20] And it is towards just such values that students have been implicitly steered in fifty years of drama lessons. One teacher proudly records a student's comments about what she claims to have learned at the end of a long workshop session: 'You try to be the best person you can be and in doing that you don't hurt anyone else'. For the teacher, this is justification enough for what has gone before.[21] If human history is the story of the gradual triumph of light over darkness then many drama teachers genuinely believe that their gently moralistic practices have a significant role to play. And it is true that for all the naïveté of some of its proponents, once harnessed to political will, the British educational revolution improved the lot of the post-war generation beyond measure. Along with comprehensive education, a key factor in the educational expansion of the 1950s and 1960s, an educational culture of self-fulfilment gave hope and encouragement to thousands whose horizons would otherwise have been confined by the stigma of failure which had been such a marked characteristic of what had gone before.

Half a century on, however, the optimism which allowed drama in schools to ride the tidal wave of educational change has all but vanished; nowadays it is difficult to sustain quite such confidence in the inevitability of human progress. The Cold War may be over, but the former Soviet Union has been superseded in some cases by bloody nationalisms most thought had been buried for ever. In the USA, average earnings for the majority have been falling for years, and in turn-of-century Britain inequalities of wealth are back to what they were before the Second World War. Malnutrition amongst the poor has returned and, as I write there is, once again, a profusion of beggars on the streets of London. One-third of British children live below the poverty line and in one of the poorest London boroughs, forty per cent of children live in households with no-one in paid work.[22] For the first time in modern history, across all social classes in the Western world, today's generation can probably expect *less* for its children than it did for itself.

In education, too, when so many of the old certainties lie in ruins, we can no longer entertain quite such an innocent faith in the benign march of progress. The non-evaluative, horticultural accounts of teaching and learning are beginning to look distinctly wilted. As the old economies of the West face challenges from the Pacific Rim, there is concern that too many young people are leaving school without either the basic skills they will need to survive in a world where, we are told, flexibility and self-sufficiency will be the key to prosperity, or the technological ability to produce the goods and services that the international market demands. In Britain, this has led to an accelerating emphasis on the outcomes of education rather than its supposedly benevolent processes and the arts have seen a turning away from the developmental, self-oriented models of the age of innocence. For dance teachers, a reappraisal of Laban's methods in the 1970s has meant a gradual abandonment of the therapeutic model of modern educational dance in favour of one which acknowledges the importance of performance, while as a result of growing concern among visual artists that art education was so preoccupied with self-expression that students were leaving school visually illiterate, art history and critical studies have now far greater prominence.[23]

For some of those for whom the 1950s and 1960s were formative years this redirection may seem like a betrayal of cherished principles. Viewed over a slightly longer timescale, however, the turn which the arts took in schools during this short period is probably more accurately described as an aberration than a revolution. The sacrifice of tradition on the altar of spontaneity in the name of originality, and the elevating of the authenticity of the students' voice above everything, denies all that we know about the way new generations learn, challenge and change. Peter Abbs reminds us of Ernst Gombrich's questions to those art teachers who at that time were refusing to take schoolchildren to art galleries on the grounds that Herbert Read had put 'freshness and originality above everything':

> But why allow oneself to be influenced by Herbert Read and not by Rembrandt? Why teach the child the words of our language but not the images of our tradition? None of us has discovered Rembrandt unaided; how can any growing mind find a point of entry into the cosmos of art without being given the opportunity?[24]

In drama education, however, resistance to the idea that there might be a corpus of knowledge and skill constituting the subject of drama with which students might become progressively conversant remained stubborn and, by the 1990s, concerns were being expressed that drama might not be serving its students as well as it might. Her Majesty's Inspectors (HMI) reported that for five to eleven year olds in primary schools, drama was only marginally present, and that much of what was observed in classes was weak and superficial.[25] As for the secondary sector, although HMI acknowledged that the subject was thriving, they considered its quality there to be very variable. While those older students who opted for drama at fourteen (in Key Stage 4) were doing well, HMI considered the standards of drama achieved by many eleven to thirteen year olds (Key Stage 3) in 1995 to be too low, with work too often having 'little sense of purpose or progression'.[26] My own visits to secondary schools in the 1990s supported this view. Although I observed many lively drama lessons that were impressive for the range of teaching techniques employed, when the discussion of moral or social issues took precedence over dramatic content these same lessons frequently failed to offer students a broad and balanced experience of the subject. I found little evidence of students writing plays or of their scripts being performed, and design considerations seemed to play little or no part in most students' experience of drama in school before they reached sixteen. Sometimes I saw students repeating well-established, but limited, techniques such as 'still pictures' or 'meetings-in-role', often with considerable aplomb but with little idea as to what advance in the command of the subject of drama might look like. It seemed that for all the efforts of conscientious, hard-working teachers, students' scant knowledge of drama as a field of human endeavour and experience with its own history and conventions was belying the subject's ubiquity.

Rebuilding the subject

It is difficult to escape the conclusion that drama in schools, having launched itself with such confidence in the age of innocence is now in need of some theoretical revitalisation if it is to prosper and flourish in the cold light of the age of experience. We live in rather more incredulous times than those early pioneers and new ways of thinking about the subject and its purposes will have to be found which do not depend upon psychotherapeutic suppositions about learning and personal growth but which instead reconnect classroom drama to drama's long and diverse history as a cultural form. We must begin to relocate drama in the world.

Social anthropologist Clifford Geertz is sure that it is only because we participate in 'the general system of symbolic forms we call culture', that our participation in the particular sector of it we call art, is possible:

> The capacity, variable among peoples as it is among individuals, to perceive meaning in pictures (or poems, melodies, buildings, pots, dramas, statues) is, like all other fully human capacities, a product of collective experience which far transcends it, as is the far rarer capacity to put it there in the first place.[27]

How young people make and appreciate drama cannot escape the influence of the cultures to which they belong. Contributors to this collection share

13

the belief that teachers of the subject of drama should not only be helping students to comprehend that influence but also to extend their perceptions beyond the mere parochial. Exposure to a wide range of dramatic forms not only stimulates creativity but also *enfranchises* students by allowing them to participate in that particular sector of 'the general system of symbolic forms' that we call drama. This book proposes that drama education is therefore, in some significant part, about *cultural induction*. We share our knowledge and understanding with students so that they can develop a critical framework within which they can enjoy plays; we share our skills – as directors, actors, designers and playwrights – so that they can practise the craft of drama for themselves. And we give them the means to challenge what they find.

The implications of accepting the principle of a programme for the teaching of drama in schools of broadly this kind are profound. On the one hand, I am in no doubt that acknowledgement of school drama's congruity with the profuse history of theatre in the world has the potential to offer students of all ages an altogether wider and more eclectic experience of the subject than before. Also, anchoring the subject firmly within the knowledge-based curriculum should go some way to addressing inspectors' concerns over purpose and progression and offer a resolution to long-standing problems with assessment. In the past, answers to students' questions about how they are getting on in drama have sometimes been less than transparent. Now, criteria for success can be made clear to students and discussed openly with them with regard to what they need to do as individuals to achieve it; evidence suggests that this kind of candour is both enabling and motivating.[28]

On the other hand, opening up the field in this way will certainly place new demands upon teachers. Fifty years of understanding drama as a therapeutic or pedagogic process will have persuaded some specialists that they have little need to be conversant with the history and conventions of the theatre. A significant number of teachers in Britain have simply slipped across to drama from English departments; others may have experienced a teacher training in drama where, in the haste to acquire the approved classroom techniques, there was little time for tuition in subject skills and knowledge. In 1992, only nineteen per cent of drama lessons in secondary schools were taught by teachers with first degrees in the subject.[29] One unfortunate consequence of this self-denying ordinance is the widespread assumption that drama is the kind of lesson anyone can teach. 'Drama is not dependent on specialists', wrote an advisory teacher in the 1980s; 'it is intended for *all* teachers', a view endorsed in 1997 by the authors of a drama handbook who praised the efforts of the writer in question for bringing drama 'further within the reach of the non-specialist teacher'.[30] Secondary drama teachers will be familiar with the result of this 'anyone can do it' attitude to their subject, as a medley of colleagues with slack timetables are drafted in to make up the odd lesson. The unfortunate truth is that so long as drama classes remain open to the criticism of having 'little sense of purpose or progression' most teachers probably are competent enough to mind them. Drama will only acquire self-respect as a subject when it can claim suitably qualified specialists and there is no escaping the implications that this requirement will have both for initial training and continuing teacher education.

This book, then, begins a process of realignment. Each of the following chapters explores how aspects of the subject of drama, understood in the ways outlined above, might be approached. Readers will doubtless have their points of agreement and disagreement with individual contributions, but the principle underlying them all is consistent – the need to offer those we teach a curriculum which is coherent, rigorous and progressive. Wherever we live, drama is a fundamental part of our lives, and increasingly so as countless dramatisations are carried by satellite to all corners of the world. If drama is to maintain and strengthen its place in schools in a way which acknowledges this pervasive presence, then the task of laying the foundations of such a curriculum is one that can no longer be delayed.

Notes

1 C. Geertz (1983) *Local Knowledge: Further Essays in Interpretive Anthropology*, New York: Basic Books, pp. 99, 109.

2 A trial may be seen as a special kind of dramatic narrative. It has characters, clearly arraigned moral positions and, like a play, it takes place in real time. The huge popularity of televised murder trials in the USA suggests that they perhaps satisfy a fundamental yearning to see justice done, a desire similarly reflected in a fifth-century Athenian theatre audience. The extent to which those involved in a trial may be said to be 'performing' is another matter.

3 M. Esslin (1987) *The Field of Drama: How the Signs of Drama Create Meanings on Stage and Screen*, London and New York: Methuen, p.36.

4 Producer: 'Oh, yes? So you think ours is a profession of lunatics, do you?', L. Pirandello (1954) *Six Characters in Search of an Author*, trans. F. May, London: Heinemann, p.8.

5 True even for the most ascetically Brechtian performance. The *Verfremdungseffekt* simply makes this contract explicit.

6 Many drama-in-education techniques – 'teacher-in-role', for example – fall into this category.

7 W. Shakespeare *The Life of Henry the Fifth*, Act IV.

8 For example, Molière's teacher, Tiberio Fiorelli, *was* Scaramouche.

9 See K. Robinson (1995) *Education in/and Culture*, Strasbourg: Council of Europe Cultural Policy and Action Division, p.11.

10 By 1540, imitations of the Roman comedies of Plautus and Terence were being performed in grammar schools, academic burlesques that became known as School Plays. The first fully developed play written specifically for children is probably *Ralph Roister Doister*, completed by the schoolmaster Nicholas Udall in 1553. A year before his death, Udall became headmaster of Westminster School.

11 W. Shakespeare *Hamlet*, Act II, sc. ii.
12 D. Hargreaves (1982) *The Challenge for the Comprehensive School*, London: Routledge & Kegan Paul, p.152.
13 In 1992, drama was being taught by a specialist teacher in seventy per cent of secondary schools and in 1996 nearly sixty per cent of students questioned in an Arts Council survey said they had taken part in drama in lessons that year. See Arts Council of Great Britain (ACGB) (1992) *Drama in Schools: Arts Council Guidance on Drama Education*, London: ACGB, p.2 and J. O'Brien (1996) *Secondary School Pupils and the Arts: Report of a MORI Research Study*, London: Arts Council of England, p.5.
14 D. Hargreaves (1982) *The Challenge for the Comprehensive School*, London: Routledge & Kegan Paul, p. 152.
15 According to the Department for Education and Employment, 79,833 students in schools and further education colleges were entered for GCSE examinations in drama in 1996; 39,691 were entered for music. Music is compulsory for students in the first three years of secondary school.
16 For a history of the rise of drama-in-education, see D. Hornbrook (1989 [1998]) *Education and Dramatic Art*, 2nd edn, London: Routledge, part 1.
17 P. Slade (1958) *An Introduction to Child Drama*, London: Hodder & Stoughton, p.2.
18 H. Finlay-Johnson (1911) *The Dramatic Method of Teaching*, London: James Nisbet, p.19.
19 H. Read (1943) *Education through Art*, London: Faber & Faber, p.1.
20 For the classic account of this view, see H. Butterfield (1931) *The Whig Interpretation of History*, London: Bell.
21 B. Edmiston (1991) 'Planning for flexibility: the phases of a drama structure', in *The Drama/Theatre Teacher* 4(1), p.10.
22 See A. Giddens (1996) 'There is radical centre ground', in *The New Statesman* (29 November).
23 The Critical Studies in Art Education (CSAE) project was set up in 1981 with funding from the British Arts, Crafts and Schools Councils. Its aim was to find ways of balancing students' experience of making their own art in school with knowledge, understanding and enjoyment of the wider art world. See R. Taylor (1992) *The Visual Arts in Education: Completing the Circle*, London: Falmer Press, p.5.
24 E. Gombrich (1984) *Tributes*, in P. Abbs, *The Symbolic Order*, London: Falmer Press, 1989, p.9.
25 In 1990, HMI found that fewer than half of primary classes had any drama experience and that of those that did only a small number achieved sufficient breadth and depth. See Department of Education and Science (1990) *The Teaching and Learning of Drama*, London: HMSO, p.7.
26 Office for Standards in Education (OFSTED) (1996) *The Annual Report of Her Majesty's Chief Inspector of Schools: Standards and Quality in Education, 1994/95*, London: HMSO, para.60, p.19.
27 C. Geertz (1983) *Local Knowledge: Further Essays in Interpretive Anthropology*, New York: Basic Books, pp.108–9.
28 See Office for Standards in Education (OFSTED) (1994) *Improving Schools*, London: HMSO.
29 Figures from the Department for Education and Employment. A further nine per cent had Bachelor of Education degrees with drama as a main component. It is difficult to imagine this situation being allowed to develop in, say, mathematics or science. Even in the arts some eyebrows might be raised if it became apparent

that students of fifteen and sixteen were being taught music by a teacher with no particular musical accomplishments, or art by a teacher who knew nothing of art history and who could not paint or draw.

30 See J. Neelands (1984) *Making Sense of Drama*, London: Heinemann, p.7 and N. Kitson and I. Spiby (1997) *Drama 7–11: Developing Primary Teaching Skills*, London: Routledge, p.13.

2

STAGES OF THE WORLD

Sita Brahmachari

A little autobiography

When one seeks humanity, one seeks oneself. Every theory is
something of a self portrait.

André Leroi-Gourhan[1]

I am the daughter of an English woman from the Lake District and an
Indian man from Calcutta who met in Edinburgh and married in Grassington,
Yorkshire. I was born in Derby in the 1960s. Throughout my early education
I experienced a confusing silence in relation to my cultural identity. This
silence, which was intended, well meaningly, to dissolve difference, also
served to negate my father's and therefore my own identity. I could only
assume that my father's Hindu culture had no part to play in my own
learning at school. Confusion reigned as I celebrated Christmas in school
and at home, but Diwali in isolation at home with family friends.

This confusion was compounded by the complex relationship our family
had with the rest of our community. At New Year, following a custom which
undoubtedly has its origin in a superstitious and fearful attitude to foreigners,
my father, who was the 'darkest' man in the village, had the dubious pleasure of
delivering coals to every house to bestow luck on each family for the following
year. One year, while we trudged through the snow, I asked him what we were
doing. He said simply, 'We are carrying out a tradition.' 'But why do we have to
do tradition?' My father thought for a while before answering cheerily,
'Because we are foreigners.' This silenced me for some time.

As I grew up I slowly began to understand what the words 'tradition',
'culture', 'foreigner' and 'race' meant. When my cousin visited from India as
part of an international dance troupe and performed dances in Bharata
Natyam and Kaṭhakaḷi in our front room, or my father read us the poems of
Rabindranath Tagore, or we paid family visits to India, I began to feel links
to other traditions. These dances and stories inspired and stimulated my
child's mind and yet remained unexplored territory in my formal education.

A move to Shropshire, secondary education and a violent shift in identity;
from the tactful silence of my country primary to an onslaught of 'Paki-calling'

at the school gates. The only time this blatant racism was tackled directly was in drama. Yet, in my class, an African-Caribbean boy and I remained conspicuously silent. The exploration of racism through naturalistic improvisation served as a constant reminder of the racist at the gates and further alienated me from my classmates. Our anti-racist dramas failed to transform the 'Paki-callers', nor did they raise my confidence. Rather they served to silence me completely during school hours, although at home I was happy and talkative and continued to explore with my brother and sisters the complexity of our dual identities as a source of celebration, creativity and constant negotiation.

On a recent visit to a drama festival in Shropshire I was heartened to see students' performances inspired by an exchange with Punjabi actors and dancers. Drama education has certainly moved on since the 1970s, both in rural and city schools. However, interaction with artists drawing on non-European traditions remains sporadic and I sense that there is still little documented material available for teachers wishing to build for their students a fully integrated, aesthetically grounded, multicultural curriculum.

Opening up the field

Throughout its history drama in schools has played an important role in confronting issues of racism, prejudice and social injustice. Theatre-in-education companies, too, using a mix of performance and workshop, have been instrumental in offering students opportunities to explore the origins of racial tension. Carefully structured role-play encourages students to speak out against bigotry and to challenge their own pre-conceptions about each other and the world in which they live. However, the success drama teachers have had in examining what theatre director Jatinder Verma has called the 'social phenomenon' of racism must be weighed against a rather less thorough exploration of the hybrid *aesthetics* of multiculturalism.[2] Students 'in role' may vicariously experience intolerance but they rarely have the opportunity to address the ever changing complexities of cultural identity. While it has provided a powerful means of countering racial prejudice and casual stereotyping, school drama has shied away from investigating the particularities of peoples, histories and artistic practices.

Perhaps drama teachers, like theatre practitioners, have been hesitant to emphasise cultural difference, fearing that it will reinforce stereotypical attitudes. Unfortunately, in the contemporary idiom, it is not uncommon for the word 'culture' to stand in for the more politically charged, 'race'. The danger of this substitution is that culture comes to be understood, like race, as a static and undynamic characteristic denoting difference. By this account, the artistic practices of Britain's diverse cultures remain 'other', 'foreign', outside the mainstream.

In this chapter, I wish to propose an alternative picture, one which does

19

not, in Paul Gilroy's words, 'see culture flowing into neat ethnic parcels but as a radically unfinished social process of self-definition and transformation'.[3] I share Gilroy's view that we must escape:

> the typically anti-racist practice of peering into the murky pool of English culture in order to locate evidence of its monolithically racist character. The desire to make art out of being both black and English . . . should be seen as a micro-political task of recoding the cultural core of national life.[4]

The changing faces of racism in this, or any other country, will not be neglected in my proposal for a curriculum which sets out to address this 'micro-political task'. However, it has become clear to me in the years following my own unfortunate experience of secondary drama, that what limits the important work that drama teachers do in countering notions of cultural and racial supremacy is the fact that such explorations are invariably locked into the conventions and forms of European theatre. The absence of culturally diverse dramatic forms of expression in the drama classroom confirms students' perception that naturalism, seen daily on our television screens, is the only form of dramatic expression of any interest. The fifteen year old who has learned Kaṭhakaḷi dance theatre from the age of five (through, say, a community arts project) sees no opportunity to contribute her craft to the drama class. Within the narrow parameters of spontaneous improvisation, Kaṭhakaḷi is effectively a foreign language, one which the student quickly learns is out of place, or at most an exotic diversion, within the conventions of the drama lesson. 'In the context of the arts', writes Jenny Francis, 'lack of acknowledgement of the contribution of Afro-Caribbean and Asian culture to the historical as well as the contemporary mainstream continues to marginalise the importance of non-European cultures.'[5] If we are to develop an aesthetically-based multicultural curriculum, we must be careful to counter notions of cultural supremacy and inferiority by making sure that we offer naturalism as only one among many dramatic languages about which all students have a right to learn.

Another obstacle to a genuinely multicultural drama curriculum is the historical compartmentalisation of the arts in European culture. For most world cultures, drama is the place where dance, music and text unselfconsciously meet. Forms of artistic expression – drama, dance, poetry, music, painting, or combinations of them – are intertwined and deeply rooted in the cultures from which they spring. Understanding this aesthetic unity will be essential for students embarking on an investigation of the dramatic function, structure and content of world drama.

So, it is clear that if we are to make our classrooms and drama studios truly multicultural, then we face some challenges. First, the European tradition has to be made *explicit* by consciously articulating its sources and inspirations in a way which demonstrates its debt to world theatre. We might begin by investigating the artistic influences on practitioners such as Brecht, Artaud, Brook and Mnouchkine, who have been inspired by *non*-European sources. Second, the dialogue between drama and the other arts should be re-opened and a theatre aesthetic reclaimed for our students. We must not just accept the relationship between classroom drama and the theatre but consciously *embrace* that relationship. Finally, as teachers, we must be prepared to learn some aspects of our subject anew. Like the musician perfecting an instrument, the subject of drama is a lifelong learning process for us as well as for our students. The drama teacher of the future may be a specialist in one or more cultural art forms – Noh Theatre or Yoruba mask drama, for example – possibly pooling that specialisation with others in a region. Above all, we will need the confidence to put our apprehensions behind us and plunge into unfamiliar waters.

The drama traditions of Britain's own communities and those of the many cultures to which they are the heirs may provide the key to some of these challenges. As I know myself, for those students of African, Caribbean or Asian origins living in Britain, acquaintance with dramatic traditions from the stages of the world is not a nicety or fancy; they cannot start to forge their own identities if they are only given role models from a dominant culture. Apart from anything else, the absence of world dramatic traditions from British drama classrooms suggests a failure to recognise the important contribution that these students, and the cultures they represent, can bring to education in drama. Thus, the Punjabi performers in Shropshire may point the way forward to the building of a more genuinely multicultural curriculum, one which unites anti-racism with an aesthetic experience which draws on vastly different performance styles. This is not so radical a proposal. In music and art in English schools students are already required to learn about 'world music' and 'world art'; I am suggesting no more than that the same principle should be applied to the subject of drama.

I never saw theatre before

As an educationalist working in the theatre I have tried to build bridges between student audiences and the work they come to see. The teaching programmes I have developed have been designed to help teachers and students engage with the work of black and Asian companies by encouraging them to explore the dramatic traditions of different cultures and the contemporary interpretations of those traditions.

Some years ago, I conducted some research with a group of sixteen- and seventeen-year-old London students, all of whom were studying for a GCE advanced level qualification in theatre studies. I wanted to find out how their very different cultural backgrounds affected their experience of a play. In

21

part, this investigation was inspired by one of the students, Ebun, who had been born and educated in Ghana until the age of thirteen. Ebun said that she had performed in plays at school in Ghana and had seen street players but considered these experiences unworthy of her present conception of drama: 'The first theatre I saw was *Thérèse Raquin* at the National Theatre. In Ghana we don't have theatre like here. I never saw theatre before coming to this country.'

Ebun negates her experience of Ghanaian street theatre because it does not take place in a darkened building where everybody is quiet. By her own admission, her conception of theatre had been learned since she began her drama education in Britain where she had acquired a very specific idea of drama, one rooted in European notions of high culture. Ebun rejects her past experience because she sees little resemblance between the street players in Ghana and what she has learned in drama. The processions, masked dancers, drumming and singing of African theatre clearly bear little resemblance to anything she has seen or been encouraged to perform in drama.

The students saw a production of *Resurrections* by Nigerian writer Biyi-Bandele Thomas, performed by Talawa Theatre Company with an all black British cast.[6] The play is set in Nigeria and explores the theme of corruption and the Yoruba belief in the interrelationship between the living and the dead. The production employed a number of Yoruba dramatic conventions including the use of a storyteller, choral rhythm work and movement and the characterisation of animal demons in the shape of vultures. A number of songs and chants were also performed in the Yoruba language.

Interviewed after the performance, a sharp distinction emerged between the responses of the students. Tony, a London-born English boy, described the difficulty he was having commenting about the production because he saw himself as having no way of evaluating the work or drawing parallels to anything else he knew or had experienced. While he thought his drama education had been 'multicultural', in that it explored the racism experienced by people in the class and he had learned about the Civil Rights Movement, he still found it difficult to engage with the performance. In contrast, Efua, a student of Nigerian parentage, was extremely excited by the play, in particular the portrayal of one character, Mebude, who, she said, resembled her own mother. Efua was upset by the responses of some of her friends who dismissed the performance as 'false'. 'They thought she [Mebude] wasn't acting well but I wanted to tell them that that's exactly what a proud Nigerian woman acts like.' Efua felt very defensive about the production which she believed was undervalued by some of her peers simply because they were unable to engage with its conventions.

Of course, it could be argued that in Efua's case, her understanding of Yoruba culture was grounded from birth. However, the performers of *Resurrections* were predominantly second and third generation British actors some of whom had learnt about Yoruba traditions through the rehearsal process. With this in mind, we should ask ourselves: to what extent is it possible for students and teachers without personal knowledge of the symbolic world of a specific dramatic tradition to absorb and understand its particular meanings and resonances? Mohammed's response to *Resurrections* may provide some answers to this question. In the students' written reflections on the play, it was apparent that those who had knowledge of other non-European dramatic traditions (in Mohammed's case, Bengali theatre) were better able to explore the cultural context of the production and the aesthetic practices employed. They were also able to recognise some familiar ground, such as the use of the storyteller, the choral work, the relationships between man and the gods, and the fluid chronology of the play. It seemed that if students were familiar with another, non-naturalistic, dramatic tradition they were able to engage with new ones with greater freedom, even if the dramatic traditions had little else in common. A comparison might be drawn with the well documented phenomenon that the bilingual speaker learns new concepts and languages more speedily than the monolinguist.

Susmita Banerjee, a British-born dancer who first trained in Bharata Natyam, Kathakali and a number of Indian martial arts forms, experiences the same sense of freedom when approaching African dance and drama. For Banerjee, the study of a range of forms is part of the process of artistic inquisitiveness which can inspire new thinking and it is in this space of 'unknown territory' that her most creative work takes place. Other contemporary African and Asian artists like Peter Badejo, Shobana Jeyasingh, and Keith Khan, whose work notably draws on a diversity of cultural traditions and performance theories, share this belief.

This is not to advocate a study of the stages of the world as that of an exotic 'other' but as a means of exploring the exchanges which have, and are, taking place between peoples of different cultures and histories. Many black and Asian practitioners are already drawing on the traditions to which they are connected to create a new dramatic language which will unite these traditions with their particular identities as black and Asian artists in Britain today. It is a practice perhaps better described as *interculturalism*, that 'dialectic of exchanges of civilities between cultures' which, according to Patrice Pavis, allows us to appreciate the 'unexpected transfers' of cross-cultural production.[7]

The hourglass of cultures

Anthropologist Clifford Geertz, reflecting on Yoruba line carving, suggests that intense work of this kind grows out of a distinct cultural sensibility 'in which the meanings of things are the scars that men leave on them'.[8] Or, as Raymond Williams once observed, culture is the way in which people write themselves into the land. All students of drama, whether they live in

London or the Lake District, should have the critical tools to view the cultural practices of their own reality in relation to the 'scars' left by others. They need to develop, in other words, a cross-cultural aesthetic. In an inter-cultural drama education, students like Ebun, Tony, Efua and Mohammed should be able to place Ghanaian street theatre, Yoruba story-telling and Kaṭhakaḷi dance theatre intelligibly alongside a production of Zola's *Thérèse Raquin* at the Royal National Theatre and, in the process, see how they might write themselves into this British dramatic landscape.

Gilroy stresses that in order to establish a cross-cultural aesthetic we first need to review 'outmoded' notions of cultural identity and race which have been the prime focus of multicultural drama education in the past. 'Black creativity has been excluded from the aesthetic citadels of modernity and post modernity', he argues, 'and this wrong can be redressed by the corrective re-construction of the Western canon'.[9] Gilroy's notion of 'diaspora identity' allows teachers and students to move beyond the politics of oppression which, as we have seen, can lead to the silencing rather than to the empowerment of students.[10] Instead of flattening all peoples into the same mould, 'diaspora identity' explores the connections between peoples through history, time and place, freeing us from ethnic absolutism and enabling us to discover our historical, social, cultural and artistic links:

> [Diaspora's] cross-cultural poetics allows for a complex conception of sameness and an idea of solidarity that does not repress the differences within in order to maximise the differences between one essential community and others. . . . Foregrounding the tensions around origins and essences that Diaspora brings into focus, allows us to perceive that identity should not be fossilised or venerated in keeping with the holy spirit of ethnic absolutism. Identity too becomes a noun of process. . . . Its infinite openness provides a timely alternative to the authoritarian implications of mechanical, clockwork solidarity based on outmoded notions of race.[11]

The idea of diaspora allows for a symbolic understanding of cultural and historical commonality and difference and, most importantly, offers a space to create, explore, develop and invent cultures and identities. A study of dramatic traditions from the stages of the world acknowledges the diverse cultural inheritance of those we teach while at the same time allowing students – all students – to view this shared heritage as integral to British identity as it changes and develops. 'The point is not to negate nationalism through inter-culturalism', argues Rustom Bharucha, 'but to incorporate the immediacies of particular histories . . . within an intracultural framework of thought and action, at once coherent and respectful of difference.'[12]

A brief examination of twentieth-century Western drama reveals that interculturalism has already had a significant impact. Antonin Artaud was influenced by the Balinese theatre, Brecht by the Peking Opera, Yeats by Noh Theatre and Grotowski, Mnouchkine, Schechner and Brook by Asian and African theatre. Many companies playing in Britain today are informed by non-European traditions. Yet when students see the work of companies like, say, Shared Experience or Theatre de Complicité, the artistic practices from which these companies draw inspiration may not be apparent to them. This hidden canon is, in itself, a form of appropriation – for Bharucha, a new form of imperialism or 'cultural tourism', in which the intercultural theatre practitioner plunders the 'other' culture for its artistic technique with no real interest in engaging with the belief systems, history and sociology out of which the artistic practices have grown:

> There is a new 'ism' in theatre today that needs to be strongly questioned. Substituting, however nebulously, the older category of internationalism, interculturalism is opening up new possibilities of relationships between cultures that seem to transcend the specificities of history, race, language and time.[13]

In the past, the pursuit of universals, essences which transcend culture, much preoccupied some theorists of classroom drama.[14] In exploring different cultural and artistic formations we should aim instead to give students insights, however limited, into the sensibility of peoples and in so doing allow them to place their own perceptions of the world in the context of these new interactions. At the same time, while there is much to be gained in the exploration of cultural exchange through the arts, there are some aspects of cultural traditions which are so distinct, so highly encoded, that those who are not themselves inscribed into these artistic practices may never gain any significant insights from an exchange. As drama teachers, we are thus presented with something of a dilemma. In celebrating the diversity and difference of interculturalism we must be careful not to lay ourselves open to the accusation of cultural tourism, of picking this and that piece of exotica to decorate our dramas. What we are looking at is not so much appropriation, nor even, perhaps, intercultural exchange, but, in Pavis' words, 'a kind of *réglage* (fine tuning) between different contexts and cultures . . . a mediation between different cultural backgrounds, traditions and methods of acting'.[15]

Pavis offers us a model (see Figure 2.1) which examines the way in which the *mise en scène* of a performance – the totality of the stage picture – transmits a 'source' culture to the public and 'what operations come into play in this cultural transfer using theatrical means'.[16] The series of eleven filters facilitates the progress of the dramatic tradition and culture, like tiny grains of sand, from source to target culture. These filters, Pavis argues, will be necessary 'until the conceptual tools' for interpreting the performance of cultures have been further developed:

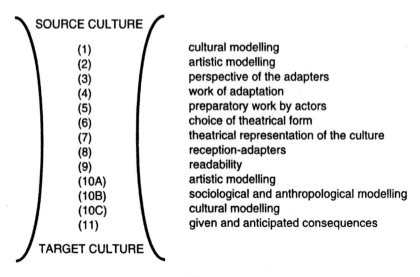

SOURCE CULTURE	
(1)	cultural modelling
(2)	artistic modelling
(3)	perspective of the adapters
(4)	work of adaptation
(5)	preparatory work by actors
(6)	choice of theatrical form
(7)	theatrical representation of the culture
(8)	reception-adapters
(9)	readability
(10A)	artistic modelling
(10B)	sociological and anthropological modelling
(10C)	cultural modelling
(11)	given and anticipated consequences
TARGET CULTURE	

Figure 2.1 The hourglass of cultures[17]

> In the upper bowl is the foreign culture, the source culture, which is
> more or less codified and solidified in diverse anthropological, soci-
> ological or artistic modelizations. In order to reach us, this culture
> must pass through a narrow neck. If the grains of culture or their
> conglomerate are sufficiently fine, they will flow through without
> any trouble, however slowly, into the lower bowl, that of the target
> culture, from which point we observe this slow flow. The grains will
> rearrange themselves in a way which appears random, but which is
> partly regulated by their passage through some dozen filters put in
> place by the target culture and the observer.[18]

With this model Pavis articulates the risks involved in attempting to
explore unfamiliar dramatic traditions. The hourglass represents a kind of
mill, so that there is always the danger that in the grinding journey to interpretation a 'deformed substance' may be produced resulting in the dramatic
traditions of the source culture losing all specificity and significance to
everyone. On the other hand, if the hourglass is no more than a funnel, it
will absorb the initial substance indiscriminately without reshaping it, and
this reshaping process is integral to the artistic process of interpretation and
performance. 'There is no theatre in the crucible of humanity where all
specificity melts into a universal substance', he argues. 'It is at the crossing
of ways, of traditions, of artistic practices that we can hope to grasp the
distinct hybridization of cultures, and bring together the winding paths of
anthropology, sociology and artistic practices.'[19]

Bharucha's concern is that for too long interculturalism has been one-way traffic – the West plundering the East. In our classrooms the picture may be rather more complex. Arts teachers, at least those in multicultural schools, witness the hybridisation of cultures developing both in daily life and in the creative work of their students. What may be happening in some schools amounts to the up-ending of the hourglass itself. For Pavis, the appropriation of another culture is never definitive: 'It is turned upside-down as soon as the users of a foreign culture ask themselves how they can communicate their own culture to another target culture.'[20]

The hourglass of cultures, I propose, offers teachers a model for the teaching of world drama which is both flexible and realistic. A project on the Caribbean tradition of Jonkonnu (a traditional Jamaican mask drama performance with diaspora links to Africa), for example, may need to adapt very little in order to make the process 'readable' in a school with a large number of African-Caribbean students; in a less culturally mixed school it may be necessary to place more filters between source and target cultures. Whatever the context, the model helps students develop the critical vocabulary of a cross-cultural aesthetic so that each time a student meets another aspect of culture in performance the process of adaptation will be needed a little less.

Making: knowing and adapting Indian drama

I return to the question I asked my father as a four year old in the Lake District: why do we do tradition? As a child I wanted to know about Kathakali and Bharata Natyam and the poems of Tagore because they seemed to say something about who I was. As human beings we like to know how we are *connected*: what habits, thoughts, qualities, aspirations and artistic forms join us with our forefathers and mothers. This is not simply a matter of curiosity; it is in our attempts to understand these connections and disconnections that we forge our own identities:

> Tradition implies movement or action through time. Performance traditions like religious or literary ones are best thought of as inherited collections of established ways of feeling, thinking and doing that are passed down through generations and, just as importantly, consist of the active and often contentious process of transmitting what has been passed down.[21]

The intercultural drama student cannot make progress without first making the attempt to engage with the all-important traditions of the source culture – for Pavis, these are the stages of 'cultural and artistic modelling' (see Figure 2.1) – and there is probably no better way to help students gain insights into the sensibility of a people than by familiarising them with the stories which inform the plays that are made, performed and watched in that culture.

If we choose Indian theatre as our source culture, then it would be appropriate to begin by introducing students to the epic poems, or *puranas*, which to this day are vehicles for thousands of Indian legends, beliefs, teachings and characters, and of which the *Rāmāyana* and the *Mahābhārata* are, of course, the two most famous. The religious themes of the *puranas* enable Indian people continually to renew their vision of the world and their relationship with the gods while the stories themselves provide a continuum of interpretation and re-interpretation. The spread of theatre across India did not depend on the existence of a playwright but on the re-interpretation of the *puranas* by different performers who were required to dance, mime, sing and speak the stories in their own idiosyncratic ways. Students should be encouraged to experiment with the oral story-telling tradition and to retell the stories they have learned in different contexts -- one group I worked with, for example, drew parallels between Shakespeare's Romeo and Juliet and Rama and Sita from the *Rāmāyana*. Analysing their own reactions to the beliefs and ideals represented in the stories, students have the opportunity to perform the roles of the 'adapters' and 'actors' of the hourglass of cultures, while knowledge of a number of epic stories should encourage them to explore dramatic theatre forms and contexts with which they may be unfamiliar, leading them to the sixth element of Pavis' model (see Figure 2.1) -- 'choice of theatrical form'.

Performing: using the Nāṭyaśhāstra

The Nāṭyaśhāstra is a treatise on the art of acting and performance attributed to Bharata Muni sometime between 200 BC and 200 AD.[22] Originating in the élite temple performances of Sanskrit theatre, the techniques outlined in the Nāṭyaśhāstra are still evident in Indian theatre forms, and many contemporary Indian theatre practitioners are returning to it for inspiration. Bharata Muni describes *abhinaya* (acting) as creating a feeling of bliss, *rasa* or *ananda*, in the eyes of the spectator, 'by revealing various mental states of the characters'.[23] He delineates three forms of *abhinaya*: *angica abhinaya* (physical acting in which meanings are ascribed to movements of hand, eye and body, an entire vocabulary of gestures), *vachika abhinaya* (acting through words, including speaking poetry, singing and making music), and *aharya abhinaya* (a focus on the actor's awareness of presence and ability to create an impact on the audience through masks, costume and stage properties). While the suggestions made in this section can only touch upon the vast amount of knowledge contained in this ancient compendium of theatre, I think the Nāṭyaśhāstra contains a number of performance conventions which may be useful to teachers wanting to challenge naturalism in the intercultural drama classroom. In one school, a group of thirteen year olds spent two terms concentrating on each form of *abhinaya* separately before attempting to marry each element of *abhinaya* in a single performance.

Of central importance to traditional Indian theatre is the close relationship which exists in performance between drama, dance and music. Stories are dramatised, not predominantly through prose, as in the West, but through song, mime, and dance theatre. It is the responsibility of the actor to actualise the world (human, natural and supernatural elements) and to create for the audience the shifts in time and place which occur in a dramatisation. In the Nāṭyaśhāstra, the *angica abhinaya* outlines the way in which a whole physical language of gesture can be created by the performer and through which gods and animals, human emotions, the natural world, even inanimate objects like furniture, can all be expressed.

In my experience, the easiest way to approach *angica abhinaya* with students is through an exploration of the emotional and devotional themes of the *puranas* and, perhaps, the contemporary poetical dramas of Rabindranath Tagore. In Kaṭhakaḷi and Bharata Natyam dance theatre, the gestures are specific to the particular poem or myth with physical signs for whatever has to be communicated – sun, moon, time, space, hours of the day. Although students cannot expect to master this complex gestic language in a few drama lessons – competence in such highly encoded forms can take Indian actors years of training – a basic introduction to the vocabulary is quite possible. One way of giving students used to an over-dependence on verbal communication in drama confidence in actualising the world through the physical is to begin by using Indian martial art forms. The dance-dramas of Kaṭhakaḷi originated in the martial arts, and by practising these, students should be able to develop their physical acting skills as well as gaining greater insight into the stories.

Once students have learned some basic gestic vocabulary they may then begin to use it to explore contemporary stories and themes which are not contained within the great epic works and are therefore without specific gestures. In this way, learning about the tradition is not an end in itself but a means of stimulating creative ideas about cultural exchange. Students should be encouraged to create their own gestic language to express contemporary situations, or themes, which they wish to explore in their drama lessons. By this stage, students should have grasped some of the fundamental elements of Indian theatre and had a chance to experiment a little, so this is a good time to introduce them to the work of intercultural practitioners, like Shobhana Jeyasingh and Susmita Banerjee.

Vachika abhinaya concentrates on spoken language and music and so offers a good opportunity for collaboration with other departments. In English, students might study the poetry of Rabindranath Tagore and develop their own poetry based on the story they are studying; in music, students can experiment with mantras, work with a tabla player or explore the use of percussive instruments like cymbals, often an integral part of leading a performance. In Kaṭhakaḷi music there are six different rhythmic patterns, each of which can be performed slowly, at medium and fast speeds; a sudden change in the pattern indicates a shift in the emotional level of the performance. The prologue in Sanskrit drama traditionally takes the form of a *poorvaranga*, a selection of introductory songs or dances which prepare the audience for the play. Here, students can script and compose their own musical scores and perform the *poorvaranga* chorally. When people attend productions of Svang theatre (a popular folk tradition), they speak of hearing the theatre rather than seeing it. An exploration of such traditions might lead to the creation of whole sections of sung narration.

Narrators perform a key function in Indian drama. The most prominent of these, the *sūtradhāra*, is present on stage throughout the performance:

> In the absence of a definite pre-written text working with an eclecti-cally assembled production script, it became necessary that someone chose the story of the performance, organise the elements of poetry, music, dance etc. The *sūtradhāra* is also a performer and controls the rhythm of the performance on stage by a pair of cymbals or other means. It is the *sūtradhāra* that tells the exposi-tionary aspects of the story, comments on the dramatic action and performs some roles.[24]

The other narrator, the *vidūṣaka*, is an independent character who can appear whenever required:

> He carries the unique function of relating the episodes and charac-ters of a story from a mythical or imaginary context, unfamiliar in time and place to the contemporary situation of individuals. He has the satire wit and audacity to comment on topical or local events and people. The *vidūṣaka* is representative of the voice of the spec-tators and therefore ensures contemporary relevance.[25]

As well as serving the drama itself, the device of the narrator may also help to bridge historical and cultural gaps between the story and the student learners. In the hourglass of cultures, the narrator enhances the 'readability' of the performance, allowing students to place their own 'reception adapters' into the work to ensure clarity and contemporary relevance (see Figure 2.1).

Until India came under colonial rule, there was no attempt in either the Sanskrit or later Indian theatre to simulate reality. Traditionally, Indian audiences have no expectation of any unity of time and place nor even of a chronological timescale; the passage of time is indicated through song and dance. The fluid chronology of the plays is representative of the way in which individual stories are conceived as part of the wider world. The practice of *kakshyavibhaga* (the imaginary division of the performance area) is created by the third form of acting described in the Nāṭyaśhāstra *aharya abhinaya*. The actor marks circular, or linear, patterns on the stage to create different locations and changes of scene. Students who have predominantly experienced naturalistic staging may find it liberating to explore the power of the performer in demarcating the stage space and this element of the Indian theatre tradition may also challenge preconceived ideas of structure in dramatic performances.

By now students should be familiar with a variety of stories, practices and performance styles derived from the Indian theatre tradition. Their presentations of episodes from the *puranas* should include a broad understanding of forms such as Kaṭhakaḷi, Bharata Natyam and Chau, and their performances should reveal a knowledge of gestic language, movement and rhythm. Sections of plays might be sung and danced, providing an opportunity for the drama teacher to work with arts colleagues. In the hourglass of cultures, students will have made critical choices about 'theatrical representations of the culture' and 'choice of theatrical form'.

Responding: intercultural theatre in Britain

From the Sanskrit theatre to the present day, Indian actors have traditionally begun by invoking the power of a god to bless the performance or, in the case of Kaṭhakaḷi theatre, to ask forgiveness from the mother earth for the disturbance caused by the dancing. This practice of *mangalacharana* reminds us once again of the sacred nature of the theatre in India and its role in linking ordinary people to the gods. The symbolic placing of Indra's staff, or *jajara*, on the stage before a performance is intended to bring actors and spectators together in an act of respect for the play which is about to begin. The marketplace, field or school hall is transformed by these rituals into a magical and mythical space. This focus on the performer's preparation, and the ceremony and ritual surrounding the performance itself, may help to give students an insight into the important role they play as actors in the story and their responsibility to the audience to whom they perform. An examination of key aspects of the tradition, such as the role of the *vidūṣaka* commentary, for example, may be a cue for students' own intercultural exploration of the relationship between ancient Indian myths and their relevance in contemporary Britain. These perceptions will be deepened and broadened if they are also able to place their own work alongside that of professional intercultural theatre groups. Watching plays like Ruth Carter's *A Yearning* (performed in 1995 by Tamasha Theatre), based on Lorca's *Yerma* and set in the Punjabi community in Britain, will help students view their own exploration of form and content in the context of wider developments in intercultural performance in Britain.

In this example of an intercultural drama project I have tried to show how students can learn elements of gestic language and some of the techniques and philosophies of an unfamiliar aesthetic by getting to know the stories. Once students have come to know a 'source culture' a little in this way, they have the conceptual tools to incorporate some of the techniques and practices into their own presentations. If they go on to extend this knowledge and understanding to the dramatic traditions of the many different stages of the world, they are beginning to develop a dramatic vocabulary which will enable them both to respond to the symbol systems of many cultures and to develop their own voices. If they can become confident of the process of critical evaluation then the aesthetic decisions from which they develop their work and steer their understanding will be well informed. For Tony, struggling to make sense of *Resurrections*, he will at last have the critical tools to assess the production which draws on cultural and artistic practices to which he had formerly been a stranger.

Towards an intercultural drama curriculum

The problem of 'cultural tourism' remains. In our desire to represent a diversity of cultures in drama, how do we avoid offering students 'token tasters' in the Bharata Natyam or African mask drama? As teachers, we know that to become accomplished in any one of these forms can take a lifetime's commitment; in introducing students to the stages of the world we are clearly not aiming to create specialists in one form or tradition. Nevertheless, we must be careful to avoid the isolated, non-integrated, session on multicultural drama, however inspirational, for this is an approach which may simply reinforce the assumption that non-European theatre is an anomaly in the drama curriculum.

We can mitigate against this perception of unfamiliar dramatic traditions as examples of 'the other' by seeing students' progress as a spiral of learning continually broadened at each interaction. The successful creation of a fully integrated intercultural drama curriculum will depend to a large extent on the effectiveness of the relationship between its different elements. Such a curriculum can be helpfully divided into five interlocking categories:

    ritual
    classical
    devotional
    folk/popular
    modern[26]

Within this simple framework, students learn about, experience and perform the dramas of different cultures from across the world *and* explore the significance of these traditions to their contemporary lives in Britain today. After exposure to a diversity of aesthetic forms, they should then be in the position to integrate these forms into their own dramas and so extend them beyond the limitations of naturalism.

In my discussions with other drama teachers about the challenges presented by the introduction of an aesthetically grounded intercultural curriculum, the need for more materials and support is always high on the agenda. Information about the cultural context of plays, guidance on specific performance traditions and techniques (such as those in the Nāṭyaśhāstra), video footage of intercultural companies at work, and, most importantly, opportunities for teachers and trainee teachers to work alongside experienced practitioners; all will be necessary if the intercultural ideal is to stand any chance of being realised in the ordinary drama classroom. Without resources like these to support a sustained, integrated programme, many teachers fear that projects of the kind I have outlined in this chapter will remain on the margins of drama education in schools and students like Tony will be unable to make sense of what they see and hear within their conception of the subject of drama as a whole. One way of tackling this very real problem is by developing partnerships with black and Asian theatre companies and practitioners. In London and other big cities, where the establishment of such relationships is relatively easy, I have witnessed some highly successful initiatives based on links between artists and teachers. Sadly, these interactions remain largely undocumented. It is my hope that teachers and theatre practitioners can be persuaded to record successful partnerships in detail in the future, so that they can be made available to the wider drama community. This is one way of beginning to build a resource base for the kind of work I have described here.

As well as enormously extending the breadth of students' knowledge and understanding of their subject, a drama curriculum which explores the aesthetics of multiculturalism may bring us as teachers closer to our aim of countering racial myopia than the issue-based drama of the past. While the latter set out to challenge stereotypical attitudes about race, the former encourages students to explore and express distinct sensibilities, moving beyond the simple oppositions of prejudice and oppression. An aesthetically grounded multicultural curriculum offers students the conceptual and practical tools through which to explore and find their own creative space within a historical and cultural continuum.

For some drama teachers, in Britain at least, I suspect that what I am proposing will be new ground. However, as ever more rapid communication causes our world to shrink further and further, I am in no doubt that the time has never been more ripe for the kinds of interventions I am suggesting. We can no longer simply subscribe, tacitly or otherwise, to the notion that Western naturalism, so extensively propagated by television, has won the day. Maybe we do all have some learning to do and some courage may be needed to brave the unknown, but the rewards will be great. And the drama teacher and his/her class will not be lone explorers. They will be joining a formidable band of cultural theorists, intercultural theatre practitioners, sociologists and anthropologists – not to mention those colleagues up the corridor in the music, dance and art departments.

I began this chapter by acknowledging that the theory I have set out here is something of a self-portrait. However, I believe it is a portrait and a basis for teaching the subject of drama which is pertinent for teachers and students of drama in contemporary Britain and, by extension, in all countries where drama flourishes. For me, a multicultural approach to the arts has been a personal journey; for others, it may be the surest way to promote those values of tolerance, sensitivity and understanding of which drama education has traditionally been such a vocal champion.

Acknowledgement

I am indebted to Susmita Banerjee, choreographer and dancer, John Martin, Director of Pan Project, London and Jatinder Verma, Director of Tara Arts, London, for their contributions to this discussion.

Bibliography

Banerjee, U. (1992) *Indian Performing Arts*, London: Sangam Books.
Brandon, J. (ed.) (1993) *The Cambridge Guide to Asian Theatre*, Cambridge: Cambridge University Press.
Deshpande, V. (1987) *Indian Musical Traditions*, London: Sangam Books.
Gargi, B. (1991) *Folk Theatre of India*, Calcutta: Rupa.
Krishna Rao, U. (1990) *A Dictionary of Bharata Natyam*, London: Sangam Books.
Menon, K. (1991) *A Dictionary of Kaṭhakaḷi*, London: Sangam Books.

Notes

1 André Leroi-Gourhan, in Pavis (1992) *Theatre at the Crossroads of Culture*, trans. J. Daugherty, London and New York: Routledge, p.1.
2 J. Verma (1996) 'Towards a black aesthetic', in *Performing Arts International* 1, p.10.
3 P. Gilroy (1995a) *Small Acts: Art of Darkness*, London: Trentham Books, p.61.
4 Ibid., p.76.
5 J. Francis (1990) *Attitudes among Britain's Black community towards attendance at arts, cultural and entertainment events*, a qualitative research study prepared for the Arts Council of Great Britain, London: Networking Public Relations, p.23.
6 The Biyi-Bandele Thomas production of *Resurrections* was performed by Talawa Theatre Company at the Cochrane Theatre, London in autumn 1994.
7 P. Pavis (1992) *Theatre at the Crossroads of Culture*, trans. J. Daugherty, London and New York: Routledge, p.2.
8 C. Geertz (1983) *Local Knowledge: Further Essays in Interpretive Anthropology*, New York: Basic Books, p.99.
9 P. Gilroy (1995a) *Small Acts: Art of Darkness*, London: Trentham Books, p.78.

10 'Diaspora' has been used to describe the dispersion of the peoples throughout the world since the Babylonian exile of the Jews in 586 BC.
11 P. Gilroy (1995b) '"To be real": the dissident forms of black expressive culture', *Let's Get It On*, London: Institute of Contemporary Arts, p.156.
12 R. Bharucha (1993) *Theatre and the World*, London: Routledge, p.156.
13 Ibid., p.1.
14 See for example, D. Heathcote (1980) 'From the particular to the universal', in K. Robinson (ed.) *Exploring Theatre and Education*, London: Heinemann, pp.7–51.
15 P. Pavis (1992) *Theatre at the Crossroads of Culture*, trans. J. Daugherty, London and New York: Routledge, p.6.
16 Ibid., p.184.
17 Ibid., p.4.
18 Ibid.
19 Ibid., p.6.
20 Ibid., p.5.
21 F. Richmond, D. Swann and P. Zarrilli (1990) (eds) *Indian Theatre: Traditions and Performance*, Honolulu, HI: University of Hawaii Press, p.4.
22 See M. Gosh (1967) (trans and ed.) *The Nāṭyaśhāstra*, Calcutta: Manisha Granthalaya. The Nāṭyaśhāstra is an 'encyclopaedia of knowledge concerning Sanskrit drama and theatre, the most comprehensive work of its kind to survive anywhere from ancient times . . . . broader in scope than the other great text of ancient dramaturgy, Aristotle's *Poetics*. The work consists of numerous chapters, beginning with the origins of theatre. Within its scope are a multitude of topics, such as theatre architecture, acting, costuming, make-up, properties, dance, music, play construction, poetic composition, grammar, composition of theatre companies, audiences, dramatic competitions, the actor community, and ritual observancies' (F. Richmond *et al.* (1990), pp.34–5).
23 N. Jain (1992) *Indian Theatre: Tradition, Continuity and Change*, Delhi: Vikash Publishing House, p.25.
24 Ibid., p.52.
25 Ibid., p.54.
26 Richmond, F., Swann, D. and Zarrilli, P. (eds) (1990) *Indian Theatre: Traditions and Performance*, Honolulu, HI: University of Hawaii Press, p.10.

3

CREATIVITY IN CONTEXT

Sharon Bailin

The Romantic bequest

For the past fifty years, drama education in schools has been underwritten by a particular philosophical perspective concerning persons, culture and education, a form of Romantic naturalism which views the person in his or her natural state as essentially good and culture as potentially damaging to this natural goodness.[1] From this perspective, education becomes a liberation and development of what is within us rather than an acquisition and assimilation of what is without. It is a picture that has been highly influential in education in general at certain times and, although its popularity has waned in recent years, its hold on drama education has been unusually tenacious.

At the centre of this picture is an account of creativity which emphasises psychological processes within the individual and de-emphasises significant achievement and the making of products. What is required in order to foster creativity is the liberation of natural, intuitive ways of understanding, protection from the influence of external cultural understandings and the encouragement of the kinds of divergent mental processes which can break the hold of conventional ways of thinking and acting. The educational manifestations of this view include a focus on creative processes of thought (seen in terms of novelty), the spontaneous generation of ideas, freedom from constraints, and the suspension of judgement. These processes are believed to transcend specific disciplinary contexts.

In this chapter I shall argue that such a view of creativity is radically defective, that it is based on unsupported assumptions and considerable conceptual confusions, and that creativity can be coherently viewed only in terms of significant achievement within identified contexts. I shall argue, further, that the pedagogical practices in drama which this view has engendered undermine the skills and knowledge which make such achievement possible.

Creativity without context

Creativity tends to be inscribed in a number of different ways in everyday speech. We speak of *creative persons* – 'Tom Stoppard is a creative play-wright' – *creative processes* –'Tom Stoppard thinks creatively' – and *creative products* – '*Arcadia* is a creative play'. Whereas traditionally the notion of creativity was associated primarily with the latter and was applied to great achievements and quality productions, the Romantic view emphasises the former two, seeing creativity in terms of the inner qualities of individuals connected with how they think.

Certain traits of personality, or cognitive attributes, are held to make certain individuals creative. Some theorists hold that some people simply are naturally more creative by virtue of such traits; others believe that everyone possesses such traits naturally to some extent and that they can be developed through training in creative ways of thinking or through protection from constraining external influences. In either case, it is supposed that we can identify creative individuals in terms of such traits. They think divergently, they are fluent in generating ideas, they are flexible in their thinking, they are spontaneous, they are unconventional, they are risk-takers – to name several commonly ascribed attributes. Such individuals are thought to be creative regardless of the specific area in which they are working. If they happen to be artists, then they will be creative artists; if they happen to be scientists, they will be creative scientists; if they are teachers, they will be creative teachers. Creative individuals are creative even if they are not working in a particular area – even if they never actually create anything. Being creative, then, is related not to what one has achieved but to the kind of person one is and the way one thinks.

The claim that individuals can be creative even if they never actually create anything rests on the assumption that those who do actually create works considered to be of value (Shakespeare, Einstein, *et al.*) accomplish this by engaging in a particular process of thought, a process which is essentially the same regardless of subject matter. Creative individuals are held to be those with the requisite cognitive and personality traits to excel at this process.

What are the characteristics of this creative process of thinking? How is it different from ordinary, non-creative thinking? Ordinary, non-creative thinking is believed to be convergent, taking place along established patterns, and confined within specific frameworks. It adheres to the logic and rules of the framework and is essentially selective, evaluating ideas according to prevailing standards. Ordinary thinking is also marked by rigidity and habit. Thus, students engaged in improvising a scene in the drama lesson will ordinarily choose a common subject and a conventional form – a television soap opera, for example – and will evaluate proposed ideas according to how well they conform to this conventional model. Because of this, a potentially innovative departure from naturalism may be rejected on the ground that it is not 'realistic'. Creative thinking, on the other hand, is thought to involve breaking out of such habitual ways of thinking. This cannot be accomplished by the use of logic, since the logic of the framework is what keeps one trapped. Instead, creative thinking involves leaps of imagination in which prevailing logic is defied and new connections are made between previously unrelated elements. Adherents to this view would argue that the plays which constitute the Theatre of the Absurd, for example, could not have been written by adhering to the logic of the prevailing framework of theatre conventions since logical plot structure was one of the defining characteristics of that framework. What must have been required for the creation of this innovative genre was a leap of imagination which *defied* logic.

It follows that irrational processes are held to play an important role in creative thinking since they loosen the hold of conventional logic and allow new, unanticipated connections to be made. Thus advocates of decontextualised theories of creativity stress the importance of chance, dreams, intuition and unconscious processes. Samuel Taylor Coleridge's account of the composing of the poem *Kubla Khan* in a dream is a classic example:

> The author continued for about three hours in a profound sleep, at least of the external senses, during which time he has the most vivid confidence, that he could not have composed less than from two to three hundred lines. On awakening he appeared to himself to have a distinct recollection of the whole, and taking his pen, ink, and paper, instantly and eagerly wrote down the lines.[2]

This emphasis on the intuitive and spontaneous has led to the creative process being seen as fundamentally generative and non-evaluative. It involves producing a large number of ideas without judging them, since our criteria of judgement would lead to the rejection of unusual, creative ideas. Judgement becomes an impediment to creativity. Students engaged in an improvisation will be more creative (so the argument goes) if they *withhold* their judgement of the ideas generated, and the more unjudged ideas they generate, the greater the likelihood of an authentically creative outcome.

The idea that creativity must involve a process which suspends judgement and defies logic contributes to a further assertion, namely that creative works are not simply continuations and extensions of relevant traditions, but rather exhibit a radical break with previous products and a discontinuity with these traditions. Thus the modes of operating which are useful within the conceptual framework of a particular tradition at a particular time cannot lead to innovation since such innovation necessarily involves violating the rules of the framework. Bertolt Brecht's well-known theatrical *Verfremdungseffekt*, for example, would be understood as a radical departure from 'that willing suspension of disbelief' coined by Coleridge a century earlier,[3] and so discontinuous with tradition.

Finally, because the creative process is considered to be, of necessity, free and uninhibited, involving the breaking of rules and established patterns, the conventions, skills and knowledge of particular traditions are regarded as constraining, locking one into the prevailing conceptual framework and inhibiting innovation. This drive towards decontextualisation has been very evident in drama education, where a curious dichotomy has been erected between 'drama' and 'theatre', with the former associated with spontaneous experience and expression and the latter with the techniques necessary to communicate with an audience. Educational value has been invested solely in the former, very much in keeping with the Romantic grounding of the drama-in-education philosophy. In the 1960s, Brian Way maintained that the provision of educational drama opportunities 'becomes possible only if we discard the limitations of theatrical conventions and consider drama as a quite different activity, calling upon different skills, different standards of judgement and entirely different results',[4] while by the 1980s we have the Canadian drama education theorist, Richard Courtney, citing with approval the views of his British colleagues, Peter Slade, Brian Way, Dorothy Heathcote and Gavin Bolton, who 'love theatre – but in its place, and that is not in the classroom'.[5] The craft skills of theatre are thus withheld from students on the grounds that they interfere with the spontaneity of the dramatic experience, bring into play the intellect rather than relying on intuition and focus on communication rather than creative expression.

In search of creative persons

So, is it actually reasonable to suppose that when we call someone creative, we are making reference to their capacity to create, irrespective of whether they actually have created anything, and that this capacity to create can be understood in terms of a particular set of cognitive and personality traits? It seems clear that when we call Shakespeare or Einstein creative, we are not referring to aspects of their personality or to how they think. We need know nothing about their personal attributes in order to make such a judgement. We call them creative because they created *Hamlet* and the theory of relativity. Our primary ascription of creativity is in virtue of *achievement*.

If this is the case, then the only way to make sense of the assertion that creativity resides in personal attributes is as an empirical claim, a claim that creative people – that is, people who come up with creative achievements – do, in fact, possess certain traits, and that these traits are causally related to creative achievement. The problem with this claim is that there is no unequivocal empirical evidence which clearly links any particular set of cognitive or personality traits with actual creative achievement.

This absence is not surprising given an understanding of what is involved in acts of creating and becomes quickly apparent if we focus on attempts to identify creative individuals. A standard test item used in 'creativity tests' is to have the subject generate as many uses as possible for a common item, such as a brick. The subject is rated on the number of uses generated (a measurement of fluency) and the novelty of the uses (a measurement of originality). There is no measure of quality. Generating a large number of unusual uses is taken to be an indication of creativity. There is no reason to believe, however, that scoring highly on such a test is in any way an indication of the capacity for creative achievement. The ability to generate large numbers of novel uses is irrelevant to many creative activities and would seem to have very little to do with the type of activity in which Shakespeare or Einstein engaged; we have no reason to expect that either would have scored highly on such tests. Shakespeare's creativity lay not in generating a large number of unusual words, but rather in coming up with appropriate words in specific contexts and juxtaposing and combining words to create desired effects. His creativity was connected more with making aesthetic judgements and choices than with randomly generating novel responses. Similarly, Einstein was not engaged in generating as many unusual theories as he could, and then choosing among them. Rather, he was creative in coming up with a theory which solved a scientific problem.

In view of the difficulty of linking creativity with cognitive abilities, investigators have tried to identify creative individuals by their personality traits. Such attempts have fared no better than the creativity tests. Some of the traits proposed as characterising the creative personality are independence of mind, non-conformity, tolerance of ambiguity, and low sociability. Yet there are just too many notable exceptions to this rule. Copernicus, for example, was an extremely timid individual who bowed to authority, and Darwin was a patient, dogged collector of details. Neither fits the proposed model of the creative personality, and yet the fact that each was creative cannot be denied. What such generalisations falsely assume is that all creative tasks are of a similar nature and that there will be one personality type who will be creative. Instead, it seems to be the case that as the nature of the creative activity varies from discipline to discipline, so too will the personality type likely to flourish there. Copernicus, with his reverence for authority, may well have been precisely the type of person required to perform the synthesis which resulted in the Copernican system, while Darwin's methodical nature probably aided him in making the painstaking compilation of data which led to his theory of evolution.[6]

The claim that creativity is primarily an attribute of persons rests on the belief that there is a specific process or way of thinking involved in all acts of creating, a kind of thinking which is generative, divergent, non-logical, rule-breaking and non-evaluative. This belief is difficult to sustain. There seems, rather, to be a variety of processes involved in creating and these include thinking which is convergent as well as divergent, logical as well as unusual, evaluative as well as generative, and rule-bound as well as rule-breaking. In fact, these kinds of thinking are not easily separated.

Making judgements

Let us look, for example, at the idea that creative thinking involves the suspension of judgement. I would argue that judgement is very much involved throughout the process of creating, that one evaluates all the time, and that, indeed, one *must*. The initial recognition of a problem as a problem, or identification of an area for exploration, is very much a product of judgement, as is the determining of a general direction for solution or way of proceeding. It is because one has expertise in an area and is immersed in its intricacies that one develops the judgement that makes it possible to see certain phenomena as in need of explanation or certain directions of exploration as viable. Moreover, even the realisation that a new approach is required or would be fruitful, and the resultant departure from established patterns, questioning of presuppositions or breaking of rules, is the result of judgements based on one's knowledge of the area and the stage reached in its exploration. And knowing where to look for solutions to problems – even what kinds of ideas would *count* as solutions – also requires judgement, as does knowing when one has reached a solution or when a work is completed.

In drama, a director developing a new interpretation of a play requires considerable judgement at every step of the interpretive process, from recognising the script's interesting possibilities, to judging the aptness of possible interpretations, to predicting the likely effect on an audience, to judging the feasibility of execution, to deciding on the particular form in which the interpretation will be manifested, to developing the interpretation in production. Thus, Ian McKellen's innovative 1992 interpretation of Shakespeare's *Richard III*, with its setting in a fictional, post-war, fascist England, could not have been a case of random novelty involving unconstrained generation. Rather, it must have arisen from his thorough understanding of the play's text and themes and incisive judgement regarding the evocative power with which those themes could be presented for contemporary audiences in the chosen setting.

If this view about the central role of judgement is correct, then the idea that creativity involves generating a large number of ideas without evaluating them is mistaken. One must judge even in the process of generating ideas, or the results would be chaos rather than creation. In his study of poets engaged in the act of composing, David Perkins found that the most highly-rated poets did not search through many alternative words, but usually considered only one or two options.[7] Perkins explains this phenomenon in terms of the way we do mental searches. Because we are able to search according to multiple criteria, we are able to go right to appropriate possibilities without generating exhaustive lists; we evaluate in the process of generating. And it seems to be the most highly skilled poets, the ones with the most highly developed poetic judgement, who are least in need of generating long lists of words. They can go right to the most effective possibilities. Perkins argues that there is a quality–quantity trade-off operating, where people can either come up with numerous solutions of lower quality or few solutions of higher quality, but that they have difficulty generating both quantity and quality. He claims, further, that the problem of uncreative solutions to problems does not stem from lack of fluency, as the decontextualised view suggests, but from insufficiently clear and high initial standards.

Another difficulty with the idea that creative thinking is very different from ordinary, rational thinking is that it misrepresents not only the thinking that goes on during creating, but ordinary thinking as well. Our usual way of thinking is not, in fact, all that rigid, habitual and convergent. Thinking always has a generative dimension; we do, in fact, overcome blocks to solve problems, go beyond the information we are given, fill in gaps, and think divergently every day. In addition, ordinary thinking does not generally take place within rigidly bounded and highly rule-governed frameworks. Rather, frameworks overlap, shift and have indefinite boundaries so that there is no need for positing an irrational leap to explain how we can cross or transcend existing structures. Such steps can be seen, rather, as a feature of a gradual, reasonable and not particularly unusual process of thinking. This account of the process of creating is substantiated by the research of both Perkins[8] and David Weisberg.[9] Weisberg found no evidence of divergent thinking, unconscious processes, or leaps of insight in his own empirical studies of individuals solving problems, in his analyses of the methods and products or creative 'geniuses', or in his examination of other empirical studies. Instead, the evidence he adduced seems to indicate that the thinking involved in creating is incremental in nature, involving a step by step procedure of modification of previous ideas based on increased information. Perkins' work led to similar conclusions. His studies of individuals engaged in creative endeavours as well as his analysis of the psychological literature demonstrate how ordinary thinking processes such as noticing, recognising, searching, remembering, and evaluating can, together, contribute to a creative result.

What these various arguments seem to point to is that the kind of thinking which is involved in creating and that which is considered normal are not of a fundamentally different kind. As I argue elsewhere, extraordinary means are not necessary in order to achieve extraordinary ends; it is the skill with which ordinary thinking processes are used and the purposes to which they are put which enable outstanding results to be achieved.[10] Crucially, what is special about creativity lies in *what* is achieved rather than in *how* it is achieved.

Knowledge, skills and planning

I have suggested that the idea that creativity involves thinking in a radically new way and breaking all the rules of the prevailing framework is based on the belief that creative achievement is characterised by a radical break with past traditions. But this assumption is also highly questionable. It may be more accurate to regard the originality of created works as lying on a continuum. At one end is originality which takes place within the constraints of the tradition; at the other lies originality which involves an alteration in some aspects of the constraints themselves. Even for products which are highly innovative, continuities and connections with the tradition are always in evidence. Innovations involve building on and attempting to deal with problems posed by the tradition. Thus, Brecht's *Verfremdungseffekt* was not a result of arbitrary novelty, but involved attempting to deal with a specifically dramatic problem, breaking down the kind of illusion characteristic of naturalistic theatre. Indeed, such continuities with the tradition *must* exist. There have to be some elements of the previous framework in light of which the innovation will have meaning and consequence. The significance of a created product must ultimately be judged against the background of existing traditions, both in terms of how the work conforms to and how it departs from these traditions, and in terms of how well it solves existing problems and opens up possibilities for new types of solutions and new directions for exploration. Ernst Kris makes this point well:

> We have long come to realise that art is not produced in an empty space, that no artist is independent of predecessors and models, that he no less than the scientist and the philosopher is part of a specific tradition and works in a structured area of problems. The degree of mastery within this framework and, at least in certain periods, the freedom to modify these stringencies are presumably part of the complex scale by which achievement is being measured.[11]

But the Romantic, decontextualised view of creativity sees creating as an essentially free activity. Thus it views the skills and knowledge of specific disciplines as potentially inhibiting to creativity because they lock one into rigid, habitual modes of operation and prevent one from thinking in new ways. This thesis is based on a view of creativity as some entity or quality existing within the individual which needs to be let out or freed, as Brian Way makes clear in his argument for drama in education:

> all people are fundamentally creative; the arts are an outlet for this creativity if – and only if – they are viewed from the standpoint of the doer and from that person's personal level of readiness and experience, no matter how primitive this level may be.[12]

What is necessary in order to foster creativity, Way and others would argue, is free expression. Any external influence hampers spontaneity of expression and constitutes an imposition from without rather than a liberation of what is within.[13] There is some plausibility in Way's statement if it is meant simply to indicate that everyone has some capacity to engage at some level in activities which involve creating. But we usually mean more by creativity than simply engaging in creative activities, since we distinguish the products of these activities by their creative value. Not all creations, that is, are equally creative.

So, what reasons would there be for arguing that knowledge and skills are inhibiting to creativity? One reason is the belief that creativity is necessarily spontaneous and unplanned and that knowledge and technique are relevant only where there is advanced planning. A student is being creative if reacting spontaneously, whereas if she has planned how to achieve a certain effect using skills and knowledge the outcome is no longer spontaneous and therefore not creative. The substance of this belief is that creativity necessarily involves spontaneity, imagination and the generation of novelty, but that these are a logical impossibility if the end is conceived beforehand. The problem with such a view is that it becomes difficult, if not impossible, to explain how control is exercised in the creation of a work. If there can be no foreknowledge of ends, on what basis are critical judgements made as a work proceeds? How could a theatre director, for example, make the myriad decisions required at every step of the rehearsal process? A more plausible account suggests that there is a considerable variety of starting points from which a work may begin and that the creative process cannot be characterised in terms of any lack of foreknowledge. The critical control which is exercised in the process of creating a work of art, for example, is the product of a variety of factors, one of which is surely the skill of the artist.

Another reason that skills in particular are considered to be inhibiting to creativity is that they are regarded simply as *habits*, an assumption based on the idea that skills, once learned, become automatic, operating below the level of conscious awareness, and fixing pre-determined ways of seeing and behaving. It follows that if students in drama are taught skills of dramatic representation or presentation, they will be locked into the ways of presenting or representing implied by these principles or techniques and this will interfere with the spontaneity and creativeness of their dramatic responses. The portrayal of skills as habits is not, however, accurate. While a habit involves the performance of an action blindly, without thought, skill involves care, vigilance and criticism. A skilled dramatic performance is one which is not purely automatic and totally inflexible but is able to adjust to changing circumstances. There are, of course, certain habitual elements which constitute a part of most skills, but skills go beyond this to include judgement as well. A painter is skilful not only in terms of the brush strokes he or she employs, but also in terms of how those brushstrokes are used in a specific painting – how the painter makes adjustments according to the way the work is progressing. Similarly, a pianist's skill goes beyond technical proficiency at the keyboard to involve judgements about tempo or volume. And the skill of the actor involves not only proficiency at movement on stage or voice projection, but also the ability to understand a character, to create a believable presence on stage, and to find concrete symbols for abstract ideas and emotions. The example of an experienced driver manipulating her vehicle through traffic illustrates the falsity of assuming that, because we are not consciously aware of our skills as we practise them, control cannot be exercised. The driver makes adjustments according to the changing traffic conditions and such adjustments are possible precisely because of the skills of the driver.

Many of the skills manifested in the arts exemplify this type of implicit knowledge. As an artist becomes increasingly proficient, both technical expertise and critical judgement become assimilated into physical responses. Moreover, aspects of critical skills can be improved with practice, and it is proficiency in certain more fundamental aspects of a skill that allows students in the arts to go on to higher levels of achievement. If expression must necessarily be in a medium, then control of the medium is a prerequisite for expression. This liberating possibility of skills is certainly evident in drama, where control of the voice and body is a prerequisite for dramatic expression and greater control enhances the possibility for more subtle and refined expression. Such skills need not interfere with the authenticity of the actor's response since they quickly become internalised, freeing him or her to concentrate on the interaction. Paradoxically, it is this repertoire of assimilated skills which allows an actor to react with spontaneity; the larger the repertoire, the greater the possibility for spontaneous responses.

Perhaps the long-standing suspicion of skills in drama education rests on a concern that any teaching of technique will amount to the inculcation of a set of rules or dead conventions; by setting up certain stereotypical gestures as the correct way to portray an emotion, for example, or by persuading students that a guiding principle, such as 'never turn your back to an audience', is an inviolable maxim. Certainly there are grounds for criticising the performance clichés of the Speech and Drama movement against which many early advocates of spontaneous dramatic self-expression were reacting but this approach is not synonymous with the teaching of skills. In fact, an actor who can portray sadness only through some learned conventional gesture is not very skilful. Rather educational effort should be directed to helping actors to draw on their own experience, observation and knowledge as well as technique in order to find fresh ways of representing and portraying.

Constraint and imagination

Perhaps the most fundamental problem with the proposition that skills and knowledge inhibit creativity is that it assumes that creativity implies total freedom and fails to accept that it is possible to be creative within constraints. The truth is that all artistic creation takes place within constraints of some sort. The majority of artists are not radical innovators of form but rather work within the limits of technique inherent in a particular style.

In drama, creativity is not therefore of necessity confined to spontaneous improvisation but is possible in all aspects of students' dramatic work. The act of playwriting, for example, even when it does not involve the creation of a new genre, is not a mechanical process. It involves the creation of a playscript which portrays images of human experience and visions of human possibility crafted in such a way that they can be brought to life through production. And some plays do this in a highly creative manner, revealing new insights, uniquely touching our sensibilities, or crystallising ideas or feelings in novel ways.

Directing a play is also an arena for students' creative achievement. Because a script is usually pre-determined and fixed, there are constraints upon the creating from the outset. Nonetheless, there is considerable leeway in how the script is brought to life on stage, and this provides possibilities for originality and freshness. Although a script may be seen as a blueprint for a theatrical production, within the confines of what is actually presented in the script there is vast scope for interpretation.[14] The interpretation of the characters, both overall and at any particular moment, and decisions about the message of the play and the means of conveying it, rest ultimately on the judgement of the director. In the theatre, a particular production may differ radically in interpretation from past productions of the same play; if innovative treatment creates a fresh vision, then the new production would be considered very creative. But even in productions where a play is treated in what is generally agreed to be a conventional way there will still be unique interpretations guiding elements of what transpires. There may be a striking portrayal, an incisive interaction, a moment of action or stillness which conveys a fresh perception. If the script is animated in a manner which enhances its dramatic values and brings original insights to the play, then such productions will also be considered creative.

Similarly, there is considerable scope for creativity for actors working with scripts. Many of those in drama education who have espoused Peter Slade's disparaging view of theatre as 'a bubble on the froth of civilisation',[15] have come to see acting for an audience as a kind of purely technical signalling, failing to recognise that acting, like playwriting and directing, may be more and less creative. Indeed, a distinction is often drawn between acting purely technically and acting in an imaginative manner, where the former refers to a performance which is superficial, reliant on a repertoire of conventional gestures and responses, lacking in depth, genuine feeling and real insight into the character portrayed, while the latter involves the creation of a unique and believable character with a depth of feeling and real understanding. It is often pointed out that an actor may be technically proficient in terms of skills of presentation and performance but yet lack these other qualities.

Imagination, then, is clearly a key aspect of creativity. Some would say that it is creativity's most important feature. While conceding that skill is not necessarily inhibiting to creativity, an objector to my line of thinking here might still claim that imagination is more central to creativity in that it transcends skill – someone can be skilful without being creative if they are not imaginative. I would argue, however, that imagination and skill are closely interconnected. There is imagination manifested in the execution of skill and skill involved in the development of an imaginative vision.

This point can be demonstrated with respect to acting. The contrast between acting purely technically and acting with imagination is based on a narrow sense of the term 'technique'. If technique is limited to movement on stage, control of the voice and body, projection and similar proficiencies, then the ability to act imaginatively and effectively must be viewed as something more. Yet surely the ability to understand a character and to create a believable presence on stage is also part of the actor's skill. Such a characterisation comes not purely from a pre-existing abstract vision, but rather from the actor working with the script, the director and the other actors and developing the characterisation through technical abilities and acting skills. Once this is recognised, we can see that imagination and skill are not easily separated. The same holds true in the case of directing. We expect the imaginative element of directing to be reflected in the interpretation which is embodied in the production. I have suggested that this interpretation is very much a product of the director's skill. He or she must bring out the dramatic values inherent in the script and doing so is largely a matter of solving the problems which the script presents. What emerges in the actual production as the director's imaginative vision is not an arbitrary flight of fantasy, but a carefully worked through entity based on work with the script and the actors combined with a sound knowledge of dramatic principles.

The situation is parallel in the case of playwriting. We might want to connect the imagination reflected in a play with the insight into humanity which is expressed – with the relationships, the emotion, the vision. Yet this vision is expressed in the dialogue of the characters, in the choice in words and in what is said and not said; in the stage movement indicated and envisaged; in the setting suggested; in the dramatic structure created. It would be misleading to think of the imagination of the playwright in terms of some abstract, decontextualised vision which can then simply be expressed by means of the playwright's skilled use of language and dramatic techniques. Rather, the former is developed through the latter. The vision is a dramatic vision, and the imagination of the playwright is a dramatic imagination.

The preceding arguments are clearly applicable to creativity which remains within the rules of the prevailing form. But it might be argued that although skill may not hamper creativity of this sort, it will be an impediment to innovation which involves breaking some of the rules. Such fears are unfounded. On the contrary, it is only an understanding of the rules and conventions, of the reasons for them and of what is at issue in complying with them which enables an artist to know when to violate these rules. A novice director may inadvertently block an actor with her back to the audience, thus losing her lines upstage; an experienced director, on the other hand, well aware of the rules of stage movement and the reasons for the general injunction against turning one's back to an audience, may choose to defy this rule in order to achieve a particularly startling effect of focus. Similarly, skills and knowledge in no way inhibit radical innovation in the sense of going beyond established frameworks. Many great artists have done precisely this, and the majority have not been artistic innocents, unsullied by the skills of a prevailing style, but have been masters of these skills. It is, in fact, this mastery which puts the artist in a position to know when the techniques will no longer suffice to express a new insight or point of view, to know when the possibilities of the present form are exhausted. New ground is broken through critical judgement, but this judgement is itself based upon a repertoire of acquired and assimilated skills and knowledge.

Culture and tradition

Peter Abbs has reminded us that our creative activity takes place, not in a private world of self-absorption, but in a cultural context of public symbols, and that it depends on these for its possibility and its continuance:

> As soon as we sing, make stories, narratives, dance, paint, we not only express and satisfy bodily rhythms we also enter into and depend upon what is symbolically available, on what has been done by previous practitioners and on how much has been effectively transmitted. Art comes out of Art, as Mathematics comes out of Mathematics. . . . The development of the sensory mode as a means of apprehending the nature of human experience depends upon the availability and range of these artistic grammars.[16]

As a consequence, Abbs recommends that as arts educators we should be introducing students to these grammars, to the tools, techniques and traditions of the various art forms. 'The arts thrive best', he suggests, 'not in private cul-de-sacs but at the busy cross-roads of symbolic life'.[17]

Reference to tradition may conjure up images of repressive and stultifying constraints on innovation in the minds of those committed to spontaneous free expression, but this is to misunderstand the nature of traditions. The kinds of traditions of enquiry and practice at issue here are not static, monolithic collections of facts, artefacts and procedures, but multiple, dynamic and evolving. Even a radical innovator like Igor Stravinsky

(1947) acknowledges the importance of tradition, which he describes as 'a living force that animates and informs the present'.

> Far from implying the repetition of what has been, tradition presupposes the reality of what endures. It appears as an heirloom, a heritage that one receives on condition of making it bear fruit before passing it on to one's descendants.[18]

Traditions evolve continually, and this change grows out of the attempt to deal with the problems inherent in a tradition as well as in response to various influences in society and culture. Truly creative innovation – change, that is, which is effective, useful, and significant – is not a product of arbitrary novelty, of uninformed intuition, but emerges out of a profound understanding of the nature of the tradition and of its principles. This point is expressed eloquently by Israel Scheffler:

> We need not pretend that these principles of ours are immutable or innate. It is enough that they are what we ourselves acknowledge, that they are the best we know, and that we are prepared to improve them should the need and occasion arise. Such improvement is possible, however, only if we succeed in passing on, too, the multiple live traditions in which they are embodied, and in which a sense of their history, spirit, and direction may be discerned.[19]

I have tried to demonstrate in my argument here that the Romantic account of creativity implicit in many drama education practices is highly problematic. Creativity is not an entity existing within individual psyches which needs to be liberated and protected from the stultifying influences of culture, but rather has to do with quality production taking place within cultural forms and traditions. In order to be creative, students require the resources which will enable them to engage knowledgeably and skilfully with these traditions. In the case of drama, this means acquiring the skills and knowledge of dramatic art as well as an understanding of the multiple and diverse dramatic traditions past and present which are the embodiment of creative achievement. Such traditions have within them tensions and contradictions as well as the mechanisms for criticism which make evolution possible. Critical judgement is not inhibiting to creativity but central to it.

Notes

1 For an account of drama education's roots in Romantic naturalism, see D. Hornbrook (1989 [1998]) *Education and Dramatic Art*, 2nd edn, London: Routledge, Chapter 1.
2 S.T. Coleridge (1816), quoted in J. Beer (ed.) *Samuel Taylor Coleridge: Poems*, London: J.M. Dent, p.163.

49

3 In S.T. Coleridge (1817) *Biographia Literaria*, ed. G. Watson, London: J.M. Dent, 1975, p.169.
4 B.Way (1967) *Development through Drama*, London: Longman, p.6.
5 R.Courtney (1980) *The Dramatic Curriculum*, New York: Drama Book Specialists, p.viii.
6 Isaac Newton once claimed that his main advantage was the power of patient thought.
7 D. Perkins (1981) *The Mind's Best Work*, Cambridge, MA: Harvard University Press.
8 Ibid.
9 R. Weisberg (1986) *Creativity: Genius and Other Myths*, New York: W.H. Freeman.
10 See S. Bailin (1994) *Achieving Extraordinary Ends: An Essay on Creativity*, Norwood, NJ: Ablex, p.12.
11 E. Kris (1952) *Psychoanalytic Explorations*, New York: International Universities Press, p.21.
12 B. Way (1967) *Development through Drama*, London: Longman, p.3.
13 For a classic account of this position, see R.W. Witkin (1974) *The Intelligence of Feeling*, London: Heinemann.
14 As Andy Kempe points out in Chapter 6.
15 P. Slade (1954) *Child Drama*, London: University of London Press, p.337: 'Child Drama is a part of real life. . . . It is quite different from any conception of theatre, which is a small – though attractive – bubble on the froth of civilisation'.
16 P. Abbs (1989) 'Aesthetic education: an opening manifesto', *The Symbolic Order*, London: Falmer Press, pp.7–8.
17 Ibid., p.81.
18 I. Stravinsky (1947) *Poetics of Music*, New York: Vintage Books, pp.58–9.
19 I. Scheffler (1967) 'Philosophical models of teaching', in R. S. Peters (ed.) *The Concept of Education*, London: Routledge & Kegan Paul, p.124.

4

CRAFTING DRAMAS

David Hornbrook

An arts entitlement

For teachers of art and music in schools, the idea that students should make progress in their subjects – get *better* at them – is uncontroversial. It is true that few art teachers these days would want to mark their students' drawings out of ten, as was once common practice, and I am sure that most music teachers would see an individual student's climb through instrumental grade examinations as marginal to the business of music education. Nevertheless, and while acknowledging all the problems of assessment in the arts, arts teachers are no different from other teachers in that they want all their students to achieve their full potential. So, while progress in the arts may not be linear in the same way as it might be said to be in mathematics, it is accepted that the paintings produced by eleven year olds should show some development from those originating in the nursery class and that they should be able to sing more consistently in tune and with a more subtle sense of rhythm than when they were younger.

The 1982 Calouste Gulbenkian Foundation report of an enquiry into the arts in schools in the UK, *The Arts in Schools*, called for 'forms of evaluation and assessment which are compatible with the different forms of work which go on in schools',[1] and firmly endorsed the principle that schools were no less accountable for students' progress in the arts than for their attainment in other areas of the curriculum:

> The basic demands from parents and employers are reasonable enough. They are for a) adequate teaching of certain skills, b) continuing improvements in the general standard of educational attainment, c) adequate information to be made available about pupils' actual achievements and personal potential.[2]

These are demands that, in my view, the students themselves would be equally reasonable in making.

It was the introduction of a National Curriculum for England and Wales in 1988, making art and music compulsory, which helped to focus these two, suddenly privileged, arts subjects on the whole question of progression and assessment. Myopic though the new curriculum was in conception, and however ineptly introduced, by the end of its first decade frameworks for the teaching and assessment of art and music in schools were in place which had been widely consulted upon and which were broadly acceptable to teachers in the field.

For all its creaky archaism, the National Curriculum meant that for the first time students had an *entitlement* to an education in the arts – or at least, in some of them. The government's 1995 revised Order for Art, for example, laid down that eleven to fourteen year olds should be learning in school the creative and imaginative skills needed 'to express ideas and feelings; record observations; design and make images and artefacts'. To help them develop 'visual literacy' they had the right to be taught 'the different ways in which ideas, feelings and meanings are communicated in visual form' and introduced to artists from 'a variety of cultures' working in 'a variety of genres and styles'.[3] In music, the same students could expect to be 'performing, composing, listening and appraising' in a way which would help them to grasp the development of musical ideas and recognise and use the basic elements of music; teachers were to introduce students to music of all kinds, including that 'from cultures across the world'.[4] Assessment in art and music was organised around exemplification material gathered from a very wide range of sources suggesting the sort of work that might be expected of the majority of students in a particular age group. The primary level art portfolio produced in 1997 shows that seven year olds are capable of handling most familiar art techniques – drawing, painting, printmaking, sculpture, portraiture – and examples of infant artwork include a fabric design based upon a study of African textiles, computer generated portraits and designs inspired by David Hockney and Piet Mondrian.[5]

Examining self-expression

Drama has been more reluctant than other arts subjects to embrace a conception of progress and attainment. Many prominent voices in drama education in the 1980s and 90s inherited a deep mistrust of the idea that students might need to develop certain skills to practise the arts and that these might be identified, taught and learned. For many years there had been a profound antipathy in some quarters to what were disparagingly referred to as 'theatre skills'.[6] For these reasons, drama's exclusion from the 1988 National Curriculum produced surprisingly mixed feelings; a sense of grievance was offset by one of relief. Marginalised perhaps, but at least drama would now be left alone to pursue its own idiosyncratic purposes away from the spotlight of publicly understood and nationally audited arrangements about what students should be able to do, know and understand.

The reasons for this aversion to the teaching of theatre skills are easy to trace. Early proponents of drama in schools had explicitly rejected the idea that the new activity was anything to do with theatre training or academic knowledge. In the bright, concrete and glass, post-war world of education, it was understood that drama teachers were concerned, not with the practices of the theatre, but with drama as a tool for social and personal development. This new sort of drama was not to be confused with the stuffy antics of amateur dramatics or the old Speech and Drama movement with its choral-speaking medals and elocution examinations. Forty years on, the wedge Peter Slade drove between the professional world of the theatre and his freely expressive classroom drama in the 1950s was, for some practitioners at least, still firmly in place:

> *Theatre* necessarily takes children towards learning the skills of theatre performance. By skills I mean voice production, the use of stage space, learning lines, lighting, prop making, design, acting and so on. *Drama*, on the other hand, dispenses largely or completely with this body of knowledge in favour of the affective exploration of the children's experience of the world.[7]

For all this, the fledgling discipline was not long able to avoid the demands of accountability made by the education system upon which its legitimacy was, irksomely, dependent. Pressure for some kind of agreement about what students were actually expected to learn in drama came in the 1960s with the introduction in England and Wales of the Certificate of Secondary Education (CSE).[8] Understandably anxious to gain a foothold on an examination which gave their subject much-needed status, the first drama syllabuses devised by teachers began to emerge. But free expression is difficult to assess and it is not immediately obvious how a student might get better at the 'affective exploration of the world' or what criteria a teacher would use to discern different degrees of personal development. The dilemma facing teachers and examination boards was well put in a 1974 Schools Council report on examinations in drama, which took Slade's distinction between 'drama' and 'theatre' as given:

> To examine or assess drama would imply the imposition of a structure which is not necessarily obvious or desirable. An examination syllabus moves towards an end product, whereas drama is not concerned with such a result. . . . Drama lacks an accepted or easily identifiable body of knowledge which is the mainstay of examination syllabuses in most subjects.[9]

More often than not, attempts to resolve this conundrum involved something of a sleight of hand. Syllabuses were produced in which the high-minded social and developmental aspirations proclaimed in introductory paragraphs were simply ignored when it came to the question of assessing outcomes. Hence, aims like, 'The general development of self-awareness and sensitivity . . . which should create self-confidence and tolerance and allow pupils to become useful members of society', or, 'To heighten the students' perception and awareness of themselves and to become more sensitive to the needs of other people',[10] could be found supporting syllabuses which required the study of twenty-two playwrights.

Out of this muddle a pattern began to take shape in which improvisation became the dominant form. In the 1970s, one CSE examination board produced a syllabus, praised by a commentator for being 'about the boldest and least prescriptive and least theatre-biased scheme'[11] he had yet seen, allocating eighty per cent of the marks to improvisation. By the time the General Certificate of Secondary Education (GCSE)[12] replaced the CSE in 1986, the former heavy weighting towards topics like 'the actor through the ages' had disappeared. The new drama syllabuses, some now depending entirely upon improvisation for assessment purposes, more accurately reflected their broad, personal and social aims, such as 'good group cooperation' (an aim which, at one time, was common to them all).[13] Indeed, by the end of the 1980s, the pendulum had swung so far away from theatre skills and knowledge that the words 'play' (as in 'a play'), 'actor' and 'theatre' were banished altogether from some syllabuses.[14] It is difficult to imagine such extraordinary linguistic contortions being thought either desirable or possible in any other art form.

Meanwhile, the first General Certificate of Education (GCE) advanced level examination in drama for eighteen year olds had been introduced – significantly entitled 'Theatre Studies' – and, by the early 1980s, was being taught increasingly widely.[15] Access to the pleasures of sixth-form teaching was now a possibility. Many drama teachers, however, working with students of this age for the first time, had now to find ways of dealing with exactly that 'accepted or easily identifiable body of knowledge' that had been so energetically disowned only a decade before. Aspects of the subject such as stage design, Jacobean Theatre and the theories of Antonin Artaud had to be taught at levels consistent with that required for university entrance. For many, possibly most, of these A-level pioneers, it is doubtful that their training in post-Sladian drama teaching methodologies – 'teacher-in-role', 'mantle of the expert', and so on – had prepared them very thoroughly for these fresh challenges.

Despite this reality, the antipathy towards skills and knowledge continued to make itself felt. In 1993, the chair of the British drama teachers' national association, National Drama, praised teachers for their examination achievements (including those in Theatre Studies) but still saw no contradiction in simultaneously warning of the danger of redefining drama 'as a body of knowledge made up of theatre crafts, genres and skills'.[16] So, practically speaking, drama teachers were now faced with the dilemma of trying to hold and reconcile two apparently incompatible views of drama. On the one hand were the principle of non-intervention in students' 'affective exploration' of their own ideas and the belief that there really was no body of knowledge and skills that could be identified with their subject: on the other, a growing sense that the Theatre Studies syllabus was exposing how poorly students had been prepared for its demands by the improvisation-dominated drama curriculum in lower years. One symptom of this tension was a tendency, in the planning of lessons and projects, to mix up specific aspects of drama with general topics or issues. In one comprehensive school I visited in the early 1990s, for example, the scheme of work for drama showed pupils doing 'bullying' in the winter term and 'mime' in the spring. Meanwhile, in lessons themselves, 'affective exploration' was sometimes extended quite beyond its capacity to promote learning. Another school revealed a Theatre Studies class reading through a scene from *The Cherry Orchard* and then being asked to divide into groups to discuss ideas for lighting it. The outcomes were disappointing, not only because the students had no access to any stage lights, but also because they had been *taught* nothing about how theatre lighting achieves its effects.

But the result of attempts to square this epistemological circle is probably nowhere better illustrated than at the very core of the drama lesson itself, in that ubiquitous product traditionally the focus for assessment in drama: the devised improvisation. Ever since Peter Slade first asked children to 'find a space', students in drama classrooms all over the world have been asked to get into small groups and improvise dramas. The devised improvisation remains overwhelmingly the predominant *modus operandi* of the drama class: satisfying as it does so many of the field's precepts, it has become, over the years, simply the natural way of doing things. Yet for all its popularity, the devised improvisation, seen in the context of world drama, is a very unusual form indeed. Having no writer, no script, no director, no stage manager (everyone, in theory, does everything), it is uniquely undifferentiated in its production. Then, although it is also likely to be *about* something in a big way – racism, homelessness, drugs (the result of the influence of the 'issue' in classroom drama), it will also, paradoxically, for all the gravity of its subject matter, be short – usually no more than twenty minutes or so at the most and often considerably less. And finally, and most significantly for my argument here, it may be successfully created by a group of students who have never done drama before or who have developed no particular theatrical skills. It cannot be said that these conditions remotely characterise theatre production anywhere else.

The skills and knowledge of drama

If we extract the wedge that Peter Slade so unhelpfully drove between the kind of drama that goes on in classrooms and that which happens in theatres and on television, then it immediately becomes clear that drama, like art and music, *does*, of course, have its own 'body of knowledge made up of theatre crafts, genres and skills', and that this knowledge is as relevant and applicable, at an appropriate level, to education in the primary school as it is to sixth-formers. Once this unity is accepted, then it is evident that the main outcomes of the drama lesson must relate to progress in the field of drama (as opposed to the understanding of social or moral issues) and that the principles of developmental self-expression cannot be applied to any form of drama much beyond spontaneous improvisation or role-play. Students will not simply *intuit* how to light a performance, any more than they are likely to perform well without being taught at least the rudiments of acting or direct without studying the way in which stage pictures are organised. The limitations of the devised improvisation as a vehicle for the expression of what students can achieve then become manifestly apparent. It is a form which rarely stretches able performers and effectively excludes those whose strengths lie in less public, but equally valid, aspects of the subject of drama, such as playwriting or design.[17]

Good drama teachers are natural egalitarians and are often justly proud of the success they have with students who fail elsewhere; accepting the place of skills means also accepting that some students will inevitably become more adept at them than others. But, putting his case for differentiation in arts education, Ken Robinson reminds us that 'individuals have different capacities in different modes of practice and understanding'.[18] My point is that this important commitment to equality of opportunity is best achieved by a broad curriculum which acknowledges the many *diverse* ways students can achieve in drama rather than by confining everyone to a few practices with which the majority seem comfortable.[19] We should not forget that some students do not find the small, undifferentiated group a stimulating format for their creativity. The solitary student who has no particular interest in, or ability at, improvisation – the one whom in the 1970s, I remember, we saw as such a problem and were always trying to 'get involved' – will not flourish in a drama curriculum where spontaneity and camaraderie are valued above all other attributes. Yet it is sometimes just those students who have the independence of mind to be genuinely original and creative – given a suitable context. The skills and knowledge of a good drama curriculum must be sufficiently broad for *all* students to achieve their potential, in the same way as, in art, the potter and the sculptor must be allowed to flourish as well as the painter.

But also, if students' experience of drama in schools is to constitute a genuine entitlement, then it is difficult to argue that the portfolio of skills and knowledge they acquire should be any less wide-ranging than that offered in art and music. That portfolio must certainly be premised upon an understanding that drama is a worldwide phenomenon, and in this respect its compilers might do worse than beginning by adapting a statement or two from the Order for Art quoted at the beginning of this chapter. As part of their entitlement, students in drama should be introduced, shall we say, 'to the work of theatre practitioners from a variety of cultures working in a variety of genres and styles'. It is difficult to overestimate the challenge presented by such a simple statement to traditional ways of doing things in drama classrooms from which theatre skills have been exiled.

When all these arguments have been made there will still be some for whom skill is simply felt to be a low-order human activity; in drama education's long-standing antipathy towards theatre skills it is difficult not to sense just a whiff of aesthetic snobbery. Skills can be regarded as mechanistic and uncreative, low status when set against the opportunities offered for individual self-expression by the 'creative' arts. Thus, when Malcolm Ross worries that the UK National Curriculum may be sacrificing the 'aesthetic' to the 'merely technical',[20] he is unwittingly subscribing to the legacy of Romanticism which places the sensibility of the gentleman artist on a rather higher plane than that of the common technician. As Raymond Williams points out, this is an account of art in which,

> 'Art' is a kind of production which has to be seen as separate from the dominant bourgeois productive norm: the making of commodities. It has then, in fantasy, to be separated from 'production' altogether; described by the new term 'creation'; distinguished from its own material processes.[21]

I agree with Sharon Bailin that far from being an intrusive solecism, skill is actually essential to the practice and understanding of any art form.[22] The child who has not learned to hold a brush, or what effects can be achieved by different consistencies of paint, is unlikely to be able to fulfil her creative potential as a painter. The danger of taking a position which denies this fairly obvious truth is that we end up by according aesthetic value to products like paintings or dramas solely on the basis that they have been produced by children. Categories such as Franz Cizek's 'Child Art'[23] or Slade's 'Child Drama', derived as they are from psychotherapeutic theories of art, show us child-centredness straining the very language we use to the limits of intelligibility. Four year old Sophie's pastel scribbles displayed so proudly on the fridge door are valuable not because they are art but because Sophie has produced them. An important, but too often forgotten, category distinction.

Nevertheless, it has to be acknowledged that in some ways skill is a limiting concept, too easily caricatured as merely a human motor response learned and reproduced without thought or feeling. And it does seems that when we speak of an actor's ability to hold an audience's attention with a gesture or a measured silence we are talking about expertise of a different order to that same actor's skill in, say, reversing into the theatre car park. While certain skills are certainly indispensable to the practice of the arts, we need a broader and more sophisticated concept to encapsulate what we assimilate as we learn how to practise an art form.

Understanding craft

I want to show that many of the prejudices and misconceptions about the teaching of theatre skills dissolve away if we understand skill as only one element of a neglected, but rather more subtle, concept of *craft*. Skill is a component of craft but by no means synonymous with it.

The successful exercise of a skill requires that I must first have absorbed certain, specialised ways of doing things to such an extent that I am not perpetually conscious of them and then that I possess the dexterity and ingenuity to apply those ways of doing things in different contexts or to different objects. The actor negotiating the car park will not be aware of, or planning for, every movement of the clutch or the accelerator. These routines, seemingly so daunting to the learner, must become automatic, so that the motorist is free to concentrate on the millions of tiny judgements that have to be made in the process of navigating the car from one place to another. I cannot call myself a skilled driver unless both these components are in place – the learned, mechanical routine and the adroitness and judgement needed to manoeuvre. This simple combination applies to all skills. If I choose to put up some shelves in my house, I will certainly need to be able to use a screwdriver and an electric drill, but I will also have to make judgements about the size of the wood, the space available, and so on. Similarly, in the theatre, the actor who remains always conscious of the movement of the rib cage at every breath will be as seriously inhibited as the driver who has continuously to bring to mind the clutch-gears-clutch sequence. Breath control must be learned, must become an automatic element of the actor's technique, so that he or she is free to deploy the deftness and imagination necessary to carry the interpretation of the part.

Skill, then, is certainly essential to craft, but craft has at least two additional identifying characteristics. The first of these is the close relationship that is normally understood to exist between craft and *art*. While craft is different from art, it nevertheless shares many of the same features, so that when we use the word 'craft' we are somehow *suggesting* the arts in a way which the use of 'skill' does not. When we stare up at the feather-like stonework of the roofs of the great European cathedrals, we may have to be reminded that such sublimity was created, not by the school of Michelangelo, but by generations of nameless craftspeople. To speak of them as skilled is accurate but hardly sufficient. Inspired by these unsung medieval builders and designers, the nineteenth-century Arts and Crafts Movement deliberately set out to blur the distinction between the artist and the artisan by restoring an aesthetic dimension to manufacture. Designer William Morris, architect Philip Webb and painters Ford Madox Brown and Edward Burne-Jones, founded a movement aimed to revitalise the mediocre workmanship of the industrial revolution with a range of characteristic hand-made jewellery, furniture, textiles and wall coverings.[24] Ever since then, arts and crafts have been unself-consciously married in the language.

It is, of course, quite possible to be a fine craftsperson without being an artist. Boat builders in the West Indies, for example, who cut down trees and shape fishing boats from them on the beach in a tradition handed down through generations are undoubtedly practising a craft, but what they produce – that is, fishing boats of a fairly rudimentary kind – cannot meaningfully be said to be art. Certainly, they themselves would be mystified if it were to be suggested that examples of their work should be exhibited in galleries or that their enterprise should qualify for arts funding, to pick two prominent ways in which our culture endorses what it regards as of artistic worth. According to R.G. Collingwood, a key difference between art and craft is in the relationship between ends and means.

> A craftsman knows what he wants to make before he makes it. This foreknowledge is absolutely indispensable to craft: if something, for example stainless steel, is made without such foreknowledge, the making of it is not a case of craft but an accident. Moreover, this foreknowledge is not vague but precise. If a person sets out to make a table, but conceives the table only vaguely, as somewhere between two by four feet and three by six, and between two and three feet high, and so forth, he is no craftsman.[25]

It is true that artists also work within constraints. Composers are required to score for pre-determined numbers of instruments, playwrights notate for particular companies of actors with specified audiences in mind. Hans Holbein would have been in trouble if he had strayed very much from sixteenth-century conventions as he worked on his portrait of the young Henry VIII (reminding us, *pace* Williams, of the mistake of assuming artistic production to be superior to the demands of patronage). Nevertheless, as they embark upon their work, the musician, playwright or portrait painter will be likely to have rather less idea of where the creative journey will lead them than the maker of tables. It is difficult to imagine Byron writing *Childe Harold's Pilgrimage* on the basis of an agreed number of stanzas, or to believe that Caryl Churchill had a minutely detailed blueprint for *Top Girls* in her head before setting pen to paper. Yet the Bahamian boat builders cannot afford to leave the outcome of their labours to chance. If they are to survive, they must continue to produce boats which perform effectively in the short seas of the Great Bahama Bank.

The third characteristic of craft, which again makes it a more seasoned concept than skill, is the sense it implies of belonging, of membership, apprenticeship, community, continuity; the *Oxford English Dictionary* reminds us that a craft may also be 'a trade's union, guild or company'. Craft is not something done in isolation. You may acquire the technique necessary to knock up a dinghy from a kit but that hardly qualifies you as a shipwright. Like the Bahamian boat builders, you learn your craft from those who have practised it before you and when you are sufficiently accomplished you join their company. You become *identified* with the craft so that you may, without embarrassment, call yourself an architect, a silversmith, a writer, a painter, a playwright, a musician. And none of these require you to be an artist, although you may also be that.

It will be argued that arts educators are not in the business of turning out artists and drama teachers in school are not in the business of producing Equity members. Yet the fact that few students will ever become professional mathematicians is clearly not a reason for denying them the opportunity to practise the craft of mathematics at levels of complexity beyond the simple skills of addition and subtraction. In the arts, it is true that few of those we teach will become musicians or dancers so that they can claim membership in the sense I have already described. Few, that is, will enter apprenticeship, let alone become master craftspeople. However, in the context of education, membership in the broader sense is of some importance. For if we are doing anything as arts educators we are engaged in the process of acculturation; we are inducting those we teach into the culture in which they live. Providing the opportunity for pupils to practise the craft at levels commensurate with their age and ability is part of their induction into membership of the culture. Bangladeshi students, for example, might learn both the traditional Bengali *jatra* form but also the way it was incorporated into dramas on the theme of the struggle for independence in the 1960s. Culture is always a complex web of past and present, local and international.

The practice of a craft, then, is distinguished by *skill, artistic potential* and *membership*. This synthesis, I hope, will allay the concerns of those teachers who fear that a curriculum which expects students to make progress in the acquisition of quite specific drama skills is of necessity one in which they are drilled in the mechanics of voice production or required to walk around speaking poetry with books on their heads. The acceptance of the place of dexterity and ingenuity in the drama curriculum will legitimate the much maligned acting techniques, surely as fundamental to drama as instrumental skills are to musicianship, along with the multitude of other associated skills such as playwriting, theatre administration, property making and so on. Unlike the solitary travail of the poet, and although, as I have suggested above, students may make their contributions in isolation, collaborative enterprise will always be central to drama. Membership is also about forms of collaboration, most obviously of the kind associated with large, public productions, but also in the everyday classroom experience of students working together as craftspeople. It is as important not to be sentimental about these labours by pretending that they somehow constitute a special form of art as it is not to downgrade them as the mere exercise of technique. To become a competent craftsperson is no insignificant accomplishment.

Getting better at drama

A criticism sometimes made of art teachers is that they pay too much attention to those in their classes who show a natural aptitude for the subject and too little to those who find art a struggle or a bore. It is not surprising that specialists should warm to students who seem to share their enthusiasm and I have some sympathy with those art teachers who see the first three years of the secondary school, where in England art is compulsory for all, as a long selection period for those more artistically able students who will eventually opt for art as an examination subject. Certainly, part of any teacher's job is to nourish natural talent; strange would be the English teacher who did not encourage the student with a flair for writing poetry or the music teacher who was indifferent to signs of instrumental virtuosity.

Drama teachers have not, in my experience, fallen prey to tacit selection by talent. Indeed, as we have seen, drama education has managed to avoid questions of differentiation by redefining success in drama as something of which everyone is equally capable – as Lewis Carroll's Dodo might have said, in drama, 'all must have prizes'. But if we believe in education as entitlement, then all students, whatever their natural endowment, have a right to be challenged and taught in a way which encourages them to make progress. It could be said that the really fine teacher is the one who helps the least gifted succeed at something which really counts as success.

Standing in the way of this right is a Romantic strain of thought which would have us believe that artistic talent is in our genes; we are either born with it or not. For the art teacher, that talent is to be identified early on and nurtured; for the drama teacher, reluctant to distinguish between students and, possibly, in view of the antipathies outlined above, to induct them, there may be a reluctance to draw attention to a student's fluency in the subject for fear of upsetting the egalitarian dynamic of the devised improvisation.

But, as I argue in Chapter 1, art is not a genetic or psychological attribute but a cultural construct.[26] Societies decide what, if anything, to designate as 'art'. What the good art teacher actually *does* is to encourage students to explore the potential of different media, to look at the work of well-known artists and examine their techniques, to observe the world and to have the confidence to use their growing aptitude and knowledge to experiment with ideas and materials. In other words, the good art teacher knows that only by equipping students with the tools and knowledge of their *craft* will they stand a chance of fulfilling their potential as artists. And the good art teacher will appreciate that this experience of the craft is the entitlement of every student, whatever their apparent faculty.

The establishment of craft as a key component of education in the arts enables us to see more clearly how we might redefine what is worthwhile achievement in drama, even for those who do not seem to have the subject in their blood. It should be possible for all students to make progress within the framework of drama crafts and the more extensive the portfolio of activities the more opportunities there will be for students to make tangible progress in some facet of the subject. Drama's unique capacity to incorporate the other arts means that it probably offers more scope for potential student achievement than any other art form. The dancer, the musician and the designer can all lay claim to aspects of the subject of drama.

Once this conceptual bridge has been crossed, the rest is relatively straightforward. A map of the subject of drama has to be drawn and ways indicated on it for students to make progress. Like any good map, the map of drama should be as comprehensive as possible, without sacrificing clarity, so that it reveals an abundance of features and give us a clear picture of the subject's terrain.

> Etched into its contours will be plays, familiar as well as unfamiliar. Its routes will trace a rich history, crossing all the cultures of the world, in which we will be able to see the work of all kinds of actors, directors and designers. We will see Kabuki, Japanese Noh, the Maoist operas of China and the Hindu dance-dramas of India. As well as showing drama at work in the theatre and the classroom, it will reveal drama's key place on television and in the street. The map will present us with the drama of the court-room, for example, in both true and fictionalised form, and throw into relief the real-life dramas of the shipwreck and the carnival.[27]

Table 4.1 shows what this map might look like in practice for eleven to fourteen year olds in the first three years of an English secondary school (Key Stage 3). In the scheme of work outlined here, over the three years students undertake a broad and balanced programme made up of eighteen projects.[28] Each project takes the form of six, hour-long sessions and, although designed to be self-contained, possibly with an assessment outcome, some areas are revisited subsequently at a greater level of complexity. Each would include reference to representative texts and practitioners where appropriate and students would have the chance to experiment with the different forms and to visit, where possible, live productions. Every opportunity should be taken to illustrate work with examples from world drama. Themes, like 'jealousy' or 'greed' could link projects, but should never be confused with them. Knowledge and understanding of earlier areas of study will increasingly inform students' approach to new challenges as they progress through the programme. A student who had missed the Brecht project in Year 8, for example, might find herself struggling with theatre-in-education in year 9.

This particular scheme, of course, is only one teacher's choice. We all have our own strengths and interests and will produce maps which reflect them. The important thing is that students make progress, not so much in their ability to read a particular map, but in the craft needed to function confidently on a variety of dramatic terrains. The craft of drama is thus transferable between maps, enabling teachers to substitute new areas of study without upsetting the progressive development of students' confidence in the subject.

In 1992, in an attempt to fill the gap left by drama's omission from the 1988 National Curriculum, members of the Arts Council of Great Britain's drama education working group set about constructing a framework for the teaching of drama in schools which would be compatible with other subjects. The outcome of their deliberations, *Drama in Schools*, endorsed the tripartite structure favoured by dance and music,[29] and proposed that the 'the three activities which constitute the subject of drama in schools are *making, performing* and *responding*':

Making drama is the ability to generate and shape dramatic forms in order to explore and express ideas.

Performing drama is the ability to engage and communicate with an audience in a dramatic presentation.

Responding to drama is the ability to express understanding, discernment and appreciation of drama in all its forms.[30]

Progression in drama, therefore, is 'recognised by the extent to which pupils are able to make, perform and respond with increasing levels of complexity, control, depth and independence'.[31]

These three activities pull together all the elements of the craft of drama. At the culmination of a six-week project in the scheme in Table 4.1, students

Table 4.1

	Term 1	*Term 2*	*Term 3*
Year 7	Indian theatre (1)	Mask drama	Elizabethan theatre (1)
	Medieval theatre	Comedy (1)	Street theatre
Year 8	Naturalism and realism	Melodrama	Comedy (2)
	TV drama (1)	Absurdism	Brecht
Year 9	Tragedy	Contemporary plays	TV drama (2)
	Indian drama (2)	Elizabethan theatre (2)	Theatre-in-education

will be assessed on their attainment in making, performing and responding in that project. Of course, the particular nature of a project will determine the character and extent of each activity. The craft skills needed to perform Indian drama, for example, will be very different from those employed in a small piece of television drama; the amount of 'making' involved in mask drama will be considerably greater than for students studying contemporary plays. Assessment criteria will reflect this as well as the fact that throughout the programme students will also be learning other aspects of their craft. Some projects might require them to develop mime skills, or to incorporate music, dance or story-telling, or to use make-up, lighting or costume, or to design a stage setting. Making dramas includes many aspects beyond the production of a script or scenario and successful performance may well be dependent as much on competent stage management or sound operation as on the actors. The melodrama project could provide opportunities for students to learn how lighting can add to the dramatic impact of their work; in particular, perhaps, how footlights make faces look unnatural and sinister. The teacher might explain how candlelight was replaced by gas in the nineteenth century, and what effect this had on the performance style of the time; a simple science experiment will show how lime burned in a gas flame produces great brightness and students will realise why the follow spots they use to pick out performers on the stage are still called 'limes'. The craft of story-telling, which lies at the root of all dramatic cultures, would be the heart of any project on Indian theatre. Students would have the chance to practise the craft of story-telling themselves, inventing stories perhaps, or re-telling those of the great Hindu poetic narratives.[32] How engaging can they make it? What makes a dramatised story engaging for an audience?

If, as they pass through school, students are to make progress in making, performing and responding with 'increasing levels of complexity, control, depth and independence', then some agreement over what might be reasonably expected of them at different ages is the last piece of the jigsaw. The scheme outlined in Table 4.1 makes it clear that I am confident that many aspects of the subject of drama customarily left until students are sixteen or older can actually be taught much earlier. If we are aiming at a comparability of entitlement with art and music, then we should remember that it is not at all uncommon to find eight year olds in art employing and talking confidently about the techniques used by Impressionist painters or infants performing and notating their own compositions in music. It is difficult to see why equivalent levels of achievement should not be expected in drama.

Drama has some acknowledgement as part of the subject of English in the 1988 National Curriculum and the government's 1995 Order for English gives an indication of the kinds of expectations we might have of students. Seven to eleven year olds, it says, 'should be given opportunities to participate in a wide range of drama activities, including improvisations, role-play and the writing and performance of scripted drama'. The secondary curriculum should include the study of plays which 'extend pupils' understanding of drama in performance, e.g. direction, portrayal and interpretation of character' and 'show variety in the structure, e.g. tragedy, comedy, farce, setting'.[33] It is also worth noting, perhaps, that in music, fourteen year olds are expected to be able to 'plan, rehearse, direct and present performances' and 'identify how and why musical styles and traditions change over time and from place to place, recognising the contribution of composers and performers'.[34]

These few pointers suggest what students might be capable of achieving in drama. It may turn out to be more than we have supposed heretofore; as I visit schools, I continue to be amazed at what even young children can accomplish. I know one inner London primary school, for example, which every year puts on a production of a Shakespeare play. One summer I saw *A Midsummer Night's Dream* there, performed in the playground on a July evening. A whole class of ten year olds had been involved in rehearsing, learning lines, making costumes and scenery and now performed the play to parents and friends. It was a memorable occasion, and as I sat there I cast my mind ahead to when, in the September following, those children would have arrived in their secondary schools, probably to drama as a timetabled subject. What sort of experience would face them then, I speculated? Would the girl who played Titania with such verve and the boy who had laboured over painted trees and cardboard crowns in between learning his lines as Demetrius have their emerging command of the craft of drama recognised, sustained and built upon? Or would the confidence and prowess so powerfully evident in that primary school playground be allowed to lie fallow in the interests of an undifferentiated programme of role-play and improvisation? If we believe in entitlement, then this is not a trivial question.

Notes

1 *The Arts in Schools* (1982), London: Calouste Gulbenkian, p.85. The report was written at a time when concern was gathering over the Conservative government's apparent antipathy towards the arts and its predilection for 'pencil and paper tests'.
2 Ibid, p.81.
3 Department for Education (1995) 'Order for Art', *The National Curriculum*, London: HMSO, p.6.
4 Department for Education (1995) 'Order for Music', p.6.
5 School Curriculum and Assessment Authority (1997) *Expectations in Art at Key Stages 1 and 2*, Hayes: SCAA Publications.
6 In 1986, for example, Gavin Bolton had warned teachers against returning 'to the training of their pupils in theatre skills and textual study'. See G. Bolton (1986) 'Weaving theories is not enough', *New Theatre Quarterly* 2(8), p.370. As recently as 1996, an experienced practitioner was still expressing concern that attention to theatre practice meant *reverting* to 'theatre studies'. See W. Dobson (1996) 'Shooting at straw targets or how to construct a postmodern paradigm in drama-in-education', *The NADIE Journal* 20(2), pp.29–39.

7 G. Gillham (1991) 'Review: "Education and Dramatic Art" by David Hornbrook', *SCYPT Journal* 21, p.46.

8 The Certificate of Secondary Education (CSE) was introduced in 1965 for those sixteen year olds not among the top twenty per cent of the ability range already taking the General Certificate of Education (GCE) at Ordinary Level.

9 Schools Council English Committee (1974) *Examinations in Drama*, London: Schools Council, p.12.

10 Examples taken from J. Crompton (1976) 'CSE examinations in drama', *Young Drama* 4(2), pp.57–66.

11 Ibid., p.63.

12 The General Certificate of Secondary Education (GCSE), introduced in 1986, combined CSE and GCE in a single system of national examinations at sixteen-plus.

13 See A. Kempe (1989) 'Towards a common syllabus', *2D Journal of Drama and Dance* 9(1).

14 One syllabus went so far as to redefine drama as 'a problem solving activity'. It aimed, 'to foster confidence in adopting a view to human problems, ideas and attitudes' by developing in candidates 'competencies met within socially interactive processes'. See Midland Examining Group (1986) *GCSE Leicestershire Mode III Drama*, Cambridge: Midland Examining Group, pp.2–3. See also, D. Cross (1990) 'Leicestershire GCSE Drama: a syllabus with a clear direction', in *2D: Journal of Drama and Dance* 9(2), pp.18–24.

15 By the Associated Examining Board.

16 G. Readman (1993) 'Drama out of a crisis', *The Times Educational Supplement* (23 April).

17 The popularity in the 1980s and 1990s of the tableau or, 'freeze-frame' or 'still-picture' as a substitute for the improvisation as the outcome of a small group work in drama introduced more limitations. While the brevity of the telling snapshot certainly helps to contain more 'outcomes' in the space of one lesson, the tableau further diminishes the dramatic skills and imagination required of participants.

18 K. Robinson (1993) 'The arts: which way now?', in P. O'Hear and J. White (eds) *Assessing the National Curriculum*, London: Paul Chapman, p.101.

19 1995 figures from the UK National Consortium for Examination Results on the relative difficulty of examination subjects at sixteen-plus, suggest that students find GCSE examinations in drama the easiest by a long way, and twice as easy as art.

20 M. Ross and M. Kamba (1997) *State of the Arts in Five English Secondary Schools*, Exeter: University of Exeter, p.18.

21 R. Williams (1977) *Marxism and Literature*, Oxford: Oxford University Press, pp.153–4.

22 See Chapter 3.

23 The Austrian art teacher Franz Cizek, opened free classes for children at the School of Applied Art in Vienna in 1898. Cizek made a point of never interfering or attempting to correct their drawings; from time to time he would randomly select work for display. Peter Slade adapted this idea in the 1950s and applied it to drama in schools. See P. Slade (1954) *Child Drama*, London: University of London Press.

24 Ironically, this had its origins in the same kind of anti-industrial Romanticism as the Progressive Education Movement which spawned drama-in-education. In the face of mass-production, Morris and his associates wanted to restore the dignity of the medieval craftsman.

25 R.G. Collingwood (1938) *The Principles of Art*, Oxford: Oxford University Press, pp.15–16.
26 I develop this argument further, in D. Hornbrook (1991) *Education in Drama: Casting the Dramatic Curriculum*, London: Falmer Press, Chapter 2.
27 D. Hornbrook (1992) 'Can we do ours, miss? Towards a dramatic curriculum', in *The Drama/Theatre Teacher* 4(2), p.18.
28 Christopher McCullough explores the project-based approach to drama in more depth in Chapter 10.
29 In England and Wales, students in music are expected to make progress in composing and performing, and listening and appraising. See Department for Education (1995) 'Order for Music'.
30 Arts Council of Great Britain (ACGB) (1992) *Drama in Schools: Arts Council Guidance on Drama Education*, London: ACGB, p.10. See also, D. Hornbrook (1991) *Education in Drama: Casting the Dramatic Curriculum*, London: Falmer Press, Chapter 3 and (1989 [1998]) *Education and Dramatic Art*, 2nd edn, London: Routledge, pp.109–10.
31 Arts Council of Great Britain (ACGB) (1992) *Drama in Schools: Arts Council Guidance on Drama Education*, London: ACGB, p.11.
32 Sita Brahmachari shows how this might be done in some detail in Chapter 2.
33 Department for Education (1995) 'Order for English', pp.11, 19.
34 Ibid.: 'Order for Music', p.7.

Part II

MAKING AND PERFORMING DRAMA IN SCHOOL

INTRODUCTION

Dramas are prepared, performed by actors and watched by audiences. In Part II, four experienced practitioners explore those aspects of the subject of drama which involve young people in the first two of these – making and performing.

The writing of plays in the drama lesson has been curiously neglected; playwriting rarely, if ever, appears as an option in examination syllabuses. Yet it could be said that a written script, capable of multiple interpretations in rehearsal, is the form of creativity in which the craft of the maker of dramas is most fully realised. Under careful guidance, a student's writing is informed by an understanding of readership and of the practical implications of making drama live in performance.

Helen Nicholson examines the craft of the playwright in education. She argues that when students write or improvise drama they draw on their experiences as readers or audiences and as such are inevitably constrained by the ideological limits of what they know and understand – writing of plays is intrinsic to cultural practice. But at the same time they bring their own diverse experiences to bear on their writing. To gain confidence in the process, students need to become dramatically literate so that they can choose from a range of different dramatic languages to express their thoughts and feelings. By exploring and making explicit the conventions, structures and forms of different dramatic genres, the teacher of the subject of drama can enrich the process of writing and devising.

Knowledge of genre was once decisively rejected by sentimentalists fearful that theatre appreciation and textual study would pollute children's natural expression. Indeed, throughout the 1990s, it was possible for fifteen and sixteen year olds to pass a GCSE drama examination with the highest grades never having written a play and without even having read one. For Andy Kempe, however, the reading and practical realisation of plays is fundamental to the subject of drama – every drama teacher, he proposes, should be a teacher of plays. Students can be helped to overcome any prejudicial attitudes they may have to reading in the drama lesson by seeing the

71

script as a form of performance notation rather than a literary text. Calling into question the authority of the playwright as the sole determiner of meaning, he uses the metaphor of the instruction manual to explain how students can be helped to understand the perceptions and aims of the different interpretive communities involved in the making of a performance.

Drama is probably the most embracing of all the arts and students can only benefit from exploring how other forms can enrich their own devising and performing. Drawing on their collaboration in a Bristol comprehensive school, Helen Nicholson and Ruth Taylor conclude this part of the book by re-evaluating the place of performance in drama and showing how students' experience of the subject can be extended by an understanding of dance. After a discussion of the relationship of the different but complementary languages of the two forms, they focus on the way dance challenges the familiar conventions of naturalism in drama and encourages students to incorporate non-Western performance styles in their work. Finally, they show how students can use their knowledge of the cultural iconography of dance and drama to communicate ideas and how this process engages them with wider cultural and artistic narratives which may not only challenge their assumptions about content and form but also expand their conception of the possible.

5

WRITING PLAYS: TAKING NOTE OF GENRE

Helen Nicholson

> I have put words in your mouth Beatrice. Do my words fit you?
> If you are a persona I have revealed too much. If you are a
> character I have revealed too little. I have given you two
> possible moods. You are no longer just form. And I am
> curious.
>
> Deborah Levy[1]

Writing and devising

In this chapter I shall discuss the process of writing plays as an aspect of students' learning in the drama curriculum. It focuses particularly on the craft of playwriting, not as the single aim of drama education, but as part of a subject which articulates with current debates surrounding innovative forms of contemporary drama and theatre practice. As such, this chapter will assess the values associated with the craft of the playwright, and outline the opportunities and problems which arise from the process of writing plays. My goal, therefore, is not to insist on one authoritative practice which leads to writing plays, but to raise questions about the various ways in which students, when working as playwrights, communicate and shape ideas. In the course of this, I shall explore how student playwrights might be encouraged to communicate with others through drama, and to become creative participants in a wide cultural sphere.

The words with which I began are taken from Deborah Levy's script *The B File*, and identify some of the central questions which surround the process of writing plays. Those involved with drama education, in common with contemporary theatre practitioners, have raised questions about the role and authority of the writer, the place of single authorship and the potential for collaboration, and the boundaries between spectator and participant. Indeed, in drama education the very term 'writing plays' has been regarded with scepticism in some quarters, conjuring images of isolated and aloof playwrights who rigidly impose their finely honed words on others. Yet whilst this is a recognisable stereotype, both professional theatre and drama education have, in recent years, challenged authoritarian practices and sought to legitimate a greater variety of voices. In finding words to fit, the experience of making drama has generated a variety of processes, of which few might be said to conform to a traditional idea of playwriting.

In an attempt to avoid the perceived imbalance of power in the relationships between playwright, performer and spectator, much of the practice which has evolved in drama education has privileged spontaneous improvisation. Strategies such as 'teacher-in-role' and 'forum theatre',[2] familiar to drama educators, aim to dissolve the boundaries between participant and audience, and ask students to make decisions while in role about how the improvisation will progress. In the more orthodox language of the theatre, students work simultaneously and collaboratively as actors and playwrights. Such classroom practices recognise the emotional impact of drama; it is the ability of drama to stir the emotions which has had a profound influence on the debate about the appropriate forms of drama in schools. As Kate Soper has argued, if it were not for the arts' 'special powers to excite and illuminate' there would be no need for debates about 'cultural policing'.[3]

If spontaneous improvisation and role-play have been intended to challenge the cultural hierarchies of the established theatre, similar concerns have been shared by drama practitioners outside education. In relation to dramatic writing, the proliferation of collaboratively devised work, initiated during the 1950s and 1960s, was regarded by many as a more egalitarian form of working. Lib Taylor has chronicled the influence of Joan Littlewood's Theatre Workshop on writers such as Shelagh Delaney and Brendan Behan, where improvisation was intended to enfranchise performers through active participation in all the processes of making drama:

> Hierarchical structures that privileged author or 'star' were dismantled in favour of group decision-making and equality of pay. Improvisation was at the heart of her methods and she encouraged each performer to participate in the processes of research.[4]

A Taste of Honey, first performed in 1958, stands as an early testament to this way of working, where the values of 'high culture' associated with middle-class theatre were challenged through both the play's form and content. Ann Jellicoe's subsequent methods of making community plays developed this process of working, where the writer collaborated with the cast, responding to their concerns, and shaping their ideas into dramatic form.[5] If Littlewood's democratic initiatives in approaches to play-making are well-known to drama educators, it is perhaps because the period which introduced this form of experimental theatre, the 1950s and 1960s, was a time of expansion in drama education. It is unsurprising that in such a climate educators such as Dorothy Heathcote, who was concurrently developing her rationale for teaching drama, were anxious to disassociate themselves from the traditional skills associated with formal playwriting and actor-training. In the 1960s established teaching methods, which aimed to transmit knowledge rather than question ideas, were also under fire, and the processes of participatory drama were heralded as a contribution to the democratisation of children's learning.

Educational theory, political thought and theatre practice have not, of course, remained static since the 1960s. Whilst Littlewood's target was the middle-class theatre establishment, her radicalism has now been absorbed into the mainstream. What has emerged in more recent times is a new challenge to the cultural values which permeate dramatic form. A more expansive, anthropological definition of culture has gained currency, challenging the traditional duality of 'high' and 'low' culture. It is with this in mind that Jerome Bruner argues for a revaluation of the active and participatory learning practices of which he has been such a well-known advocate.

> Nothing is 'culture-free', but neither are individuals simply mirrors of their culture. It is the interaction between them that both gives a communal cast to individual thought and imposes a certain unpredictable richness on any culture's way of life, thought or feeling.[6]

The implications of Bruner's thesis suggests that creating a dramatic text is neither exclusively personal nor entirely culturally determined; it is an interactive process which is open to change and renewal. All dramatic practices, including spontaneous improvisation, are subject to a continual process of cultural re-evaluation.

The development of devised drama is a good example of how the practice of writing plays has converged with changing cultural attitudes. The process of collaborative working has led to new genres of dramatic writing, and devised drama has emerged as an important force in contemporary British theatre. Companies such as Trestle Theatre, Forced Entertainment and Forkbeard Fantasy continue to work in innovative dramatic forms, and have shifted the emphasis away from a text-led, literary tradition towards a conception of theatre as a creative art form. Devised theatre has provided an opportunity for a multidisciplinary theatre[7] – the work of Forkbeard Fantasy, for example, has frequently drawn on film as well as theatre for its sources and dramatic form – and, as Ruth Taylor and I argue in Chapter 7, the combination of dance and drama has much creative potential. Equally, however, it has led to script-based productions such as Patrick Marber's *Dealer's Choice* developed in 1994 under the more mainstream auspices of the Royal National Theatre in London. What they share is a specific interest in dramatic form, and in the process of dramatic writing in its broadest sense.

The proliferation of writing processes which lead to play production implies that there is no one single practice which leads to innovative and challenging drama. Whilst some companies have developed successful creative partnerships, particularly those whose members have worked together for many years, collective play-making is not without its difficulties, and the playwright continues to have a role in contemporary theatre. Writers such as Winsome Pinnock, Caryl Churchill and Jackie Kay, whilst welcoming some collaboration with performers, recognise the enduring importance of the craft of the playwright. Susan Croft acknowledges that although the devising process is a fruitful specialism for some, other play-wrights find it limiting: 'Others . . . felt that they had lost their own voice within the collective one, which sometimes homogenised a politically correct, accessible but rather shallow script'.[8] This concern is artistic as well as political. Whilst many playwrights would still recognise Croft's descrip-tion of the 'canonical notion of the solitary, god-like, male authority voice producing the fully-formed work of genius', there is a reluctance to adhere to particular ways of working at the expense of individual voice. Perhaps most crucially for drama education, there has been a move, in Charlotte Keatley's words, to using theatre 'as an art form, not platform',[9] where there is a renewed interest in the effects of the aesthetic languages of theatre. In an attempt to find a balance between the unstructured 'get-it-all-in-ism' of undifferentiated collaboration and the authoritarianism of the writer, play-wrights have sometimes been employed to work with a company, so that their craft can be used to shape ideas and images. Caryl Churchill describes her way of working with Joint Stock theatre company on *Light Shining in Buckinghamshire*:

> The play is not improvised: it is a written text and the actors did not make up its lines. But many of the characters were based on ideas that came from improvisation at the workshop and during rehearsal. I could give endless examples of how something said or done by one of the actors is directly connected to something in the text.[10]

This way of working suggests that the role of the playwright has developed; it takes account of *both* the spontaneity of improvisation and rehearsal *and* the specific knowledge and crafts of the playwright. It also, and perhaps incidentally, implies that the playwright is not the sole voice of authority but has, amongst others, a powerful contribution to make to the process of making drama.

If the power of drama is to affect the emotions, then this is most success-fully achieved when it is well crafted. A range of teaching methodologies in drama education acknowledge the element of craft in the drama lesson, and the many books for teachers aim to encourage students to feel the potency of carefully structured dramatic moments. However, where students are given the skills and craft to engage others in their ideas, drama education enables students both to experience an emotional response to a drama structure and to find ways of affecting others. They are not mutually exclusive, but interdependent. To ensure that this balance is maintained, students and teachers will continue to learn from the experiences of professional theatre workers. This chapter will argue that far from upholding outdated practices of establishment drama, the student as playwright is participating in such a process, and through this becomes an active and curious participant in the creative exploration of cultural values.

Expanding the cultural field

The idea that drama is integral to cultural practice is central to a discussion of the craft of playwriting. The residue of Matthew Arnold's description of the arts as culture's 'best self' continues to influence arts educators; traditionalists have upheld Arnold's values by arguing that an education in canonical works is morally improving, whereas others, notably in drama education, have favoured the more apparently natural, and child-centred, practices of spontaneous improvisation. Interestingly, this division masks shared assumptions both about the description of culture, and the practice of reading. It takes it for granted that 'culture' signifies 'high art' of the academy, and that 'readership' involves a simple transmission of establishment values. Increasingly, as more inclusive description of culture has influenced education, this essentialist duality has been usurped by an understanding that all cultural practices are, in James Clifford's word, 'inventions', which might be located in a social and historical context. As such, *all* drama is inescapably part of the cultural field, conforming to Clifford's idea that narratives are 'constructed, artificial . . . cultural accounts'.[11]

Within this redefinition of culture, the practice of play writing, to follow Jerome Bruner's argument, is not 'culture-free', but *grounded* and constituted through social interaction and cultural practice. In other words, the students' choice of material, the content of their drama, and their use of dramatic forms is informed by lived experience. Similarly, as play writing is an art form which, as Gunter Kress argues, relies on 'ideas in exchange' it requires not only self-understanding but other-understanding.[12] It follows that students, when working as playwrights, might expand their cultural horizons by reading and seeing as wide a variety of drama as possible.

Nonetheless, Pierre Bourdieu's argument that the academy has institutionalised the arts deserves to be taken seriously. In *The Rules of Art*, Bourdieu suggests that in Western cultures the arts have been appropriated by an academic élite, whose privileged 'economic and social conditions' have determined standards of aesthetic judgement. He warns that it is education which has been responsible for professionalising the arts, and that this has discriminated on grounds of class, gender and race. An undifferentiated view of 'truth', either of the artistic tradition or of self-expression, he argues, fails to locate the social conditions of production and invention.[13] For the student embarking on writing a play, and the teacher who encourages dramatic writing, Bourdieu's thesis has two interrelated consequences. First, it suggests that all creative work – including the most spontaneous – articulates within a culture and is not, as has sometimes been thought, extraneous to it, and second, that the student's approach to dramatic texts might be critical and interrogative rather than laudatory.

If the social division Bourdieu identified in artistic practice is to be eroded, and students are encouraged to participate in a diversity of cultural practices, their writing will be enhanced by experience as readers, performers and members of audiences. The aim of this familiarisation is to promote curiosity into the craft of the playwright, to encourage students to interpret what playwrights say and how they say it. In this practice of reading, the emphasis is shifted away from self-identification with roles thought to be 'morally uplifting' and asks students to question the work of others. As Charles Taylor argues, human beings are not locked into 'ethnocentric prisons', but by contrasting their preconceptions with those of others, they might enlarge their perceptions and self-understanding:

> This means that I articulate things that were purely implicit before, in order to put them to question. In particular, I articulate what were formerly the limits to intelligibility, in order to see them in a new context, no longer as inescapable structures of human motivation, but as one in a range of possibilities. That is why other-understanding changes self-understanding, and in particular prizes from some of the most fixed contours of our former culture.[14]

Taylor's argument, when applied to the creative practice of writing plays, suggests that it is not just the mechanics of playwriting which might be acquired through diverse dramatic experiences. Rather, it implies that to participate in drama as playwrights, performers or spectators is necessarily an active and creative process of learning which encourages both self-interpretation and an understanding of historical context and cultural difference. Following Bourdieu, only when the essentialism of artistic self-expression has been exposed as a myth might drama education acknowledge its responsibility, in Bruner's words, for its role in 'shaping the Self'.[15]

The acquisition of a dramatic language with which to articulate and exchange ideas is part of the process of writing plays. In the case of drama, this is not just a written language, but includes the physical, spatial and aural languages of, for example, image, gesture, movement and sound as part of the fabric of cultural communication and dialogue. And, as Wittgenstein argues, it is through language that concepts are learnt and defined, and not the other way round. According to Wittgenstein, language is not a reflection of pre-existing inner thoughts, nor an 'incorporeal process' but part of the 'vehicle of thought'.[16] Where students are given the opportunity to learn a conceptual language through practice and experience, he argues, they are able to move beyond the limits of the teacher's own horizons:

> But if a person has not yet got the *concepts*, I shall teach him to use the words by means of *examples* and by *practice*. . . . And when I do this I do not communicate less to him than I know myself. . . . Teaching which is not meant to apply to anything beyond the examples given is different from that which '*points beyond*' them.[17]

The importance of Wittgenstein's theory to the writing of plays is that it suggests that the process of learning about drama is not didactic, but dialogic and interactive. As students work as practitioners in drama, they engage in conversations which help them gain an understanding of how its languages work. They may then apply their understanding of dramatic form and artistic concepts to other contexts, and in ways which may be unexpected or unpredictable. It follows that while both students and teachers are inevitably constrained by the limits of language, the acquisition of new dramatic languages allows for greater choice and new possibilities. Taylor makes the claim more explicit. He challenges the idea that artistic expression articulates only 'already existing feelings', arguing that 'new modes of expression enable us to have new feelings'.[18]

Dramatic literacy, or the learning of dramatic languages, is not just one form of expression amongst others, but a particular way of shaping and creating ideas. The feelings, concepts and values of a culture are inseparable from the dramatic form itself. By participating in a breadth and diversity of dramatic experiences students are able to gain insights into both their inherited attitudes and those of a wider cultural sphere. Put simply, if students are not introduced to different dramatic forms, they can only draw on those which are already familiar to them. This is not an argument for inducting students into a 'better' culture, but about *expanding* the cultural field, about giving them more variety. According to Wittgenstein's thesis, this will not only extend their creativity, it will enhance their *conceptual* development.

This relationship between conceptual thought and creativity was demonstrated to me by a group of thirteen and fourteen year old students, who had been working on Lin Coghlan's play, *A Feeling in My Bones*.[19] The play addresses the issue of inheritance and cultural dispossession, and uses both poetic form and naturalistic dialogue. Having worked on the play, the students were writing their own scripts about moving to a new area as 'incomers' and experimenting with different forms of dramatic writing to create atmosphere. Surrounded by bits of paper inscribed with scraps of poetic dialogue, they revised their ideas through rehearsal, referring back to the text with a growing interest in Coghlan's dramatic craft. As I watched their work, it became apparent that they were consciously manipulating dramatic form to explore both a concept and an emotional response. I suggested that they might write about why they had chosen to use poetry in their drama. Sarah and Robert wrote these responses:

> She [Coghlan] manages to make you think about the past and history by using those poems. We wanted that in our bit about moving into the new house. To show that you haven't left everything behind when you move. Then we use ordinary language for the scene at school.
>
> It [the poetry] makes you think about how you aren't just you, but part of a bigger something. I hadn't thought of that before. It makes you feel big and small at the same time. We want people to feel that about our play. But it's a bit hard and we have had to write some bits down, which we don't usually do in drama. We've changed it quite a lot.

This evidence indicates that by extending their dramatic repertoire, Sarah and Robert have gained insights into unfamiliar concepts. Furthermore, through their own writing, they seem to have discovered how poetic and naturalistic dialogue can signify different kinds of dramatic atmosphere. In Wittgensteinian terms, Sarah and Robert have used the language of drama as 'a vehicle of thought'. It has given them a chance to reflect on their own and other's ideas, a critical awareness and, as playwrights, a new level of control. Writing enabled them to become critical readers.

As Sarah and Robert worked, they found that spontaneous improvisation was useful, but limited. Whilst they continued to use it when working on scenes which had more familiar ideas and dramatic structures, they found that they needed to compose poetic dialogue to communicate concepts which they felt required a different dramatic language. I witnessed a similar need in a class of much younger students who had worked with the dancer Susmita Banerjee, and who wished to adapt some of the images they had learnt into their drama. They, too, used a form of written notation, both to develop their thinking and to consolidate the less familiar, non-naturalistic elements of their dramatic text. To follow Bourdieu, a curriculum which aims to expand the cultural field will include in its content a wide variety of dramatic forms, without which we risk offering an education which is socially divisive and conceptually limited. The writing of plays, when informed by the kind of active and dramatic readings of texts which Andy Kempe describes in Chapter 6, encourages students to interpret and interrogate personal, social and artistic assumptions as part of the cultural practice of drama.

Genre as education

The place of writing in the drama curriculum has tended towards practices such as 'writing-in-role' or keeping journals. Whilst these responses to drama offer valuable learning experiences to the students, enabling them to reflect on and organise ideas they have already explored in improvisation, they have not usually been aimed at encouraging the craft of playwriting. In terms of the English curriculum, drama offers an important place for discussion of the relationship between spoken and written language, and an opportunity to identify the various linguistic idioms they have used in role through different modes of writing.[20] And indeed, the relationship between writing and speech is central to the playwright's craft. Curiously, however, the creative potential for including different *dramatic* genres in the drama curriculum has been neglected; where this has been discussed in drama education, it has been primarily perceived as a debate about process *versus* product, with the implication that learning about different dramatic genres is based on literary criticism rather than creative and artistic processes. Interestingly, a similar debate has been conducted in English teaching, where advocates of 'process writing' have claimed that an understanding of genre stifles the personal voice, whilst their 'genre approach' opponents have argued that students are disempowered if they are not given access to its structures and social usage.[21]

Such a debate between 'process' and 'genre' is germane to my discussion of the writing of plays, because it profoundly affects what teachers and children might do in drama lessons. It also signifies the political differences between the two schools of thought. In 'process drama', described by Philip Taylor as a 'dramatic playing activity with their teacher',[22] students' writing practices are associated with reflection on the drama, and response to it. This model suggests a liberal curriculum in which it is assumed that learning to write is, in Janet Maybin's words, 'a natural process supported by the teacher'.[23] For proponents of a genre approach, the curriculum is directed by the politics and values of cultural materialism, in which, according to J.R. Martin, 'learning the genres of one's culture is both part of entering into it with understanding, and part of developing the necessary ability to change it'.[24]

Yet whilst this contradistinction would appear to offer a direct choice to teachers, there are potential disadvantages to a rigid adherence to either perspective. As Maybin points out, despite claims that the personal voice is paramount, the process model frequently exercises informal censorship when faced with the expression of racism or sexism, for example, and thus masks its ideological commitments. The genre approach, whilst in theory more conscious of the social production of drama, risks a rather anodyne curriculum in which students might learn a lot about dramatic forms and structures, but are never really given the chance to make their own.

The challenge is to find a way of teaching dramatic writing which is *both* interactive, personal and dialogic, *and* acknowledges that drama is a cultural art form. If, to return to Bruner, cultural innocence and ideological neutrality is a myth, all script-writing is in some way shaped and informed by dramatic convention. Nonetheless, it is the interplay between established genres and contemporary discourse which gives writing its vitality and sense of individual voice. They do not have to be regarded as mutually exclusive. This might be seen in practice in Caryl Churchill's *Top Girls*, where she uses the genre of Brechtian epic to show the different political situations of the roles, but also develops a way of writing in which she betrays conventional dramatic form by overlapping the speech and dialogue of her characters. Whilst the dialogue gives the appearance of 'natural' conversation, it is carefully timed to create emotional tension.[25] When I read the first act with a group of fifteen years olds, they became interested in how to portray multiple stories and political values when devising and scripting a play of their own. They did not simply ape Churchill's use of dramatic genre, but introduced a repertoire of speech patterns from their own lives – in-jokes, snatched telephone calls, advertising slogans – to their Brechtian exploration of teenage experience.

The way different dramatic forms convey and influence meanings can be understood by students, even of a young age. Children in a class of five and six year olds I visited were adept at anticipating audience response through a variety of genres. There had been a class outing to see a pantomime version of *The Ugly Duckling*, and displayed in sequence on the classroom walls were pictures they had painted as a storyboard, with captions written in dramatic dialogue. Coincidentally, I had taken one of the class, Lauren, to see a puppetry version of the same story at the Little Angel Theatre in London. Lauren had told her friends about it, and they invited me to see their own version of the play, *The Ugly Barbie*, devised with some teacher support, complete with programme notes and biographies of the actors. The assembled cast of four Barbie dolls, three Kens and a teddy were used as puppets, the paintings and captions served as both script and backcloth, and some parts were prepared through improvisation. A rather pathetic Barbie doll had been drawn on by her owner, and was banished from the toy box, and left to wander round the countryside until she had a wash in Teddy's pond. The children mixed their dramatic styles, using the musical effects of the puppet show to express the character's sad mood, and the pantomime tradition of audience participation ('She is an ugly Barbie,' 'Oh no she's not!', and so on) to maintain involvement. I would like to think that the finale, sung with much hilarity ('There once was an ugly Barbie'), was an ironic comment on Barbie's conventional image, but Lauren told me that they had chosen it because it would cheer everyone up at the end. The puppet show was good at doing the sad bits, she said, but 'didn't make your tummy jump' when it ended happily. The creative interplay of different dramatic genres showed how these very young students had learned to interpret the effects of dramatic conventions and, by adapting them in their play, had interpreted the folk tale in their own way.

A conceptual understanding of what the craft of playwriting means entails a recognition that playwrights adapt, bowdlerise, borrow and steal dramatic genres for particular ends. They may also use the 'found' images and language of voices and situations they know well to achieve particular dramatic effects. Charlotte Keatley suggests that the job of the playwright is to 'structure images and ideas' in ways which challenge presumptions and expectations.[26] When students communicate their ideas to others through different dramatic genres, with an awareness of the effects they are creating, they have grasped the concept of craft in playwriting. Working with a group of fourteen-year-old British Asian girls, I was privileged to see this conceptual understanding demonstrated in practice. The students were devising a play about the experiences of their mothers, many of whom were alienated from official institutions in Britain because they spoke Urdu. The girls had decided to invert the power relations by using English as the language of the home, and Urdu for the scenes set in school. In one scene, they wanted to use comedy to portray a school parents' evening, in which the girls would continually mistranslate for their mothers and teachers, telling each side that they were hard working, diligent pupils. They asked me to provide examples of how comedy works in drama, in Vygotsky's terms, to give them the 'scaffolding' on which to build their understanding of dramatic writing.[27] From this, they selected a dramatic genre and comic form which they felt most suited their purposes. The result was a carefully crafted script which used dramatic irony to make their point about the power of language to exclude, but through a deliciously comic subversion of the genre of social realism. In performance, the use of Urdu in their play forced the audience to question whose 'reality' they were witnessing and this, combined with humour, enabled the girls to make a serious point. The audience was challenged through both form and content, an interplay between the conventional and the experimental; the playwrights had fulfilled Arthur Miller's dictum that the art of playwriting is about doing the expected in an unexpected way.

It has been convincingly argued that no dramatic genres or conventions are exempt from ideological considerations. As Brecht was well aware, the content of the drama, its meanings and messages, are inextricably linked to the politics of dramatic form. Brecht's answer was to lay bare the mechanisms of theatre praxis, but in the process he also invented a new dramatic genre which privileged demonstration over psychological naturalism. Subsequently, feminist and post-colonial theorists and practitioners have been particularly effective in following Brecht's lead by challenging the idea that the playwright's use of dramatic form is politically neutral. However, Brechtian theatre forms are not the only way to challenge neutrality. Plays such as Timberlake Wertenbaker's *Love of the Nightingale* make this point explicit;

she offers a feminist critique of male-authored conventions through parody. Deborah Levy also suggests that whilst no dramatic form is exempt from political readership, the playwright might exploit it for her own use: 'Form is everything. All meaning, all ideology, lies in form. The composition of my theatre is using the language of the theatre for all the meanings it can give me'.[28]

But all dramatic conventions are, as the word suggests, conventional; each genre of drama is, by definition, repetitive and predictable in form. In Western cultures, there is a hierarchy of dramatic forms, in which the literary tradition (Shakespeare, Marlowe, Shaw, for example) has been privileged over other dramatic genres.[29] The poetic, in particular, has been favoured as a high art form. But as any teacher knows who has read the performance poetry of Grace Nichols or Benjamin Zephaniah with students, or seen the plays of Liz Lockhead or James Berry, even 'literary' forms are not as bound by rules as they once were and, indeed, the boundaries and definitions of particular genres are increasingly difficult to locate. Oral traditions, music, film and the visual arts are now included within the repertoire and craft of contemporary playwriting. However, the consequences of this diverse practice mean that there are tough decisions to be made about which dramatic forms might be included the curriculum. For a teacher, the question still remains, which dramatic genres? And how might students learn to use a diversity of dramatic forms for themselves?

Where dramatic genre is part of the subject of drama, to be used creatively by student playwrights, the emphasis is placed on the *representation* of ideas. As students take control of the dramatic form, and are not manipulated by it, they gain a progressive and explicit understanding of how they, as playwrights, might construct dramatic texts as a vehicle of thought and communication. There is no right or definitive answer about which dramatic forms to include in the curriculum; I would not wish to see an established canon of 'great dramatic genres' but a changing variety of styles each with their own explicit cultural resonances and dramatic significances.

The role of the playwright

It is inherent in the craft of dramatic writing that the script only reaches its full potential in performance. Drama is a living art form, which entails practical exploration of the words on the page, and the written script constitutes only part of a performance text. How the script is read by the actors, how ideas are understood and communicated to the audience, is dependent on the rehearsal process and the context of performance. As playwrights, therefore, students work on several layers of interpretation. The process of writing is not only informed by an understanding of readership but of the practical implications of making drama live.

A script which is capable of multiple interpretations, can sustain interrogation in rehearsal, and reaches its intended audience in performance, is one where the craft of the playwright is most successfully realised. The playscript cannot be read as an immutable blueprint for a dramatic performance, because, as Wittgenstein points out, a blueprint offers a 'mere case of knowing, not seeing', and negates the role of interpretation and perception.[30] To have a conceptual understanding of what the playwright does is to realise that performers, directors, designers and audience all have a contribution to make. In the language of semiotics, the writing of plays entails an awareness of the synthesis between theatrical and dramatic signifiers.[31] Put simply, where student playwrights take account of the effects of images, movement, sounds, as well as their words, they recognise that they are only one part of the dramatic enterprise and acknowledge that their work is open to re-interpretation.

If all this seems obvious, it is because performance has conventionally begun with a playscript – sometimes perceived as the work of the god-like figure Susan Croft identified. But in contemporary theatre, the script, particularly in physical theatre or devised drama, may offer a retrospective notation of dramatic action, and the written script may reflect a mixture of dramatic languages. Where playwrights collaborate with performers and directors, the playscript may be a record of improvisation, rehearsal and technical effects as well as the playwright's choice of words. Playwriting, in this context, is an interactive process, where the role of the writer is to incorporate the experiences and ideas of the group into a play which has coherence and a sense of dramatic unity. In the drama classroom, where there is a rich tradition of collaboration and sharing ideas, such an approach to playwriting would appear to suggest that the process of writing is always a reflective afterthought to group improvisation. Yet where students move beyond their immediate and spontaneous reactions to dramatic situations, and begin to consider the craft of writing plays, the role of the playwright is more clearly differentiated. Nina Rapi, a playwright working in London, suggests that collaboration is enriched where the differences between the roles of actor, writer and director are well established:

> I don't believe in situations where roles are not clearly defined. Firm guidelines are essential, otherwise 'collaboration' becomes a power battle and a nightmare. . . . Mutual respect and clear boundaries are the key really.[32]

Rapi is specifically discussing the role of the writer in professional theatre, but her words have relevance for drama education. While teachers and their students may not always wish to assign writing to specific children in a group and in practice students are likely to act as performers, directors and designers of their work, they may usefully be encouraged to gain an awareness of the role and function of the playwright, and to separate the job of writing from others in the dramatic and theatrical process. By so doing, the work may be consciously structured, with cognisance of process, and with time to reflect on the dramatic representation of ideas.

One of the roles of the playwright is to create a script which allows actors and directors scope for interpretation in performance. Writing about the visual arts, Merleau-Ponty refers to the 'blanks' between the brushstrokes, which are as expressive as the paint-marks themselves. He relates this to language, suggesting that what is implied or left unsaid is often important in creating meaning. Where the arts invite interpretation through the 'gaps' or silences, Merleau-Ponty argues that they 'teach us to see and make us think as no analytic work can'.[33] Something of the same analogy might be applied to the writing of plays. In the craft of playwriting, the 'blanks' between the words can signify a gesture, a movement, an image, or an implicit relationship between characters. Or, as Harold Pinter's plays suggest, there might be a more complex relationship between language and silence where characters disguise their feelings through their dialogue. In this context, the role of the playwright is to be aware of the potential for a multilayered interpretation of the script in performance, and to give the necessary ambiguity which will allow the performers and directors to explore the script in such a way that it will encourage the audience to think.

The process of writing a play is often described as an exploratory journey. The outcome is unpredictable. Although playwrights might begin with an image, an idea, a dramatic structure or a particular role, this intention is revised and reshaped as the work unfolds. There is a curiosity about how the play will turn out and playwrights may be unsure where it will go. As the play takes shape, playwrights may observe new possibilities, new arrangements or unintended ideas, which cause them to revise and re-interpret their initial intentions. It is this capacity for invention, to speculate on ideas through the process of working which separates art-making from analysis. Richard Wollheim, writing about painting, suggests that the process of working within the medium causes artists to reflect and experiment: '[H]e thinks over what he has done, brings to light inadvertent features of his action, decides on how these features could be made to count for something, and resolves next time to put it into practice'.[34]

According to Wollheim, artists stand back from their work, and revise it to take account of the unexpected or unforeseen. They develop a critical eye, deleting and changing direction after observing the effects of their work before it is fully completed. In drama, this practical exploration of work in progress is often separate from the process of rehearsal, which is directed towards creating a performance. It focuses on the playscript, enabling the playwrights to reflect on how the work is developing. Through trying it out, new insights into the play emerge, and this informs the next stage of the writing or devising.

A group of twelve and thirteen year old students, some with learning difficulties, found that, by becoming spectators of their work, they had the opportunity to explore new directions in their drama. The class was working on morality plays, and had previously developed shadow puppet plays using Indonesian moral fables.[35] I had followed this work by using the play *Everyman* from the English tradition. They did not read the scripted play, but heard the story, and they had enjoyed playing with the sound of some of its lines – 'with unclean life, as lusts of lechery' was a particular favourite. I wanted them to contrast the medieval morality of the play with contemporary values, and they made a list of sins they thought would have relevance for 'Everyperson' today. After some role-playing to explore the ideas, each group took responsibility for representing one of the sins. They devised a storyboard, and through continual use of improvisation, they wrote draft scripts collaboratively. They then handed the scripts on to another group who read it for them whilst they watched. Many groups found that their characters revealed too much early on in the scene, so that, having established what the sin was, they could only keep repeating it. This left little scope for the actors to interpret the role, or to build up to a moment of dramatic climax. One group identified that they needed to know how to reveal to the audience that someone is lying, cheating or 'grassing' on mates, without other characters on stage noticing. They began to experiment with representing ideas in exchange through physical actions, using a wider range of dramatic devices. Another group decided to withhold more information from the audience because, as one girl put it, although they had considered their own moral values through writing the play, you also need the people who see it to 'ask the same sort of questions about what they'd do'. Some discovered that although they had created strong characters, they needed greater dramatic contrast between them to get their point across. Having seen the play in progress, there was a renewed discussion about why they had selected some vices rather than others, recognising that 'sin' is much more fun to portray than virtue. Through this kind of reflection on their drama, they gained an understanding of how the playwright's craft has the potential to invent, as well as reflect, cultural values.

The mechanics of playwriting, its formalities and conventions, can be useful if students intend their scripts to be read by people other than themselves. But scripts do not have to be fully worked signifiers of dialogue and action. A script may take the form of a storyboard, a series of stage directions, a poem, a cartoon strip, a scenario or one of many other forms of notation. Whilst writing can be a good way to order ideas, it is not the only way to work as a playwright. The devised work of Forkbeard Fantasy is rarely scripted in any formal sense before performance, and the playscript of their show *The Fall of the House of Usherettes*, about the history of film, was presented as a comic strip tabloid newspaper. This had the advantage of incorporating the visual images in the show, as well as the dialogue. But in itself, the craft of playwriting is not dependent on the production of a fully formed written script. The aim is not to hand in a piece of written work, but to create a play *text*, a living art form.

To delineate the playwright in this way means, by implication, that it is a role differentiated from complementary dramatic crafts. This is not to say that some students will always write plays, and others will perform them. It simply means that when they are working as playwrights, students are given the time and support to consider their use of dramatic form and to notate what they do. This is active and experiential learning, where students are given the space to experiment. Through the application of their craft, young playwrights might find new ideas and explore the unexpected.

A sense of audience and the role of the teacher

The making of drama is, of course, a complex and challenging business. My suggestion is that where students work as playwrights as part of the subject of drama, it enables them to break down the process of making drama, and make it more manageable. Students learn in different ways; some find spontaneous improvisation difficult or unsatisfying, and some have trouble writing. A fully differentiated curriculum, which takes account of students' individual abilities and experiences, will aim to develop both their strengths and address their areas of weakness.

In his theories of learning, Vygotsky argues that the role of the teacher is to provide children with a framework upon which to build. If they are offered too wide a choice, he argues, they will become confused and thus prevented from effective learning. With this in mind, art teachers sometimes restrict the palate children use, knowing that if they mix all the colours together, they usually make brown. As playwrights, students need similar structures. The teacher's role is to frame the work, to define and limit the choices that students can make. In this context, the 'palate' may be a dramatic genre or form, an image, a play or a story – a combination of form and content. It is not a matter of teaching children to write by imitating 'great' writers. When students work as playwrights, they need to focus on selected aspects of the subject of drama, so that they might mix new forms with those with which they are already familiar. It is a balance between providing constraints, which can lead to creative drama, and gradually expanding their cultural horizons. In this context, and following James Clifford's view that all cultural practices are 'inventions', part of the teacher's role is to enable students to recognise that playwrights are not an élite band of visionaries, and that there is no great mystery attached to the writing of plays.

This exploration of the place of the playwright has assumed that a sense of audience is important. Underlying this premise is the principle that students' ideas deserve to be heard. As a consequence, questions are raised about the potential ways in which they might represent their ideas, and how they might use dramatic form to communicate. This requires a subject knowledge, a dramatic literacy, acquired through experience and practice, and not haphazardly through trial and error. What this means is that where teachers gradually introduce students to a wide variety of drama within a progressive curriculum framework, they will gain an explicit understanding of how the languages of drama work. To return to the analogy of the paint-box, if they are not taught how to mix their colours, we risk undifferentiated and unstructured work which leaves the students unsatisfied. Developing a sense of audience is part of the process of learning to be inventive with drama; it encourages students to put themselves in someone else's position, and to consider how their drama might be interpreted by others.

The craft of playwriting has been neglected in education. Whilst children have been encouraged to write poetry and short stories, to compose songs and paint pictures, there is surprisingly little evidence of educational theories or methodologies which would support their development as play-wrights. In part, this must be attributed to the audience for conventional theatre; theatre-going remains a middle-class activity. But then, so is visiting art galleries and buying poetry books, and television drama is very much part of popular culture. To argue that students should become practitioners in the craft of playwriting is not to say that they should be persuaded simply to accept the cultural values of traditional theatre practice. On the contrary, it aims *both* to validate their home cultures *and* to expand the cultural field, with the recognition that practising the craft of the playwright allows new and familiar ideas to take shape.

Notes

1 D. Levy (1992) 'The B File', *Walks on Water*, London: Methuen, p.152.
2 For a description of teacher in role, see J. O'Toole (1992) *The Process of Drama*, London: Routledge, pp.82–6. Forum theatre's most famous exponent is Augusto Boal, whose book *Theatre of The Oppressed* (London: Pluto Press) was first published in English in 1979.
3 K. Soper (1993) 'Postmodernism, subjectivity and value', in J. Squires (ed.) *Principled Positions*, London: Lawrence & Wishart, p.24
4 L. Taylor (1993) 'Early stages: women dramatists 1985–68', in T.R. Griffiths and M. Llewellyn-Jones (eds) *British and Irish Women Dramatists since 1958*, Milton Keynes: The Open University Press, p.18.
5 A. Jellicoe (1987) *Community Plays – How to put them on*, London: Methuen.
6 J. Bruner (1996) *The Culture of Education*, Cambridge, MA: Harvard University Press, p.14.
7 A. Oddey (1994) *Devising Theatre*, London: Routledge.
8 S. Croft (1993) 'Collaboration and exploration in women's theatre', in T.R. Griffiths and M. Llewellyn-Jones (eds) *British and Irish Women Dramatists since 1958*, Milton Keynes: The Open University Press, p.50.
9 An interview with Charlotte Keatley, in L. Goodman (1996) *Feminist Stages*, Amsterdam: Harwood Academic Publishers, p.141. Feminist theatre practi-tioners have considered the politics of the body, and of how visual images are

read and communicated. See E. Aston (1995) *An Introduction to Feminism and Theatre*, London and New York: Routledge, pp.64–77, for a more detailed examination of this concept.

10 C. Churchill (1985) 'Light shining in Buckinghamshire', in *Plays: One*, London: Methuen, p.184.

11 J. Clifford (ed.) (1986) *Writing Culture,* Berkeley: University of California Press, p.2.

12 G. Kress (1982) *Learning to Write*, London: Routledge & Kegan Paul, p.120. Joe Winston also makes an excellent case for 'other-understanding' in drama education in 'Emotion, reason and moral engagement in drama research' (1996) *Drama Education* 1(2), pp.189–200.

13 P. Bourdieu (1996), trans. S. Emanuel, *The Rules of Art*, Cambridge: Polity Press, p.294–5.

14 C. Taylor (1995) *Philosophical Arguments*, Cambridge, MA: Harvard University Press, p.149.

15 J. Bruner (1996) *The Culture of Education*, Cambridge, MA: Harvard University Press, p.35.

16 L. Wittgenstein (1963) *Philosophical Investigations*, trans. G.E.M. Anscombe, Oxford: Basil Blackwell, pp.105–7.

17 Ibid., p.83.

18 C. Taylor (1995), p.98.

19 L. Coghlan (1994) 'A feeling in my bones', in A. Kempe (1994b) *Dramascripts Extra*, Walton-on-Thames: Thomas Nelson.

20 See J. Neelands (1994) 'Writing in imagined contexts', in S. Brindley (ed.) (1994) *Teaching English*, London: Routledge, pp.202–9. Neelands usefully offers to English teachers a variety of ways in which drama stimulates different modes of writing, but he does not list playwriting among them.

21 Teachers of English will be particularly familiar with this argument, which was initiated by M.A.K. Halliday (1985) *Spoken and Written Language*, Geelong: Deakin University Press, and developed by, for example, G. Kress (1982) *Learning to Write*, London: Routledge & Kegan Paul.

22 P. Taylor (1996) 'Introduction: rebellion, reflective turning in arts education research', *Researching Drama and Arts Education*, London: Falmer Press, p.15.

23 J. Maybin (1994) 'Teaching writing: process or genre?', in S. Brindley (ed.) (1994) *Teaching English*, London: Routledge, p.193.

24 J. R. Martin (1994), quoted in J. Maybin (1994), p.192.

25 C. Churchill (1982) *Top Girls*, London: Methuen.

26 An interview with Charlotte Keatley, in L. Goodman (1996) *Feminist Stages*, Amsterdam: Harwood Academic Publishers, p.140.

27 See J. Britton (1994) 'Vygotsky's contribution to pedagogic theory', in S. Brindley (ed.) (1994) *Teaching English*, London: Routledge, pp.259–63.

28 D. Levy (1996), interviewed in L. Goodman (1996) *Feminist Stages*, Amsterdam: Harwood Academic Publishers, p.231.

29 See the UK National Curriculum 'Order for English' (1995) *The National Curriculum*, London: HMSO, for a recommended list of great literary playwrights, such as, Marlowe, Shaw and Sheridan, thought to be suitable for children.

30 L. Wittgenstein (1963) *Philosophical Investigations*, trans. G.E.M. Anscombe, Oxford: Basil Blackwell, p.204.

31 This is not to resurrect Peter Slade's 'theatre/drama' distinction. It is common practice in theatre semiotics to separate the dramatic from the theatrical, where the former applies to the script and the latter to other performance signifiers.

32 N. Rapi (1996), interviewed in L. Goodman (1996) *Feminist Stages*, Amsterdam: Harwood Academic Publishers, p.235.
33 M. Merleau-Ponty (1973) *The Prose of the World*, Evanston, IL: Northwestern University Press, p.90.
34 R. Wollheim (1987) *Painting as an Art*, Princeton, NJ: Princeton University Press, p.24.
35 For useful guidance on the craft of puppet making, see T. Coult and B. Kershaw (eds) (1983) *Engineers of the Imagination: The Welfare State Handbook*, London: Methuen.

6

READING PLAYS FOR
PERFORMANCE

Andy Kempe

The creativity of studying plays

Shortly before starting work on this chapter, I was watching a group of four-teen year olds working on a soliloquy from *Macbeth*. The student teacher had set the task up clearly and the school students were wholly willing to engage with the work, but their initial practical explorations were stilted and seemed not to be giving any new insight into either Shakespeare's words or how they might be brought to life in performance. Only after some carefully focused interventions to draw attention to how the words sounded and the associated movements looked did a creative spark appear. Suddenly a number of different and exciting interpretations of the piece started to emerge. The experience illustrated how, without guidance, inexperienced players tend to treat words literally at the expense of the metaphorical power of the script and epitomised for me the importance of teaching students how to read a script so that they can recognise its aesthetic potential as well as its literal content. If students are to grasp the difference between reading a play and anticipating it in performance, they will need to understand both the perspective of the theatre audience and the theatre practitioner.

The traditional emphasis on improvisation in drama education has persuaded many teachers of literature also to use improvisation as a way into play scripts in English lessons. Underlying such practice may be a belief that confronting the script directly will somehow stifle the students' creative response to it. And of course, if interpreting scripts involved simply following the playwright's instructions, then theatre production would be no more inspiring than assembling kitchen units from a series of pictograms and theatre artists little more than technical jobbers. My argument here is that this is very far from the case and that improvisations devoid of a recognition of the conventions of the stage – what might be called 'the register of theatrical signs' – are unhelpful in drawing attention to what playwrights give actors, directors and designers to help them achieve an aesthetic dimen-sion in the subsequent performance of the work. Attention to such a register does not preclude creativity: it promotes it. The reader is invited to interpret the script by asking 'How will this happen on stage?' and 'What would the effect be on me if I were to experience this as an audience?'. Both interpretive questions involve creativity in that they demand that the script be played out and played *with* in a practical manner.

Drama teachers are used to focusing students' attention on visual imagery, especially in terms of the positioning of performers in relation to each other. Tableaux, or 'freeze-frames', or 'still-pictures', have been common features of drama lessons at least since the 1980s. It is certainly true that the messages read in the actor's body are infinitely variable, a point made well by Stephen Berkoff: 'There is nothing on this earth that a performer can't suggest by using his body. An actor's body is a powerful and even dangerous instrument and is capable of recreating things that a playwright cannot write down'.[1]

Yet, while the ubiquitous 'still-picture' is held to be creative in itself and to stimulate creative thinking in its interpretation, similar attention seems not to have been given to the inventiveness involved in speaking lines, or investigating the other physical signs that make up a performance. It is as if the fact that the words are pre-determined by the playwright necessarily negates the possibility of the students applying their own imagination. In fact, as Jonathan Miller (1986) points out, the script offers apparently limitless potential for originality:

> the phonetic distinctions that can make a difference to the meaning of a sentence are so small that it would take an almost infinite set of written characters to represent them all. Such a notation would be so dense that it would be difficult for the eye to distinguish the different characters from one another. It would be like trying to tell the time on a clock dial that depicted nanoseconds. And since prosody involves several independent variables, each one of which would probably require its own dense notation, the script would become well-nigh illegible. It is difficult to imagine any actor sight-reading such a 'score'.[2]

Finding a suitable way of performing a line involves considerable imaginative engagement. Add to this the other elements that make up a performance, such as lighting, costume, make-up and scenography, and one sees how tremendously creative the act of staging a play is. But these are skills that are learned by harnessing creativity rather than giving it free rein, and as drama teachers, it may be that we have been too reluctant to constrain students' spontaneity while they learn to master the medium. As I write this, I am aware of my eight year old daughter practising her guitar. She has not had it for very long and is just starting to learn. While I am sure she is playing the right notes and occasionally hitting them at the right time, it is still pretty hard to detect a tune. At present, she is operating at a purely functional level. The playing has no 'feel' to it and she seems to lack an overall concept of where the piece is going or how it hangs together. But she is not disheartened, and neither am I. We both understand that to master the instrument will take practice and that her own creativity must take a back seat for a little while until she has grasped the physical demands of the instrument. Where creativity is all, on the other hand, it seems that the acquisition of actual craftsmanship becomes a matter more of chance than intention. The question must be asked if this is all students are entitled to by way of an education in drama – or, indeed, is all that they want. Writing in the early 1980s, Brian Watkins was already noting the way in which improvisation had elbowed out the teaching of theatre skills and dramatic literature:

> The title 'Improvisation' covered a host of activities, most lacking definition, structure or understanding, but supported by inappropriately borrowed disciplines or partially-digested child psychology. . . . Increasingly classes asked for 'real plays'. . . . Sometimes it appeared that the drama teacher, sticking rigidly to dogmatic theories of educational drama, was the person least able to recognise the children's needs, much less accommodate them.[3]

It is my intention in this chapter to explore the challenges facing teachers who want to give their students an understanding of plays and help them towards a conscious and satisfying mastery of the skills required to make, perform and respond to them.

Reading plays as literature

The well-thumbed copies of Terry Eagleton's *Literary Theory* and Raman Selden's *A Reader's Guide to Contemporary Literary Theory* in English university libraries[4] are a reflection of the way in which many English courses have moved away from considering the effect literature may be having on us as readers towards discussions of how, or why, we read literature and what we mean by it. Students wanting to apply contemporary literary theory to plays, however, are likely to be disappointed by the lenses for study offered by books like these. While traditional models treated plays as simply another form of literature, contemporary literary theory has all but ignored them. So, while it is easy for students to see that plays are not the same as novels and poems, particularly if they are familiar with performance analysis, it is much more difficult for them to find theorised discussions of exactly *how* they are different and what the practical implications of these differences might be. A factor which makes the application of literary theory to plays problematic is the fact that play scripts contain a number of elements which are not literary.

In his discussion of the question 'What is literature?', Terry Eagleton cites the London Underground sign, 'Dogs must be carried on the escalator', to illustrate that while all types of writing are open to literary interpretation we would not generally see writing like this as literature because it refers to a specific, pragmatic situation rather than referring to a general state of affairs.[5] Our understanding of what is written is dependent on the context in which we read it. Taking the sign to hold, in Eagleton's words, some sort of 'cosmic significance', would be either wilfully or playfully to misread it, or mistakenly to apply an inappropriate convention of reading. Play scripts, in some respects at least, *do* tend to use language in just such a direct, specific, pragmatic way. This is most obvious in the convention of stage directions. When we read at the end of J.B. Priestley's *An Inspector Calls*, for example, '*As they stare guiltily and dumbfounded, the curtain falls*',[6] the instruction seems unequivocal. Where the stage direction differs from the underground sign is that although the instruction *appears* unambiguous, what the consequent action signifies in the context of a performance of the play is open to a much wider interpretation. Thus, while the direction as written does not look 'literary', the effect it promotes may be profound.

Post-structuralist theories of literature have explored the unstable nature of linguistic signification, some even going so far as to suggest that the reader is free to ascribe meaning to signs just as he or she pleases. Others have challenged this freedom. Wolfgang Iser, for example, suggests that the unbounded potential of the text is inevitably constrained by elements inherent in its language, the manner in which it is received and the conventions the reader has been taught to apply. Iser proposes that any text contains certain 'blanks' which the reader, or listener, must fill for it to become comprehensible: 'Blanks allow the reader to bring a story to life, to assign meaning, and by making his decision he implicitly acknowledges the inexhaustibility of the text; at the same time it is this very inexhaustibility that forces him to make his decision'.[7]

So, how is the decision to fill the blanks guided? How do we attempt, as readers or listeners, to resolve the ambiguities of the text? Knowledge of the rules of grammar, although essential, is of only partial help. Miller points out that to understand the question, 'Can you pass the salt?', as an enquiry into one's *ability* to pass the salt is to apply English grammar correctly while failing to recognise the idiom.[8] Similarly, in the theatre, reading the stage direction above and expecting that at the end of *An Inspector Calls* a curtain will mysteriously and suddenly drop from the sky would be to make a mistake of the same kind. Anyone who is versed in the way stage directions are written, on the other hand, will know exactly what is to happen at this point in the performance: an obvious point, perhaps, but one which shows how conventions are learned through experience and active teaching. The way in which we employ a shared understanding of language beyond its strict grammatical sense is even more apparent when speech is used metaphorically. Miller again:

If you hear the advice 'Put a Tiger in Your Tank' and you were to extract the meaning on the basis of English composition alone, you would in fact have to undertake an elaborate programme of cramming a striped carnivore into a motor-car petrol tank. It is only a knowledge of the English community, car-owners, and assumptions about tigers having a fierceness that might apply to the power of petrol that enable us to see that this is not, in fact, an order to go out and track tigers for the boot of the car.[9]

The filling in of the textual blanks, then, is partly informed by the way in which the different communities we know, or to which we may belong, share a register. We look to speaker and context to indicate the meaning which is being inferred. Even without being aware of the whole context in which the word 'set' is uttered, for example, if we hear it from the mouth of a cook we may suspect it refers to custard or some other culinary thickening; a naturalist, on the other hand, might be talking about a place where badgers live. Hear the word in a theatre and we will most likely assume that the conversation is about the scenery for a play. Thus, we know that the instruction, '*The curtain falls*', indicates that the audience must be given a signal that the play is now over. Theatre practitioners could actually achieve this without a curtain at all – by simply lowering the stage lights, for instance. The interpretation is thus constrained but not entirely closed; the blank has been filled, but only in that particular context.

This 'slippage' between signifier and signified multiplies in the performance of a play, for the audience has rather more than just the words of the text to interpret. It would be very handy if, like Danny Kaye in the film *Wonder Man*, we were blessed with the ability to read more than one written text at once, for performances are 'polysemic', communicating not just through spoken words alone but via a complex cluster of signs issued simultaneously. It is because of this, that applying literary theory to a play script is of limited value. The playwright, unlike the novelist or poet, is uniquely constrained by the fact that he or she is *notating* what happens on the stage.[10] And, as Miller says, how can a writer notate, precisely, the tone, pitch, volume and pace of a line of dialogue – let alone all the other elements of performance? Teaching young people how to read a play on the page involves helping them to see the potential of the multiple texts inherent in the playwright's words as they appear on the pages of script. It is here that an understanding of theatre semiotics can help reveal the processes involved in the transition from page to performance and give an insight into how an audience is invited to interpret the work.

A knowledge of how registers are shared may help us to contextualise what we see and hear. Stanley Fish argues that groups of readers form what he calls 'interpretive communities' and suggests that texts are understood according to the conventions students have been taught in order to understand them.[11] These conventions may change over time and will inevitably vary from place to place. Nevertheless, by this account, communities reach a tacit agreement that signifiers are constrained in meaning. Why whole works cannot mean just whatever we wish is because we have learnt to interpret them according to certain *rules*. Although Fish has been criticised for this approach to literature on the grounds that he fails to theorise the convention of reading of which he speaks and simply makes the assumption that everyone reads in the same way,[12] his model might be useful to us in helping students learn how to read plays.

Reading plays as instruction manuals

Like musical compositions, plays have two sets of readers – those who read the notation and those who read the performance. Or, using Fish's model, it may be said that the play script is read by two interpretive communities. The first of these is the community of actors, directors, designers and technicians who undertake to put the script into performance. Unlike poems or novels, which allow the reader to ascribe meaning to each word and phrase directly, these artists and technicians stand between the play script and that other interpretive community: the audience at the subsequent performance. Understanding the relationship these two communities have with each other and with the words of the playwright is the key to the successful reading of plays for performance.

The craft of the first interpretive community – the actors, directors designers and technicians – is to help an audience fill in the blanks of the polysemic performance text by assembling signs in a way that will elucidate rather than confuse. One task of the teacher of plays then would be to introduce students to the register of signs shared by the production team which animates play texts in performance.

Aston and Savona discuss the way in which play scripts contain two kinds of instructions for those setting about creating a performance. 'Extra-dialogic' instructions are those, like stage directions, which are written down but not spoken on stage; 'intra-dialogic' instructions are those which are implicit in the dialogue itself.[13] It is a convention in Western publishing to print 'extra-dialogic' instructions in italics to signal that they are not to be spoken but to be taken account of in staging the play. Here is an example from Chekhov's *The Cherry Orchard*:

> *Suddenly a distant sound is heard, coming as if out of the sky, like the sound of a string snapping, slowly and sadly dying away.*[14]

This instruction is not a metaphor, demanding complex interpretation; it is simply telling the sound technician what must be produced at this moment in the performance. The technician's interpretation of the words is constrained by codes and contexts which eradicate the kind of ambiguity present in figurative language. Because Chekhov is writing instructions for the team who will turn *The Cherry Orchard* into a performance, he must make some assumptions about the codes and conventions likely to be applied to them. When he writes, '*Suddenly a distant sound is heard*', he is at the very least trusting that someone will understand how this is to be achieved.

Extra-dialogic instructions can give directives to all those involved in creating a performance. It is profitable to ask students to look at a selection of stage directions, such as those that follow, and consider which members of the production team are actually being addressed and how they would go about realising the task if they were in the team:[15]

> *In front of the fire – since that is the post of vantage, stands at this moment Major Booth Voysey. He is the second son, of the age that it is necessary for a Major to be, and of an appearance that many ordinary Majors in ordinary regiments are. He went into the army because he thought it would be like a schoolboy's idea of it . . . he stands astride, hands in pockets, coat-tails through his arms, cigar in mouth, moustache bristling.*
>
> *The Voysey Inheritance*, Harley Granville Barker[16]

> *The framework of a giant Tipi forms the entire setting. Eight struts meeting in the middle with a larger gap at the front. . . . The circular floor, of canvas and an Indian motif, is padded to allow for physical work and acrobatics. In the background hangs a large circular white disc, which can be lit from behind to create moonlight, sunset, day etc.*
>
> *Hiawatha*, Michael Bogdanov[17]

> *. . .echoes. Then from behind them a great ripping of ice and creaking iron. The sound of the Soviet ice-breaker.*
>
> *Whale*, David Holman[18]

> *She wears a skimpy ochre top and short skirt. A long, narrow, rectangular, white cotton apron, hangs from the neck to her thighs. It is embroidered with a blue border, and decorated with strings of white beads. Her headdress is a high, fan-shaped, brown busby with a coloured head-band sewn with white beads.*
>
> *In Search of Dragon's Mountain*, Toeckey Jones[19]

While extra-dialogic instructions such as these seem to be unequivocal about what is required from those responsible for implementing them, what is achieved in the performance will not only be dependent upon the skills and material available to the production team, but also on the vision and imagination of the designers and craftsmen and women who realise them. Some degree of interpretation is obviously involved though it is of a different order to the interpretation the team will need to bring to those directions implicit in the dialogue itself, the 'intra-dialogic' instructions. Consider the relationship between the stage direction from *The Cherry Orchard* and the line which follows:

> *Suddenly a distant sound is heard, coming as if out of the sky, like the sound of a string snapping, slowly and sadly dying away.*

LIUBOV ANDRYEEVNA: What was that?

Imagine reading only the dialogue in a classroom exercise. Students would be able to tell that the character was reacting to something although would not know what. On stage there should be no such ambiguity, for when combined with the sound effect which the audience will hear for themselves, it becomes obvious what Liubov Andryeevna is reacting to. Giving minute extracts of play scripts to students and asking them to demonstrate what they think is being asked for is one way of showing how the craft of the writer and the production team interrelate.

Some plays, notably those from the classical, medieval and renaissance periods, rely almost entirely on the reader being able to extract a sense of setting and action from the dialogue alone; the text 'states the terms of its own staging'.[20] This may be one of the reasons why young students sometimes find Shakespeare so difficult.[21] In this example from *Romeo and Juliet*, Shakespeare does not actually write an instruction for the actress playing Juliet saying that she must pick up the empty phial and then kiss the dead Romeo, but it is clear that for her to make no physical reference either to the bottle or the presence of Romeo would make the lines nonsensical:

> What's here? a cup, clos'd in my true love's hand?
> Poison, I see, hath been his timeless end.
> O churl! drunk all, and left no friendly drop,
> To help me after! I will kiss thy lips;
> Haply, some poison yet doth hang on them,
> To make me die with a restorative.
> Thy lips are warm![22]

Asking students to experiment with different ways of making these lines 'read' in an enactment draws their attention to the signposts for action embedded in the script while at the same time demonstrating that a number of variations are possible without the scene losing coherence (a point aptly demonstrated in Baz Luhrmann's 1997 film adaptation in which it is shown that Romeo need not actually be *dead* when Juliet speaks these lines). But it is not only physical action that can be directed by intra-dialogic instructions. Sometimes, the actual sound of the words can give an actor an indication of how they should be delivered, as in this soliloquy from *Macbeth*:

> She should have died hereafter;
> There would have been a time for such a word.
> Tomorrow, and tomorrow, and tomorrow,
> Creeps in this petty pace from day to day,
> To the last syllable of recorded time;
> And all our yesterdays have lighted fools
> The way to dusty death. Out, out, brief candle![23]

On one level, as the teacher of English literature might be keen to point out, the line 'tomorrow, and tomorrow, and tomorrow' suggests a period of time extending into the future. For the actor, and the student of drama, Shakespeare's choice of vocabulary shows rather how the line should be spoken. Consider the sound qualities of the line, how difficult it is to say it quickly compared with 'Out, out, brief candle!'. While the rhythm of the line in some ways *constrains* the actor playing Macbeth – and also constrains the audience's interpretation – it also *releases* the actor to add new elements in his physical performance which can give the words added texture. Thus, although the line must be spoken slowly, that does not stop the actor saying it ironically, or mournfully, or bitterly. The fourteen year olds I was watching were working on this same soliloquy. Under the guidance of the student teacher, they began to explore these sound qualities by using the speech as if it were a piece for a chorus. This allowed them to pick out the words and phrases they wanted to emphasise by echoing or repeating them while enriching their work with abstract movements that reflected the emotional impact of the sound patterns.

For an audience, and for the actor, the experience of hearing and seeing words spoken is very different from that of reading them silently, not least because of the physical signs projected by the very act of speaking. By way of demonstrating this to students, one might ask them to say the words 'huge' and 'tiny' while concentrating on what they are forced to do with their mouth and perhaps their whole face. Then, maybe, in German – 'riesig' and 'winzig' – or in French – 'énorme' and 'tout petit'. They will see that the sizes signified by these adjectives appear to be physically represented in the process of saying them. By releasing students from their books in order to experience and experiment with the gestures and movements suggested by a play text and by encouraging students to experiment with ways of speaking the words of a script aloud, a play's potential meanings will become clearer than would ever be possible through silent reading.

I have argued here that students should be encouraged to see play scripts not so much as literary texts, like novels and poems, but rather as instruction manuals which are followed by a team of theatre artists as they transform the words of the playwright into a performance. These instructions may take the form of seemingly unequivocal commands, such as stage directions, or more subtle indications hidden in the playwright's choice of vocabulary. But, useful though this analogy is, its limitations must already be apparent. For while any number of people accurately following the instructions with a plastic model kit would produce much the same result, the same cannot be said to be remotely true for a play. The reason for this is that while play scripts certainly do contain *some* instructions, Iser's 'blanks' tantalisingly remain, and it is in the blanks, those spaces which cannot be notated, that both readers and audience may revel in aesthetic interpretation.

Interpreting plays for performance

The way in which actors, directors and designers interpret play scripts will depend on the interpretive community to which they belong. Their training, the ethos of the company with which they are working, their history, will all influence the way they set about filling the blanks in the text. At the same time, they remain constrained by the script. I have tried to show how an over-literal approach can be stultifying and unilluminating; for some, on the other hand, the temptation to let their imaginations ride roughshod over the playwright's instructions is hard to resist. Getting the balance right between interpretation and textual fidelity is the key to a successful performance. Some of the conundrums faced by theatre artists in realising a play script in performance can be illustrated by looking at the plays of Samuel Beckett. While Beckett gives the actress playing Winnie in *Happy Days* the most detailed instructions of what she must do, the power of the play *as a play* is not immediately apparent from a reading.

WINNIE: (*gazing at zenith*) Another heavenly day. (*Pause. Head back level, eyes front, pause. She clasps hands to breast, closes eyes. Lips move in inaudible prayer, say ten seconds. Lips still. Hands remain clasped. Low.*) For Jesus Christ sake Amen. (*Eyes open, hands unclasp, return to mound. Pause. She clasps hands to breast again, closes eyes, lips move again in inaudible addendum, say five seconds. Low.*)[24]

Nevertheless, by using minutely elaborate directions like this, Beckett is guiding the actress playing Winnie towards the theatrical signs he wants deployed. The precision of her execution will certainly constrain an audience's interpretation but will not close it. Room for interpretation still exists. The point that students will do well to realise is that the actress who tampers with the instructions herself, rather than working in the blanks, is *adapting* the play rather than interpreting it into a performance.

Students should also learn that even when playwrights try to control exactly what an actor does, they cannot determine what an audience will make of a performance. This is not to say that an audience's reactions are completely unpredictable. When J.M. Barrie's script for *Peter Pan* asks the audience to clap if they believe in fairies, the writer was surely pretty clear how they would respond. Predicting responses is a fundamental part of the craft of theatre production, playwriting included, but quite different from determining meaning. One way of demonstrating to students how playwrights actively position their audience in relation to the action on the stage in order to induce a response is to ask them to try out a number of extracts where the actor addresses the audience directly. Experiencing the opening scene of Peter Nichols' *A Day in the Death of Joe Egg* in which a teacher berates the audience as if they are a naughty class, or the numerous asides in Claire Luckham's fake Restoration comedy, *Moll Flanders*, will quickly show them one way in which an audience's emotions can be manipulated.[25]

To help students understand more fully how the all-important creative balance between instruction and interpretation is maintained, it will be necessary to proceed a little further in the journey theatre artists make in their realisation of a play script. Although a playwright may give more or less specific instructions regarding the use of lighting, sound, space, movement and gesture, and the actors, by voicing the lines, may find guidance on how to deliver the words, attending to these instructions alone will not wholly reveal the play, either as it was formed in the playwright's mind, or shaped by the ideas of the performers themselves. This integrity can only be achieved by considering the different facets of the play script in relation to each other in order to pick out a coherent dynamic in the play *as a whole*. Consider David Storey's play *Home*, for example. The final stage direction reads:

> *After a while the light slowly fades.*[26]

This seems to be a purely functional direction, but the lighting designer may not see it as such. He or she will surely ask 'What type of light is it that is fading?', 'How slowly is "slowly"?', 'What is the intensity of the light?', 'What colour?', 'From which direction is it coming?'. The answers are apparent a few pages before this when the character Harry says, 'The sun has set'.

Any lighting designer who sets out to bathe the stage in green at the end of the play is either missing the point or deliberately subverting the text. I am not suggesting that texts should never be subverted, but doing so requires a conscious decision based on an understanding of the conventions that are being broken. What should be informing the lighting designer of *Home*, is an understanding of the tacitly agreed theatrical register which will frame both the production and the audience's response. Given that the audience's experience of earthly sunsets is not of a green glow, such a choice would lead either to confusion or speculation as to why a convention had been broken.

Most members of an audience experience a performance holistically. They will be left with a general impression, a feeling about what they have experienced. It takes a very sound knowledge of the script to know whether the production team is following the playwright's instructions accurately, especially its extra-dialogic elements. If, in the script, a stage direction reads, '*Enter, stage left*', will it affect that general impression if the actor comes onstage right? Will the speed the actor enters matter, or what he or she is wearing? Such decisions must be made consciously by those responsible for the performance according to the significance they, as an interpretive community, attach to the action. Agreement on how the text is to be interpreted in performance is vital if the production is to be coherent. A maze of unrelated signifiers will leave an audience frustrated as they follow a succession of signposts each of which appears to lead to a dead end.

When the actors in *Home* perform the penultimate stage direction,

> *Harry has begun to weep. Jack gazes off. A moment later Jack also wipes his eyes.*

they will be well placed to predict the audience's response, but only if they have attended to an underlying dynamic in the play script and have already given the audience a series of coherent signs to read derived from it. They may ask, 'Why are these men crying?', 'In what way does their weeping connect with the fact the "the sun has set"?', 'Will the audience weep in empathy with Harry and Jack, or will they feel a sense of mocking towards them?'. The response will depend on the way the whole production has moved towards this moment.

For the teacher, showing students how the interpretation of plays is constrained both by what is written and by the register of signifying conventions available to the production team is vital to their understanding of how plays are read for performance. And in their own performances too, students need to realise the importance of attending to the signifying details. Consider the questions raised by the opening stage direction of *Home*:

> *There is a white flag pole RC and upstage a low terrace with a single step down C; and a balustrade L. A round metalwork table is set slightly off-centre L, with a metalwork chair on either side.*

Where is this play set? What resonances does the image of 'a white flag pole RC' have? What sort of characters are we being shown? Further down the first page of the script, we are told that Harry wears 'a casual suit, perhaps tweed, with a suitable hat'. What might a suitable hat be? A policeman's helmet perhaps? A sombrero? Presumably not. David Storey is trusting that the costume designer is a member of an interpretive community that will associate the casual tweed suit with the British colonialism suggested by the stage furnishings. While the teacher may have to make a class aware of the significance of some of these details, he or she may at least trust that even very young students will spot the difference between images that seem incongruous and those that seem harmonious. Simply reminding students of the fun young children get from flip books which allow them to put a cowboy's head onto a nurse's body standing on a pair of clown's shoes, is an effective way of demonstrating how inappropriately mixed signals can both amuse and confuse.

By the time they reach the end of *Home*, the play's two interpretive communities will want to have filled in the blanks sufficiently to create in their minds a coherent whole. The way the characters are dressed, the set on which they appear, the final lighting direction and the fact that both men are weeping will join all the other signifiers in a complex but intelligible matrix of meaning. Perhaps they will conclude that the play is a metaphor for the demise of the British Empire, although that is certainly not the only possibility. What is important from a teacher's point of view is that students realise that plays acquire symbolic value by attending to the visual as well as verbal and other aural signifiers, some of which are prescribed by the playwright, others by the company of technicians and performers who set out to give an audience their own interpretation of the playwright's work.

I have outlined in more detail elsewhere some techniques for helping students understand the ways dramatic signifiers are structured and interrelated.[27] One technique is to divide a script into sections and to ask groups of students to read a section and write down on slips of paper what they think are significant actions contained in it. These actions may be signalled by stage directions or by what the characters are saying and doing. A 'map' of the whole script is then plotted by laying out the slips in the order in which they appear and arrows are drawn between those actions that seem to be linked in some way so that students can see both the entire narrative of the play and, hopefully, gain an insight into its structural dynamic.

In countering traditional approaches to the teaching of plays as literature, it has been suggested that it is more appropriate to see them as 'blueprints' for performance. Such a term is misleading, however, for it implies the playwright has a completely clear vision of the performance and has supplied a set of unequivocal instructions which, if followed to the letter, will achieve the desired outcome. In fact, the process followed in building a performance from the written text is less akin to following the detailed drawings of an architect and more like a group of builders being given a rough sketch, a pile of bricks, some plugs, wires, pipes and paint and told that they are to construct a five-storey building which is to be bold but aesthetically pleasing and which should reflect its surroundings. In the practical activity suggested above, a comparison of one group's 'map' of a given script with another's would serve to illustrate this point very well. Each group will have emphasised different aspects of the 'rough sketch' and be aiming to use materials in different ways.

Finally, the effect of time on interpretation must not be forgotten. Each successive reading or performance of a play will be a product of history, so that although the words on the page will be the same ten years after a first reading of a script, the reader will have aged and will be confronting it in a new context. Nevertheless, there is still an 'organic continuity' between the first and subsequent readings; the reader's attitude may have developed, but subsequent readings of the text will still be informed by the initial reading. For Miller, there are structures of meaning *inherent* in the text. He argues that failing to recognise the way these have been previously interpreted in production leads to a fracturing of the line of communication between the playwright and the audience; the work 'appears to be quoted rather than produced'.[28] In Robert Lepage's 1996 Toronto production of *Elsinore*, Lepage played all of the characters in a heavily 'quoted' version of *Hamlet*. Revelling in the possibilities of modern theatre technology and the capacity to create and juxtapose startling and often amusing images, Lepage's production was a celebration of how his own creativity had been stimulated by the original play. However, to talk of this production as a *performance* of *Hamlet* would be quite wrong, for while it gave insights into Lepage's interpretation of the original, it resisted the play's inherent structures. Miller's argument is not that things stay the same because of these inherent structures but rather, as Trevor Pateman points out, 'structure and history are mutually necessary, not mutually exclusive'.[29] Plays, like myths, develop historically but are encountered in the 'now' of the reader or audience.

Lifting the characters from the page

In the literary tradition, John Styan suggests, there is often an assumption that fictional characters have a kind of *pre-existence*, a psychological reality which may be detected and discussed through close reference to the dialogue.[30] It is an assumption which implies that characters must somehow be cloned by performers rather than created by them. A canter through the tasks offered in the back of many school editions of plays reveals that just about any type of writing can be employed to explore the lives characters are supposed to live beyond the bounds of the script: letters, diary and filofax entries, newspaper articles about their antics – even obituaries. While exercises like this may well be useful in testing students' knowledge of the events of the play, it is difficult to see that they could give them much insight into the way the characters are played will be construed by an audience. Similarly, any amount of 'close reading' is unlikely to provide much of a vision of how the characters might look and sound on stage. Part of the problem is that all such exercises tend to treat the characters in isolation and away from the only context in which they actually exist – the world of the play. Compare these essentially literary devices with Jonathan Miller's approach.

> I start out the rehearsals treating the speeches in the text as if they are premises to let that are to be occupied by persons as yet unknown. When casting, I may have advertised for a particular type of tenant but I cannot tell exactly how they will inhabit the role.[31]

Miller's casting and the subsequent development of the actors as tenants inhabiting characters shows a recognition of what sort of neighbours they will make *in the performance*. In this model, we go straight to the world of the play, to the harmony and tensions that come to light when the assembled characters are brought to life and seen trying to, or choosing not to, get on with each other.

So, what would this alternative approach look like in practice? I start from the assumption that, in order to understand a dramatic character, it is necessary to experiment with how that character might be played against others on the stage. Students might begin by trying to voice the lines in a number of highly *in*appropriate ways. This can quickly help them to fix on what they find an appropriate reading. Reading the soliloquy from *Macbeth* quoted earlier like a radio show jingle, for example, or performing it as a rap, not only makes playing with language fun but also highlights the fact that the rhythm of the lines and Shakespeare's choice of vocabulary will simply not stand such treatment without its inherent structure cracking. Later, students could be asked to write stage directions for actors on possible interpretations of small sections of script before passing them on to others to perform. Even this simple exercise can raise quite complex questions. Take the first two lines of dialogue in *Home*:

JACK: Harry!
HARRY: Jack.

How might these lines might be spoken? Characters' names may suggest a nationality and perhaps even a rough idea of the characters' ages. The exclamation mark gives the actor playing Jack some indication of the range of possible intonations. Beyond this, there is not much to go on. When I tried this exercise, two pairs of students added these stage directions:

JACK (*Clearly terrified. Cowering on the spot*): Harry!
HARRY (*Sternly. Staring at Jack*): Jack.

JACK (*Smiling broadly and opening his arms*): Harry!

HARRY (*Embarrassed. Looks down and mumbles*): Jack.

This led to a discussion about what sort of expectations each interpretation raised about the characters' relationship to each other. Which one seems right? The class immediately agreed that, from the evidence available, both could be and that to find out would require seeing more of the script.

Character work may be further enhanced by taking account not only of what characters say, but what others say about them and what the audience sees them do. Once again, attending to stage directions is essential in order to distinguish between what it is necessary for the production team to know and what the audience will ultimately experience. Not everything will be revealed in advance. A clear example of this is to be found in Emlyn Williams' thriller *Night Must Fall*.[32] The stage direction which announces Dan reads,

> *She is followed by Dan, who saunters past her into the room. He is a young fellow wearing a blue pill-box hat, uniform trousers, a jacket too small for him, and bicycle clips: the stub of a cigarette dangles between his lips. He speaks with a rough accent, indeterminate, but more Welsh than anything else.*
>
> *His personality varies considerably as the play proceeds: the impression he gives at the moment is one of totally disarming good humour and childlike unself-consciousness. It would need a very close observer to suspect that there is something wrong somewhere – this personality is completely assumed.*

While it is essential for the actor playing Dan to know that his personality 'is completely assumed', the performance would obviously be doomed if the audience saw this straight away. For the teacher in the classroom, the point is that the student reader of the play-as-literature is similarly denied the suspense of finding out 'who done it' because he or she will already have read Williams' direction. There is more fun – and more to be learned – by experimenting with just how the actor playing Dan might play this entrance without the foreknowledge that a reading brings.

Every drama teacher, a teacher of plays?

The history of how drama in schools has marginalised the study of plays has been well charted elsewhere.[33] Statistics derived from a 1990s survey of university students, where only ten per cent could name a play they had studied at school in drama lessons, support the view that for a long time there has been a deficit in this important aspect of the subject of drama.[34] A survey of my own in 1993 indicated that while the majority of secondary English teachers in Britain saw the teaching of plays as an important part of their work, fewer than half their drama colleagues thought that the teaching of

107

plays was important.[35] Given the physical restrictions of English classrooms, it looks very likely that large numbers of secondary students are missing out on the chance to experience how the opportunities for performance and practical exploration afforded by a well equipped drama space can help them gain an understanding of the ways plays are read for performance. Experience suggests that even if it were possible to whisk an English class off to the drama studio for some practical experimentation, it is doubtful that many English teachers would feel confident about teaching plays in this way.[36] Styan may have been rather optimistic when he wrote:

> There has been a change in our approach to the study of drama. . . .
> We used to work out plots and discuss characters, and occasionally analyse verbal imagery and the style of speech. Now we know that to discover, say, the time-scheme in *Othello* (if this can ever be done in a non-realist play), or Lady Macbeth's hidden relationship with her father ('Had he not resembled/My father as he slept, I had done't'), or Hamlet's views on marriage ('Why wouldst thou be a breeder of sinners?') brings us very little closer to the play in question.[37]

I believe that the rejection of the literary model of play analysis has not been as sweeping as Styan suggests, which leaves something of a hiatus in the teaching of plays. On the one hand, many drama teachers accustomed to an orthodoxy which has rejected dramatic literature remain reluctant to include a study of play scripts in their schemes of work, while on the other, English teachers are obliged to fall back on the codes and practices of literary studies which have tended to privilege the literary content and neglect the polysemic nature of the play in performance. The picture may appear bleaker still when one realises how many drama teachers began their careers as teachers of English.

If school students are to have proper access to the subject of drama in all its breadth and diversity, there needs to be a conscious shift towards the study of plays as texts rich in potential for creative interpretation for performers and audience. In this chapter I have used some very short extracts from a number of plays and put some markers down as to how this shift might be initiated. A fuller account of such practical methods may be found in some of the more recent publications aimed at the schools' market.[38] I have argued that the decisions taken by a production team will constrain the audience's interpretation of the play in performance and suggested that this basic principle should inform the way students are taught to read plays effectively. Starting from this point, the drawing of students' attention to the way short extracts of scripts provoke visual and aural images would sit alongside a gradual introduction to whole play scripts of increasing complexity. Playing practically with extracts from Shakespeare is a very different proposition to giving a whole Shakespeare script to a class as a first (and too often final) experience of his (or any other writer's) plays. If an effective way of teaching children how to read novels is to progress from picture books, which allow them to match the written narrative against the visual images, to successively challenging narratives which demand a mental visualisation of characters and events, then a similarly progressive strategy is required in the teaching of plays.

In the subject of drama, improvisation need not be seen solely as an outlet for a student's own creativity, an end in itself, but as part of a rehearsal process which stimulates and draws on a student's imagination and inventiveness to unlock the potential of the text in performance. To attempt to detach students from the constraints of their own interpretive community, or the interpretive communities of playwrights and theatre artists, in the name of spontaneity is to do them a grave disservice. Without having their attention drawn to what makes a good play good, argues playwright Noel Greig, it is unlikely that young people will be able to make any worthwhile plays of their own. 'Limitation', he says, 'is stimulation'.[39]

Notes

1 S. Berkoff (1994) *One Man's Show*, London: London Weekend Television.
2 J. Miller (1986) *Subsequent Performances*, London: Faber & Faber, p.45.
3 B. Watkins (1981) *Drama and Education*, London: Batsford, pp.105–6.
4 T. Eagleton (1983) *Literary Theory*, Oxford, Basil Blackwell; R. Selden (1985) *A Reader's Guide to Contemporary Literary Theory*, Brighton: Harvester Press.
5 T. Eagleton (1983), p.6.
6 J.B. Priestley (1947) *An Inspector Calls*, London: Heinemann.
7 W. Iser (1974) *The Implied Reader: Patterns of Communication in Prose Fiction from Bunyan to Beckett*, Baltimore, MD: Johns Hopkins University Press, p.280. Helen Nicholson makes a similar point in Chapter 5.
8 J. Miller (1986), p.42.
9 Ibid.
10 For an exploration of the idea of 'notation' in drama, see D. Hornbrook (1991) *Education in Drama: Casting the Dramatic Curriculum*, London: Falmer Press, pp.49–50.
11 S. Fish (1980) *Is There a Text in This Class?* Cambridge, MA: Harvard University Press. See also, 'The community of discourse', in D. Hornbrook (1989 [1998]) *Education and Dramatic Art*, 2nd edn, London: Routledge, Chapter 11.
12 See R. Selden (1985), p.118.
13 E. Aston and G. Savona (1991) *Theatre as a Sign System*, London: Routledge, p.76.
14 A. Chekhov (1951) trans. E. Fen, *The Cherry Orchard*, Harmondsworth: Penguin Books, Act II.
15 See A. Kempe and L. Warner (1997) *Starting with Scripts*, Cheltenham: Stanley Thornes, in particular Units 23–30.
16 H. Granville-Barker (1987) ed. D. Kennedy, *The Voysey Inheritance*, Cambridge: Cambridge University Press, Act II, p.97.
17 M. Bogdanov (1981) *Hiawatha*, London: Heinemann, Act I, p.1.
18 D. Holman (1989) *Whale*, London: Methuen, Act II, sc.1, p.32.

19 T. Jones (1992) *In Search of Dragon's Mountain*, Walton-on-Thames: Thomas Nelson, sc.2, p.16.
20 E. Aston and G. Savona (1991).
21 Some of the problems of teaching Shakespeare in the classroom are explored, in W. Michaels (1993) 'Plots have I laid: Shakespeare in the classroom', *NADIE Journal* 17(2), pp.23–9.
22 W. Shakespeare, *Romeo and Juliet*, Act V, sc.iii.
23 W. Shakespeare, *The Tragedy of Macbeth*, Act V, sc.iv.
24 S. Beckett (1961) *Happy Days*, London: Faber & Faber, Act I.
25 See A. Kempe and L. Warner (1997), in particular Units 11 and 20. See also A. Kempe (1998) 'Reading plays', in A. Goodwyn (ed.) *Teaching Literature and Media Texts*, London: Cassell.
26 This, and subsequent extracts, are taken from D. Storey (1970) *Home*, London: Samuel French.
27 A. Kempe (1996b) 'The whole text and nothing but the text', *Australian Drama Education Magazine* 2, Brisbane: National Association of Drama in Education, pp.8–13.
28 J. Miller (1986), p.37.
29 T. Pateman (1991) *Key Concepts: a Guide to Aesthetics, Criticism and the Arts in Education*, London: Falmer Press, p.165.
30 J.L. Styan (1984) *The State of Drama Study*, Sydney: Sydney University Press, p.1.
31 J. Miller (1986), p.96.
32 E. Williams (1982) *Night Must Fall*, London: Heinemann, Act I.
33 In for example, D. Hornbrook (1989 [1998]) *Education and Dramatic Art*, 2nd edn, London: Routledge. See also, A. Kempe (1994a) 'Dramatic literature in the classroom: time for an inspector to call?', in *Drama* 3(1), pp.9–15.
34 A survey of ninety-nine postgraduate certificate of education and BA drama students at the University of Reading and Homerton College, Cambridge in 1995 revealed that, by the age of sixteen, students had, on average, studied just *three* plays. A sizeable majority of these were by Shakespeare. Only nine of the respondents could name a play that they had studied in drama lessons as opposed to English lessons. Although most of these students would have finished their compulsory education before the introduction of the English and Welsh National Curriculum, the questions remain: 'to what extent are students being given the chance to experience play texts as the basis for a performance and will such a limited range allow them to compare and contrast structure, style and setting?'.
35 The survey targeted 600 schools throughout Great Britain. From the 141 respondents, thirty-nine per cent regarded the teaching of dramatic literature purely as a feature of English literature in general. While sixty-five per cent of English teachers regarded the study of plays as essential, only forty-seven per cent of drama teachers did.
36 A point made by the Schools Curriculum and Assessment Authority for England and Wales: 'many teachers and schools are not confident in their ability to meet the drama requirements', School Curriculum and Assessment Authority (1996) *Monitoring the School Curriculum: Reporting to Schools*, Hayes: SCAA Publications, p.4.
37 J.L. Styan (1984), p.1.
38 For example, see A. Kempe and L. Warner (1997) *Starting with Scripts*, Cheltenham: Stanley Thornes and M. Fleming (1997) *The Art of Drama Teaching*, London: David Fulton.

39 N. Greig (1994), in a practical workshop at the University of Reading: 'A couple of generations of would-be chair-makers', he wrote, 'have produced a vast array of bean-bag seats. Without any guidance within their trade, they learned from the only instructive form available: the television', in P. Abbs (1994) *The Educational Imperative*, London: Falmer Press, p.117.

7

THE CHOREOGRAPHY OF PERFORMANCE

Helen Nicholson and Ruth Taylor

Learning through collaboration

This chapter originates in our collaboration as teachers of drama and dance which began when we worked together in a large city comprehensive school during the early 1990s. At the time, the work of arts educators, most notably Ken Robinson and the influential National Curriculum Council Arts in Schools project, stressed the educational value of a coherent arts curriculum.[1] Our aim was to find practical ways of working together which acknowledged and preserved subject specialisms but which also encouraged students to extend their understanding of performance by exploring the creative opportunities presented by the combination of different art forms.

In practice, our work was not confined to drama and dance; we also found ourselves sharing ideas with musicians and visual artists, and enhancing our own knowledge of art forms which do not easily sit within traditional subject boundaries.[2] However, possibly because both are *performing* arts, we discovered that the combination of dance and drama was mutually enriching in particularly productive ways, and much practice in primary schools supports this premise. As we worked with our students, we discovered that the educational traditions of drama and dance complemented each other. The subject of dance has tended to place a greater emphasis on artistic movements, technique and theatre practitioners than has drama, which, in turn, has a very strong and important tradition of encouraging students to explore themes and issues. When these two elements of learning were combined, we found that students were able to generate their own creative ideas within a framework of diverse contemporary practices and artistic traditions. The combination of drama and dance enabled our students to experiment with a wider variety of performance styles than adherence to a single art form would have allowed.

Although we did not want to remain locked into our own subjects, we also felt that neither of us had the knowledge, artistic expertise or teaching methodology required to encourage students to achieve a high quality of learning in both disciplines. Also, because we both felt somewhat constrained by our own educational experiences, which had limited us to specific styles of performance, we wanted to avoid passing on this particular inheritance to our students. In working together to devise a coherent arts curriculum, in which almost all students followed courses in drama and dance to the age of sixteen, one of our objectives was to structure a programme that would enable students to find ways of articulating their ideas in both dance and drama and to incorporate performance styles which transgressed traditional boundaries.

The culture of performance

Performance has always been present in drama education, although its description, and its place in the curriculum, have changed according to contemporary theatre practice and educational values. Many drama teachers in schools have contested the traditional implications of the term 'performance', and have sought to replace formulaic approaches to rehearsal with more participatory models of learning. Furthermore, under the influence of cultural anthropology and the practices of alternative theatre, the definition of what *constitutes* performance has expanded. Performance is now no longer regarded as solely the preserve of the theatre-going public, but has come to include a variety of art forms (such as performance art, for example) found in a range of contexts and spaces. It is with this enlarged description in mind that this chapter will re-evaluate the place of performance in drama education and, by focusing on the relationship between drama and dance, will explore the educational issues which confront teachers and their students when they work towards performance.

Performance plays a large part in the culture of young people. From an early age, children develop a wide repertoire of performance crafts based in the oral traditions of the playground, where joke telling, skipping rhymes, clapping games and nursery rhymes are learnt and repeated as part of an inherited culture. Children's play is also interspersed with more recent aspects of performance; they move easily between the traditional and the contemporary as television catch-phrases, advertising jingles, rap and pop songs become incorporated into playground games. This playground culture of rhymes and role-play games enables children to recognise and use a variety of oral structures and to experiment with different patterns of speech and genres of narrative.[3] There is a strong element of performance in these games; the movements and voices are learned and practised. Indeed, many games require a high degree of technical skill, with skipping games, for example, providing levels of apprenticeship within the form itself. Playground performance is often multidisciplinary, reflecting a shared culture which is continually renewed through song, dance and drama.

The performance traditions which children bring to school provide an important basis for their work. As part of their everyday experience, children learn by watching others, by participating as members of an audience, and through regular practice often undertaken with remarkable tenacity, until they have perfected the craft and are ready to move on to more difficult or elaborate games. Observation of children at play would suggest that there is a high level of satisfaction to be gained by 'getting it right' and, indeed, no-one performs playground games better than young children. In part, it is this culture of performance which provides a model for their future education. The mixture of artistic disciplines, the emphasis on physical and oral crafts, and the determination to succeed is evident in the games children play. But where performance is included as part of an arts *education*, children may learn to understand and interpret artistic forms, to interrogate ideas and images, to find an emotional engagement with the subject matter. Performance becomes not simply a matter of reproducing the patterns of movement, the sounds or the rhythm of voices which the particular genre requires, but of using artistic languages to represent and explore thoughts, feelings and values. Furthermore, in both popular culture and established theatre practices, performance often incorporates a range of art forms such as the visual and aural effects of movement, design, sound and voice. In drama, a collaboration with other arts provides students with opportunities to explore performance in a diversity of artistic and cultural contexts.

Although an enduring aspect of the drama curriculum, the educational justification for performance has tended to polarise around two positions. On the one hand, theatre performance has been regarded as a means of understanding issues presented in dramatic form. Tony Jackson describes the theatre as 'an educational medium and a force for social change'.[4] Others have seen performance as the more arid acquisition of theatre skills, dislocated from their artistic and cultural contexts. However, in the artistic practice of performance these seemingly contradictory positions may be revised and found to complement each other.

Where students involved in devising a performance are encouraged to draw both on their own lived experiences and on the work of theatre practitioners, they are asked to question how theatre arts communicate and represent ideas. According to Maurice Merleau-Ponty, artistic creativity involves both an understanding of the art form, and the individual experiences of the artist:

> I am receiving and giving in the same gesture. I have given my knowledge of the language: I have brought along what I already know of the words, the phrases, and the syntax. I have also contributed my whole experience and everyday events, with all the questions left in me – the situations open and unsettled, as well as those with whose ordinary resolution I am all too familiar.[5]

Applied to making and giving a performance, Merleau-Ponty's argument suggests that the process is both creative *and* interrogative, culturally grounded *and* personally felt. As such, students' experiences as members of an audience inform their creativity and their knowledge of theatre form enables them, as performers, to communicate their ideas within a wider cultural frame.

Rachel Rosenthal, who danced in Merce Cunningham's young company and taught acting for Julian Beck's Living Theatre in the 1960s, describes creating a performance as 'a bit like gardening'. Using the metaphor of 'sowing seeds' she suggests that performance is an exploratory process in which the performer investigates ideas and finds innovative forms of communication.[6] Rosenthal's experimentation with both artistic style and content have led her to unorthodox modes of representation, to forms of theatre which are multidisciplinary and multifaceted. With this kind of innovative practice in mind, contemporary theatre practitioners have experimented with new performance arts, exploring those which build on the abstract languages of dance and the narrative structures of drama. The work of companies such as Theatre de Complicité and Lloyd Newson's DV8, or the collaborations between Caryl Churchill and Ian Spink,[7] have shown that by challenging the conventions of both disciplines, performance enables them to articulate ideas in ways which subvert traditional expectations. The choreographer Lloyd Newson, for example, has frequently spoken about the need for a 'new vocabulary' for dance, and has found the verbal language of drama liberating:

> Working with words is a new medium. I feel like I have opened a new door, a new dimension, and it does make me feel, as Wendy Houston says, as though we've been mute. I've only been half talking for a long time.[8]

When combined with a dramatic narrative, the symbolic portrayal of mood and emotion in dance enables students to explore the theatrical representation of ideas and to make conscious decisions about how audience perceptions might be challenged. Under the influence of contemporary practitioners, of whom Rosenthal, Cunningham, Churchill and Newson are examples, there is a recognition of the education potential inherent in the language of performance and in the learning achieved when students work *as* performers.

Theatre dance and dramatic form

Although drama and dance share a history of live performance, the most obvious difference between the conventions of drama and dance is that drama has customarily placed an emphasis on the spoken word, whereas the language of dance expresses thoughts, ideas and emotions through movement. Indeed, the literary tradition of scripted plays has implied that the written text is the primary source for performance, and reading, rather than performing, plays has been very much part of educational practice, particularly in the English curriculum. In dance, a kinaesthetic art form, meanings are represented through physical actions, using highly codified techniques and styles.

In the performance of dance, choreographed movements use symbolism to reach an audience, a language which is based on culturally bound conventions of non-verbal communication. Perhaps one of the most intelligible of dance styles to those familiar with the narratives of drama is ballet. Its close association with mimed gesture means that its codifications may be familiar to an audience whose members understand the cultural conventions of gestured movements. A hand resting on the heart, for example, and a gesture towards another dancer signals to an audience that the one is in love with the other. In this case, provided that the language of dance has been constructed appropriately and choreographed using recognised modes of representation, the performer has both been given the required 'tools' to interpret the choreographer's intention and has conveyed the emotion in a style which enables the audience to follow the story.

However, there are many forms of dance where the emphasis on dramatic story-telling is less strong and which are more ambiguous in interpretation. The range of subject matter in contemporary dance is huge, including the more abstract work of choreographers such as Merce Cunningham. However, despite the absence of a linear narrative and accepted forms of mimed gesture in Cunningham's dance, the movement and dynamics of the choreography carry emotional resonances. In *Duets* (choreographed in 1988), for example, which consists of a series of apparently unconnected duets executed one after another, the abstract expression of the dance leaves the audience with the task of decoding and interpreting the symbolic representation of mood and feelings. This style of dance makes different demands on the audience, for, rather than adhering to a single narrative line or mimetic gestures, the *form of the dance itself* holds a multiplicity of meanings. Cunningham describes the relationship between choreographic intentionality and audience.

> I don't think that what I do is non-expressive, it's just that I don't try to inflict it on anybody, so each person may think in what ever way his feelings and experience take him. I always feel that the movement itself is expressive, regardless of intention of expressivity, beyond intention.[9]

Cunningham suggests the role of the audience is to engage emotionally with the language of expression, and interpret the work without searching for the choreographer's original meaning or intention. Nonetheless, this is not simply a subjective response to a series of dance motifs.[10] The process of reading the dance, of making it intelligible, requires an understanding of the particular language of this form of theatre dance.

One important aim of dance education, therefore, is to equip students with the means to interpret dance. The many conventions of performance can then be recognised and decoded, enabling students to create their own meanings based on their previous knowledge and understanding of the form and content of dance. The emphasis on audience response suggests that the meanings of dance are contextually and culturally grounded; they are open to re-interpretation, by the choreographer, *and* the performer *and* the audience. Indeed, Randy Martin, writing about dance literacy, argues that 'over-reading' a dance text implies that it is a 'static work' rather than a live art form.[11] In practice, an education in dance is an education in interpreting and experimenting with its symbolism and non-verbal forms of communication; it aims to make the language of dance accessible to a wider audience. Because dance theatre has evolved a complex sign system of its own, without a dance vocabulary young people struggle to make sense of what they see, to make *associations*, and are thus excluded from the creative practice of performance.

In education, the challenge to find a more inclusive model of performance suggests that the process of learning about the professional world of theatre dance should be placed in the context of the artistic and cultural understandings which students bring with them from outside the classroom. Dance in performance is an integral part of today's teenage music culture; MTV and the various music channels have turned the pop video into a visual and kinaesthetic experience which has taken the song beyond the aural. Indeed, many professional dance companies have become increasingly indebted to the electronic arts which are very much part of young people's experiences. Here the distinction between high art and popular culture has been eroded. Sally Banes comments on this development:

> Social-dancing provides a historically rich context for the wedding of music and dance. And as social-dancing from MTV to hip-hop to theatricalised tango and ballroom, dancing on Broadway – began to rivet the world's attention in the 1980s, the avant-garde took its lead from popular culture.[12]

How then, in providing an education in performance, can the gap be bridged between the abstract language of theatre dance and the instant accessibility of dance in the music video? If the practice of performance is to encourage young people to explore their thoughts and ideas and emotions, and to communicate their ideas to an audience, how might they find a language of performance which reflects and extends their own social experiences?

Jazz is one example of a dance style which, because of its various re-interpretations in black performance arts, is integral to students' social lives. The music of the Fugees, for example, has re-invented rap and reggae and simultaneously increased the demand for a dance-led music scene. Thirteen and fourteen year old students may be introduced to the style of jazz through the African-influenced style of dancing (isolations, parallel, low centre of gravity, syncopated rhythms) which accompanies the Fugees' music. The relaxed way of moving within the style gives the first suggestion of meaning: the dynamics of the movement are peaceful and calming. If the dancing is then analysed in relation to the video setting (an inner city street, the sunset-lit beach, a studio interior), more 'clues' can be read and interpreted. The students learn through practice and critical observation, focusing on the representation of ideas within a cultural framework that is already familiar to them.

In moving from popular culture to theatre art, students might consider the various interpretations of jazz dance styles by dance theatre practitioners. Judith Jamison, Alvin Ailey and the jazz influences in Christopher Bruce's work provide starting points, as their work generally has a strong narrative and, in the works of Jamison and Ailey, an overt exploration of ideas associated with the emancipation of the slaves and black American rights (Ailey's *Revelations*, for example, choreographed in 1960). These ideas are expressed using the accepted conventions of contemporary jazz dance and an abstract representation of ideas through symbolism. Whilst analysing the narrative content, and learning to adapt it for their own creative work, students learn about the historical development of jazz style; through finding clear parallels in their own social dance they become familiar with the symbolic language of dance in the theatre. This requires students to examine the principles underpinning the technique, to analyse the style and stylistic qualities of jazz, and to trace its historical development and the choreography and interpretation of meanings. It is a participatory process, wherein students experiment with their own performances of jazz dance and build on their experiences and understanding of the form.

If the performance of dance is to inform drama, it entails an understanding of the relationship between the movement of the body, the dramatic atmosphere and the representation of ideas. A particularly interesting example of this combination (which we used with students in both drama and dance lessons) is *Still Life at the Penguin Café*, choreographed in 1989 by David Bintley. The dance depicts a variety of species which are extinct, or on the verge of extinction. Although the romantic story line of the animals who seek refuge in the ark at the end of the ballet is naturalistic, their characteristics are shown through motifs and emotive images. The vulnerability of the zebra, for example, is depicted using a series of slow extensions interspersed with small, rhythmic movements influenced by African dance styles. Set against a background of physically identical women, all sporting black and white boas to depict the zebra's fur, the zebra dancer moves with a melancholic expression of resignation. This particular dance invokes the conventional imagery of animals in popular culture and by extending the metaphor, subverts a familiar representation of animals in order to draw attention to the element of protest implicit in the work.

This 'representation of a representation' increases the need for an audience to have the 'tools' with which to interpret the choreographic symbols for themselves. At the same time, the students' interpretation of Bintley's work is not a detached process of analysis, but a creative journey, where understanding of the form of representation is shown through their own dance and devised drama. As they embark upon this journey, it is important that students have the confidence to experiment without fear of being judged 'right' or 'wrong'. The responsibility lies with the students, as choreographers and performers, to ensure that the ambiguities inherent in the form are presented in such a way that there is scope for the audience to re-interpret their work.

Dance theatre differs from drama in its particular languages and systems of codification. Because the references to everyday use of mime and gesture in dance can be close or distant, the term 'literacy' is more commonly applied to dance than to drama. In turn, the application of the conventions of drama to dance can make it less abstract and more explicit in terms of narrative, role and exploration of ideas. Where they inform each other, dance and drama encourage the exploration of implicit and multiple meanings, and enable students to make performances using culturally recognised frameworks of representation and symbolism.

The context of production

A collaboration between drama and dance offers an alternative to the dramatic convention of naturalism. Television has made young people very familiar with naturalism, so that for most students, soap operas and mini-series are what they recognise *as* drama – with the accompanying tradition of melodramatic representations of contemporary social issues.[13] Whilst not wishing to negate the significance of this major dramatic genre, our collaboration aimed to offer students the chance to extend their artistic repertoires by working within forms of performance with which they were less familiar. Seen in the context of world cultures, naturalism offers a potent but limited means of representation. While our reasons for introducing students to a wider language of performance was in part an ambition to introduce them to a wider range of artistic forms from a diversity of contemporary and historical contexts, we also wanted to show how different styles of performance *in themselves* communicate ideas and values. Although the naturalistic acting styles of television drama are well suited to the exploration of social issues, for example, and it is integral to the genre that moral decisions are invited from the audience, they do nothing to explore the more metaphorical representation of cultural values through myth, ritual or poetic and abstract narratives. Ngugi wa Thiong'o, writing about the politics of African theatre, argues that it is through language, including the abstract and verbal languages of performance, that cultural values are created and reproduced:

> Communication between human beings is also the basis and process of evolving culture. In doing similar things and actions over and over again under similar circumstances . . . certain patterns, moves, rhythms, habits, attitudes, experiences and knowledge emerge. . . . Over time this becomes a way of life distinguishable from other ways of life. They develop a distinctive culture and history.[14]

Ngugi wa Thiong'o suggests that the form and style of communication is inseparable from the values of a particular culture. The implication of his argument is that unless we introduce students to a range of performance styles they will remain limited to their immediate cultural horizons. For Ngugi wa Thiong'o, whose specific project is to decolonise African theatre practice, this constraint is part of the process of liberation; his advocacy of a nationalist and patriotic theatre would have very different political resonances in Britain. What is transferable to other contexts is his identification of the relationship between artistic form, the style of performance, and cultural values. In drama education, it has become accepted that performance genres, such as naturalistic drama and epic theatre, interrogate ideas and values. However, performance may also be a public expression of collective beliefs and an important means of cultural affirmation or resistance.

Working with a group of sixteen year olds on African theatre as part of a collaborative project, the value of integrating drama and dance in performance became clear. The aim was for the students to produce a performance piece which would focus on the use of collective memory and oral traditions in contemporary African theatre of resistance. The starting point was a scene from Ngugi wa Thiong'o's play, *Ngaahika Ndeenda*, in which the dramatic action is developed through dance and song.[15] As our students began to explore the scene and find appropriate styles of performance, they discovered that the form of the performance was inseparable from the content; dance was used to invoke memories of the past and aspirations for the future. The play led the students to research both the crafts of the performers and the context of production. Their preconceptions about the significance of performance was challenged as they learned of plays, dances and songs which had been banned by colonialist rulers, and how the traditional crafts of the performers had been adapted to tell a story of the Kenyan people. They realised that the lines, 'In those days, We used to dance in the Kineenii forest', meant more than some picnic pastime; this was performance at the centre of a struggle for human rights. In learning the dance and the songs, and by finding acting styles which suited a form of dramatic story-telling which is often poetic, choral and monologic, they were able to explore both the cultural and artistic context of the play. By working physically with the form, they found that the rhythms of the dance and songs signified a collective affirmation of a cultural tradition.

Our aim was not, however, for the students to achieve some kind of 'authentic' performance of Ngugi wa Thiong'o's play. Rather, we wanted them to learn about this particular form of theatre through practice, and to apply their understanding to their own work. In choosing Marina Gashe's poem, *The Village*,[16] as a starting point for their own performances, we hoped that students would address issues of the theatrical representation of Africa in the West. The poem is rich in visual images and potential for movement, and the students wove together choric dialogue with dance. However, it was the experience of working on Ngugi wa Thiong'o's play which led them to understand that Gashe's 'Old women dark and bent', and 'Young wives like donkeys', were not to be represented as elements in a Romantic pastoral idyll; they were aware of Ngugi wa Thiong'o's criticism of officially sanctioned, exported stereotypes of African rural culture. Their final piece, in which they employed a range of performance styles – freedom songs, Mwomboko dance and mime – was framed by a traveller's commentary through which, interestingly, the students chose to interrogate Western images of Africa through the use of slides and naturalistic dialogue.

We were aware of the risks of cultural appropriation, and of the dangers of mistranslation, but to explore this aspect of drama without consideration of performance style and form would be to miss the point. In the students' final performance, however, the mix of naturalism and symbolic languages of movement, song and poetry allowed them to evoke a distance between one set of cultural values and another. As such, they were not attempting to 'be Africans', as some travesty of authenticity in the conventional, post-Stanislavski sense of the term, but to use the abstract languages of theatre to tell an important story. It required us to introduce students to appropriate acting styles, dance forms and song; they needed a 'grammar' of performance which was both intelligible and contextually grounded. In Clifford Geertz's words, it was a question of 'blurring the genres' in order to encourage students both to learn from African theatre practice and to reconsider their perceptions about a particular social context and the cultural significance of performance. And although issues of representing 'other' cultures were far from resolved, as Ngugi wa Thiong'o has commented, in a climate of mutual respect, there is much to be gained from exchange.[17]

This project demonstrated to students that the values of a culture and the practice of the arts are interdependent. It is through the symbolic languages of the arts, as Geertz has identified, that experiences, memories, beliefs and thoughts have a public significance: 'In order to make up our minds we need to know how we feel about things; and to know how we feel about things we need the public images of sentiment that only ritual, myth, and the arts can provide'.[18] If meaning-making is dependent on language, language not only describes experience but is also constituted by it. In this context, telling stories in dramatic form, recognising and using the symbolism of performance, is part of a process of exploration. As the interplay between personal feelings and cultural values, the symbolic languages of performance are integral to, and grounded in, both the social production of art and the public act of communication.

The place of performance

Performance, we have argued, is embedded in a social context and carries cultural significance. Making a performance which reaches and involves an audience depends, therefore, on some understanding of theatrical convention and an awareness of the cultural expectations brought to the specific performance event. By the same token, the intelligibility of a performance is guided by the conditions of production and reception, the crafts of the performers and the use of recognisable theatrical devices. In practical terms, this means that students' experiences as members of an audience inform their work as performers. As such, the critical observation and creative interpretation of performers' crafts form part of the process of learning to communicate with an audience.

The ability to 'read' a performance is dependent on the recognition and interpretation of theatrical signifiers. However, many studies of the relationship between the performers' intentions and audience reception suggest that there is no straightforward or transparent meeting point between them. Rather, it is argued, audiences *interpret* a performance, both individually and collectively, by drawing on both their cultural understanding of the art form and their personal experiences. Audiences inevitably 'read' a performance from a particular perspective – what Hans-Georg Gadamer has described as their 'horizon of expectation' – but the performance itself may open up new horizons and unforeseen possibilities. Reading a performance is not, therefore, an entirely arbitrary or subjective process but neither is it a simple matter of uncovering a stable or fixed meaning. Susan Bennett describes the act of spectatorship in terms of a dialogue, which both affirms cultural expectations and challenges audience perception: 'Cultural systems, individual horizons of expectations, and accepted theatrical conventions all activate the decoding process for a specific production, but, in turn, the direct experience of that production feeds back to revise a spectator's expectations, to establish or challenge conventions, and, occasionally, to reform the boundaries of culture'.[19]

Applied in an educational context, this argument takes on a particular significance. As members of an audience, students learn to recognise and interpret the cultural conventions of performance which they may use creatively in their own work to invite and stimulate audience response. As they become increasingly aware of the different effects of artistic representation, they are able to manipulate form with increasing dexterity, drawing on what they know as *readers* of performance texts.

In this context, the choreography of performance takes account of a critical appreciation of performance crafts and of their contribution to the signification of meaning. It is a process of discovery, where students learn to recognise that their work will be interpreted within a framework of reference brought to the performance by the audience. Or, to borrow Wittgenstein's phrase, it involves an awareness of how the linguistic 'signposts' of performance might be used to communicate with others. Reading symbolic languages, according to Wittgenstein, is a dialogic experience which *guides* the audience; it is the artistic text *itself* which teaches students the effects of gesture, voice, movement, pace, dramatic timing, motif, and so on. The word 'signpost' is particularly useful in this context; performers, working collaboratively with directors, choreographers and designers, create the signposts which are then available for the audience to interpret. In educational terms, where students are likely to choreograph their own performances, a critical literacy of theatre is directed towards giving students greater artistic independence, through an application and adaptation of the 'vocabulary' of dance and drama.

The practical application of theories of production and reception, particularly when they are used to expand students' artistic repertoires, leads to a reconsideration of the place of performance texts in the curriculum. In dance education this is well established; in drama the case for critical appreciation has been less clearly defined. Teachers of drama do offer models of performance in their lessons, however, most notably through the practice of 'teacher-in-role', where, by taking a part themselves, they can steer the action and direct the learning. This technique is not usually used to teach the craft of performance, although its naturalistic acting style offers a perspective from which to interrogate the content of the drama and can be an effective way of extending students' linguistic registers. Furthermore, as Joe Winston points out, the 'teacher-in-role' employs theatrical conventions such as 'gesture, costume, gait, tone of voice, symbolic objects' which may be used to engage students' emotions.[20] Indeed, by learning from teachers and other performers, students might gain the confidence to experiment with the physical crafts and symbolic languages of performance for themselves and identify how their understanding of audience reception influences their own creative work.

Much radical theatre performance has transgressed established artistic categories by bringing together dance, drama, music and visual spectacle. Some of the most striking challenges to conventional theatre in Britain were the carnival-like performances of community theatre groups in the 1970s and 1980s, where the fusion of styles and blurring of genres invited political comment. The place and the style of these performances, the profusion of theatrical crafts employed, the use of caricature and satire, meant that this form of alternative theatre became (to borrow Baz Kershaw's phrase) a form of 'cultural intervention'.[21] Theatre practice which draws overtly on local knowledge in this way shows students how performers' assumptions about the audience's everyday experiences can infuse the piece. It also demonstrates how a performance style might itself be used to confront social issues.

As part of our collaboration, we used a project about community theatre with students aged twelve and thirteen to explore the relationship between place, audience and performance crafts. Using the exaggerated and parodic styles of street theatre, the work aimed to create a dramatic narrative which showed the significance of carnival to a particular community and to tell the stories of the characters involved. The project began with research into the cultural significance of street theatre, its representation by Brueghel in medieval times, video footage of Caribbean carnival, and the observation of contemporary street performers in Bristol and London. The students discovered that street theatre frequently contains an element of protest, often through the inversion of hierarchies or the satirical representation of establishment figures. This appealed to their sense of comedy enormously, and they collected images and motifs to incorporate into their own work. Coincidentally, during the project there was a school trip to see Dylan Thomas' *Under Milk Wood* at a local theatre and, at their suggestion, the opening speech of Captain Cat provided them with a model which began their own performance narrative.

The performance piece showed the day of the carnival framed by an observer who, like Captain Cat, commented on the action. Flashback sequences showed the recent histories of the characters and illustrated the motivation for each part of the carnival, such as the settling of old scores and the celebration of past events. The carnival itself was a dance, in which movement was choreographed from the 'found' images of a street scene. The dance was devised and performed by small groups of students, while other members of the cast created the background sounds of an excited, participating audience. In this way, the class were the audience for their own performance; the structure gave opportunities for group work, in both dance and drama, whole class role-play and the performance of a dramatic script.

The students who participated in this work demonstrated their understanding of different performance styles which they used for a variety of artistic and dramatic purposes. Their experiences as audiences had come from a similarly wide range of sources: live theatre, video extracts, photographs, carnival itself and the 'found' images of the street which they interpreted in dance and drama forms. This gave the students new experiences of the arts which, when combined with observation of everyday life, stimulated and informed their creative practice. Furthermore, watching performances also provided an important frame of reference for interpretation and appreciation of their own and each other's work. The ability to use a critical vocabulary of performance to describe the choices they made enabled the students to be explicit about their learning, and reinforced their understanding of movement, gesture, voice, motif and dramatic focus. As part of the rehearsal process, we encouraged them to support each other by acting as critical observers, adding ideas as choreographers or directors. Preparing to present their play to an audience, however informally, provided a real context for their work; the student performers gained ownership of the artistic form, and felt an emotional commitment to its success.

The relationship between theatrical representation and audience response offers both intellectual and creative challenges; it extends students' 'horizons of expectation' by encouraging them to recognise familiar ideas, values and feelings and by opening new ways of seeing. It is, in Gadamer' words, one way in which their 'range of vision is gradually expanded'.[22] Furthermore, and importantly, where classroom practice includes an element of performance, students are encouraged to situate themselves in relation to the expectations of a perceived audience. In the process of exploring the place of performance, students learn to question assumptions, to depend on each other, and to share mutual responsibility for the work.

Languages of performance

Underlying this discussion of the educational opportunities presented by performance is our view that neither drama nor dance has a *universal* language of performance, despite the fact that they both are present in cultures throughout the world. This not only raises questions about the interpretation of performance. It also implies that a performer's task – to create theatrical signs using voice and body – is only meaningful in collaboration with an audience which, broadly speaking, shares similar points of reference. In drama education, and particularly where a range of art forms is included in the drama curriculum, the acknowledgement that the language of performance is contextual rather than universal has two interrelated consequences. First, it suggests that no one style of acting or rehearsal methodology has the capacity to represent and convey a diversity of ideas and values. Second, it recognises that the craft of the performer is contingent on context, and is intimately connected to the particular genre, style and form of performance.

Philip Zarrilli, in his discussion of the theory and practice of acting, makes the point that an understanding that all languages of acting are provisional rather than universal opens the way for more diverse and differentiated practices of performance. He argues that Western approaches to actor training have been dominated by psychological naturalism, a method

125

which articulates with culturally specific theories of self-hood. As such, the emphasis on the authenticity of feeling, individual motivation and intentionality reproduces specific ideas about the relationship between character, role and dramatic action which, whilst useful in some styles of performance, has limitations. In reconsidering the actor's craft, he suggests that the abandonment of the search for a universal language of acting is liberating: 'Rather we can spend our energy on the continuing challenge of searching for languages of acting which best allow one to actualize a particular paradigm of performance in a particular context for a particular purpose'.[23] In terms of drama education, which is not ordinarily concerned with actor training, the recognition that approaches to role, to rehearsal and to dramatic representation derive from culturally specific values and attitudes suggests that a variety of performance paradigms might broaden students' perspectives.

Despite the powerful influence exerted by directors and choreographers such as Stanislavski, Brecht, Cunningham and Bruce on performance practice, their work too indicates a provisional rather than universal language of theatre. The emotional involvement and political commitments to which their practices aspire represent a specific set of expectations and assumptions. As Philip Auslander argues, deconstructive theories of both acting and self-hood have explored the values which underwrite these paradigms of performance and have drawn attention to the ways in which performers create meanings through the body.[24] In a reconceptualisation of performance as a physical act of communication, the body is located as the primary instrument of expression. This does not mean that performance entails a simple repetition of learned techniques; it requires both emotional and intellectual engagement with the languages of performance, described by Merleau-Ponty as 'embodied agency'. In his essay 'Eye and Mind', Merleau-Ponty suggests that the intellect and the emotions are contingently and reciprocally implicated in expressive acts: 'It is by lending his body to the world that the artist changes the world into paintings ... not as a body as a chunk of space or a bundle of functions but that body which is the intertwining of vision and movement'.[25] Furthermore, as feminist and postcolonial performance theorists have identified, the body is not a neutral 'chunk of space', nor is performing a matter of just 'being yourself'. The body, in performance as elsewhere, carries with it a weight of cultural signifiers which are read and constructed according to individual and societal values. In this context, a performance is a dialogue between artists and audience; actors and dancers communicate through the body, and the audience re-interprets the symbolic languages of performance.

Jerome Bruner argues that meaning-making is shaped by those traditions which have become a 'culture's toolkit of ways of thought'.[26] However, neither cultural values nor artistic styles stand still; the juxtaposition of different performance traditions is one way of interrogating or affirming orthodox ways of thought. As a public language of dialogue and exchange, the arts offer new ways of feeling and thinking. For Merleau-Ponty, artistic creativity is a process of research:

> A language which gives our perspective on things, thus putting things into relief, opens up a discussion over things which does not end in itself but itself invites research and makes accumulation possible. What is irreplaceable in a work of art ... is that it contains, better than ideas, *matrices of ideas*.[27]

In an educational context, the performing arts offer a very practical and direct way to explore personal values and cultural attitudes. This is not just confined to theatre practice which sets out to alter perspectives; myth, ritual, story and the abstract representation of emotion, all give insights into the 'matrices of ideas' which constitute artistic practice. For young performers, the accumulation which Merleau-Ponty describes is not a check list of performance skills but a more subtle acquisition of performance crafts explored in the context of the cultural and artistic representation of ideas. The choreography of performance, in the way in which we understand the process, aims to engage students both emotionally and intellectually. Because performance involves taking risks and as an imprecise art holds many ambiguities, it is perhaps appropriate to end on a note of uncertainty. Actress Fiona Shaw comments on the 'magic of suggestion' and the 'vulnerability' which is implicit in all performances. Echoing her quotation of Touchstone in Shakespeare's *As You Like It*, in the process of exploring the languages of dance and drama with young people, we have found 'Much virtue in if'.[28]

Notes

1 For a rationale for combined arts, see National Curriculum Council Arts in Schools Project (1989) *The Arts 5–16: Practice and Innovation*, London: Oliver & Boyd.
2 We are thinking here of a range of art forms, including, for example, pop video, puppetry, masque, Aboriginal dreamtime, Noh Theatre, Kabuki and many others.
3 For a discussion of the performative qualities of playground games and children's picture books see H. Nicholson (1996) 'Voices on stage', in M. Styles, E. Bearne, V. Watson (eds) *Voices Off: Texts, Contexts and Readers*, London: Cassell, pp.248–63.
4 T. Jackson (ed.) (1993) *Learning Through Theatre*, London: Routledge, p.4.
5 M. Merleau-Ponty (1973) *The Prose of The World*, Evanston, Northwestern University Press, p.11.
6 R. Rosenthal (1985), cited by E. Lampe, in 'Rachel Rosenthal creating her selves', in P.B. Zarrilli (ed.) (1995) *Acting (Re)Considered*, London: Routledge, p.304.
7 Memorably in *The Lives of the Great Poisoners* (1990) and *Hotel* (1997).

8 G. Carter (1993) 'Gary Carter talks to Lloyd Newson', *The Dance Theatre Journal* 10(4), p.9.

9 Quoted in J. Lesschave (1985) *The Dancer and the Dance: Merce Cunningham in Conversation with Jacqueline Lesschave*, London: Marion Boyars Publishers, p.106.

10 Cunningham's emphasis on the expressivity of dance form, drawn from Suzanne Langer, has been contested by Miwa Nagura, who argues that it is read through an understanding of the cultural symbolism of Western contemporary dance. For a fuller discussion, see M. Nagura (1996) 'Cross cultural differences in the interpretation of Merce Cunningham's choreography', in G. Morris (ed.) *Moving Worlds*, London: Routledge, pp.270–87.

11 R. Martin (1996) 'Overreading the promised land: towards a narrative of context in dance', in S. Foster (ed.) *Corporealities: Dancing Knowledge, Culture and Power*, London: Routledge, pp.177–98.

12 S. Banes (1994) *Writing Dance in the Age of Postmodernism*, Hanover and London: University Press of New England, p.336.

13 For example, the popular BBC television soap opera, *EastEnders*, has variously tackled issues such as rape, paternity rights, alcoholism and mental illness.

14 Ngugi wa Thiong'o (1981) *Decolonising the Mind*, London: Heinemann Educational, p.14.

15 Ibid., pp.95–8.

16 L. Hughes (ed.) (1970) *Poems from Black Africa*, Bloomington and Indianapolis, IN: Indianapolis University Press, p.47.

17 This is a complex argument and much the concern of Sita Brahmachari in Chapter 2. Ngugi wa Thiong'o argues that the European appropriation of African arts, as examples of primitivism, is to be resisted, but offers a more optimistic alternative of intercultural dialogue, within a climate of mutual respect, as a means of avoiding cultural stagnation. See Ngugi wa Thiong'o (1993) *Moving the Centre*, London: Heinemann Educational, pp.12–24.

18 C. Geertz (1973) *The Interpretation of Cultures*, New York: Basic Books, p.82.

19 S. Bennett (1990) *Theatre Audiences: A Theory of Production and Reception*, London: Routledge, p.180.

20 J. Winston (1996) 'Emotion, reason and moral engagement in drama', *Research in Drama Education* 1(2), p.197.

21 B. Kershaw (1992) *The Politics of Performance: Radical Theatre as Cultural Intervention*, London: Routledge, p.68.

22 H.G. Gadamer (1975) trans. W. Glyn-Doepel, *Truth and Method*, London: Sheed & Ward, p.302. See also, Dan Urian's use of an audience's 'horizon of expectations' as an element of his spectator's guide in Chapter 8.

23 P.B. Zarrilli (1995) 'Introduction: theories and meditations on acting', in P.B. Zarrilli (1995), p.16.

24 Philip Auslander argues that, despite their differences, Brecht and Stanislavski designate the actor's self as the *logos* of performance which gives the audience access to 'human truths'. For a fuller discussion, see P. Auslander '"Just be yourself"; logocentrism and difference in performance theory', in P.B. Zarrilli (1995), pp.59–67.

25 M. Merleau-Ponty (1974) trans. J. O'Neill *Phenomenology, Language and Sociology*, London: Heinemann, p.283.

26 J. Bruner (1996) *The Culture of Education*, Cambridge, MA: Harvard University Press, p.19.

27 M. Merleau-Ponty (1973), p.90.

28 W. Shakespeare, *As You Like It*, Act V, sc.iv. From an interview with Fiona Shaw in L. Goodman (1996) *Feminist Stages*, Amsterdam: Harwood Academic Publishers, pp.142–6.

Part III

WATCHING AND
UNDERSTANDING DRAMA

INTRODUCTION

The concept of audience has received comparatively little attention from writers on drama education. The supposition that students will learn more from their participation in 'acting out' than from the more reflective and distanced experience of sitting and watching has remained largely unquestioned.

If the subject of drama is to be broadened and extended in the ways proposed in preceding chapters, then the audience becomes a highly significant component. It is worth remembering that outside the classroom few of us take part in plays but all of us watch them. The development of semiotics and theories of reader response has helped us understand how meaning is interpreted through the systems of encodable and decodable signs, no less in dramatic performance than elsewhere, and there is much that can be learned from developments in English and media studies where the relationship of texts to the society which produced them on the one hand and which reads them on the other is well advanced.

Dan Urian believes that our neglect of students as potential audiences has helped the theatre become the home of a cultural and social élite. At the same time he acknowledges that many young people are 'put off' by the theatre and that it is sometimes difficult for teachers to know how to contextualise students' experience of performance in a way that enables them to become a critical audience without imperilling their enjoyment. After examining some theoretical accounts of spectatorship – and acknowledging that no account can ignore the pervasive influence of television – he offers a comprehensive spectator's guide designed to help students and teachers interrogate their experience of a dramatic performance. The guide breaks new ground in covering not only familiar elements of theatre – text, acting, design and so on – but also the audience's relationship with the production before the performance begins and after it is over.

They may not be theatre-goers, but it is estimated that half the adult population of Britain watches plays on television. The ever-present electronic screen and its influence on drama and culture is Jane Gangi's subject. In her essay on drama and media ecology, she shows how the drama

131

curriculum must take account of the influence of television and use it to enhance students' experience of drama in schools. Tracing the shifts in forms of communication from the oral tradition to the technological revolution of the twentieth century, she argues that television has created a beguiling new epistemology of naturalism which is in danger of inducing a culture of passivity. Drama teachers share the task of making students aware of the degree of manipulation which lies behind television's easy familiarity and are uniquely placed to help students develop the skills of critical interpretation.

Finally, Christopher McCullough shows how a project on Brecht's *Mother Courage and her Children* can put into practice some of the themes of the book and help students to develop the dramatic vocabulary they will need as the makers, performers and watchers of plays. He argues that simply to do drama is not in itself radical and that if students are to grasp – and possibly challenge – the meanings of the world they find themselves in, then the habit of critical reading is essential. Using Brecht's *Modellbuch* as a guide, he shows how profoundly different interpretations of even a short scene from the play are possible. Only by appreciating the dramatic potential of different readings and interpretations is real engagement with the text possible; only by having the craft and vocabulary to implement those interpretations, he argues, is radical creativity likely.

8

ON BEING AN AUDIENCE: A
SPECTATOR'S GUIDE

Dan Urian
translated by Naomi Paz

Challenging the inheritors

The last few decades have seen important developments in drama studies. As well as initiatives in the fields of theatre history and research, new areas of interest have also emerged, such as performance studies, drama and theatre-in-education and drama therapy. Despite this proliferation, and despite the fact that many countries now have drama education in their schools, theatre audiences are in decline and theatre-going steadfastly remains a minority pursuit.

For young people, theatre has a respectable 'adult' image. Also, many see drama as a 'highbrow' art aimed 'naturally', as it were, at select groups.[1] Jean Duvignaud calls the target population of the theatre *héritiers* (inheritors), and notes that 'it could be claimed that the theatre audience has not changed to any great extent since the seventeenth century'.[2] The culturally privileged go to the theatre and the theatre creates texts which suit them. The result is a vicious circle of self-affirmation in which theatre remains the property of the hegemonic elements of society who use it to affirm their status and for whom performances serve as a social meeting place. In Israel, for example, people of Western origin – generally well educated, secular and affluent – gather 'naturally' at the theatre, whereas for those from a non-European background (both Jews and Arabs), theatre is seen as élitist and not easily accessible. This social distinction is reinforced by the difficulty the latter groups have paying the high price of theatre tickets. It is important to note that in Israel, theatre is perceived by its audiences as a place for the discussion of important political and social problems (of which there are plenty); those who do not reach the theatre, remain outside the arena of debate. There are good cultural, aesthetic and political reasons for insisting on drama education in schools.

Nonetheless, the twentieth century witnessed an important revolution – in

Martin Esslin's words, 'the drama explosion'.[3] While the 1920s and 1930s may only have seen the better-off at performances of new plays, and even then only in the big cities, since the Second World War everyone, almost everywhere that television exists, can watch several dramatic texts a day. This revolution is giving drama education a new impetus. Teachers in many different countries are employing a variety of strategies to bring children and young people closer to the art of theatre, in particular by getting them to see plays.

For some teachers, developing the craft of spectatorship is likely to be a matter of sharing with their students their own knowledge and understanding of drama acquired, perhaps, over many years. For the newly qualified drama teacher, however, trying to find a way of structuring students' experience as spectators without simply confirming all their prejudices, the mass of material now available on audience response may prove more of an inhibition than a help.[4] Some schemes may seem 'academic' and boring, with little apparently to intrigue and interest young people. And then there is the challenge facing those teachers for whom drama is not even their field of expertise. I am not suggesting here that the student spectator must, of necessity, acquire a large amount of theatrical knowledge – 'cultural capital' – before being able to enjoy the performance of a play; an experienced and sensitive spectator may not necessarily have had any formal education. It is just *because* theatre is perceived as a highbrow art, *apparently* requiring a great deal of prior knowledge and understanding from those responding to it, that some teachers feel daunted by the task of preparing students to make the most of a visit.

It is my contention that guided spectatorship can bring the theatre audience closer to a performance. Guided spectatorship is not intended to restrict students to a particular approach or conception of drama, but rather to introduce a dialogue with the work; the aim is to create an informed spectator. One difficulty of such a programme, of course, is the tension that may develop between the students' enjoyment of a performance – surely the primary condition of an encounter with an artwork – and the demands of the tasks involved in deciphering and commenting upon it. Such tasks may impinge upon students' motivation and confirm suspicions that theatre is not for them. In this chapter, I am offering a framework for spectatorship, in what I hope is accessible language, which aims to give confidence to those teachers uncertain of quite how to approach a theatre visit with their students.

Theatre, cinema and television

Theatre existed for thousands of years without the need of study programmes to help audiences appreciate what was being presented. The reasons for the contemporary theatre spectator's need for guidance are, in part, connected to the changes undergone by the art of drama itself. Film and television have made dramatic texts the public property of all.[5] Live theatre has thus become an art belonging to the pre-electronic past, and for those used to watching television and cinema it can easily appear to be old-fashioned and irrelevant. For one thing, television and cinema are able to enlist the best directors, actors, designers and musicians, and television viewing habits may lead to young spectators demanding from theatrical drama precisely what they find in electronic drama – a demand that theatre, because of its own unique nature, cannot and does not need to fulfil. Since the rise of television there has been no shortage of articles mourning the death of theatre as an artistic institution. Nonetheless, in many countries, theatre continues to be the art most in demand. Moreover, despite the chronic economic crisis in which most theatres invariably seem to find themselves, the overall number of theatrical productions has actually *grown* in the last few decades, especially if we include those whose cultural 'legitimacy' had been somewhat doubtful in the past, such as light entertainment shows, musicals and stand-up comedy. In France, for example, about 200 theatrical productions were staged in 1970, whereas in 1988 the number had risen to 1,300, despite the fact that the relative percentage of the population attending the theatre in France had dropped by almost half during the same period.[6]

The starting point for any project which aims to bring students closer to the theatre must inevitably be the knowledge they will already have acquired through watching cinema and television. Fortunately, such 'dormant' knowledge can be easily converted to a common platform, facilitating explanation of such dramatic terms as 'plot', 'characters', 'dialogue' and 'subject'. Outwardly, there is great similarity between the live and recorded dramatic arts, particularly in what Roman Ingarden calls the 'main text', the dialogue spoken by the characters. These similarities can be extended to the other dramatic components – plot, characters, and so on. There are also, of course, large and important differences between theatre and the other media, principally in what Ingarden terms *Nebentext*, or the 'side-text'.[7] A play's stage directions (*Nebentext*) guide actors and designers, whereas directions in a film script guide the work of the camera and the editor. Thus, when we examine the theatre text more closely, we find that it is characterised by the peculiar conditions of spectatorship that exist in the theatre, which greatly differ from those in a cinema and from the circumstances of watching television at home. Guided spectatorship draws attention to the shared aspects in order to arrive at the unique characteristics which make up the art of theatre, most particularly, of course, the fact that it is a living communication between actors and audience in a shared space. The special quality of the actor-audience relationship in theatre spectatorship, as well as the social circumstances and components involved in a theatrical gathering, constitute important motives for theatre-going.[8]

The dormant dramatic knowledge possessed by young people and adults is extremely wide and varied. Most young people watch television and go to the cinema and develop critical tools for dealing with the broadcast texts. 'Children growing up nowadays who see several hours of drama on television each day', notes Martin Esslin, 'must be infinitely more effectively conditioned to accept and understand dramatic conventions than earlier populations who may have had far fewer opportunities to experience dramatic performance'.[9] Esslin claims that what theatre, cinema and television share is the 'dramatic', and that intensive watching enriches the spectators' knowledge of plot construction, character design, use of dialogue and other dramatic components.[10] The same narrative can be presented live to an audience or filmed with a camera.[11] Also, research has shown that the attitude of television viewers to televised drama is not a passive one, as has often been claimed.[12] Television viewers often participate in different ways, becoming involved through surveys, letters to the broadcasting channel or television journals. Although the differences between the media are important, over-emphasising these may be strategically unwise, particularly when dealing with young audiences. Part of the pleasure in an approach that utilises the familiar is the students' discovery that they know things already, much as Monsieur Jourdain, in Molière's play *Le Bourgeois Gentilhomme*, discovers to his great joy that he has been speaking prose his entire life. Students find both purpose and pleasure when they are guided to activate their television knowledge in the study of theatre. What is important, for our purposes, is that they are acquiring a dramatic vocabulary which can be used in drama education.

A theatrical *Baedeker*

Several questionnaires, maps and tables on the subject of spectatorship have been published in recent years. Taken together, they constitute a summary of knowledge regarding the 'reading' of theatre productions.[13] Some describe the play's components, or the inclusive system of theatrical signs (synchronic), while others combine this data in a presumed track of spectatorship, from entering the theatre building up to and including leaving it (diachronic). Each one directs the spectator towards those components of the theatre experience which otherwise may not have been noticed or thought to be of importance.

In bringing these various models of spectatorship together, I have used the idea of the tourist guide book. Just as a tourist guide directs the traveller to cultural sites and items in the described region, my spectator's guide offers a route through the experience of watching a play while also making clear the possibility of alternative routes. Travellers on this theatrical journey can choose some parts of the plan and omit others. For the theatre spectator, the choice should be affected principally by the play, or plays, chosen;

there is no point in stopping off at a group of questions relating to lighting when confronted with a play staged outdoors in daylight, for example, or at a discussion of scenery and costume when observing a classroom improvisation. The 'tourist' in the theatre is quite free to alter the order of questions and to begin and end at any point. The guide is a tool which, like a tourist guide, allows routes to be chosen according to the aims of the teacher and the questions raised by a particular performance.

The guide aims to provide a clear and concise approach to the craft of spectatorship. Several of the ideas suggested are those of other researchers and teachers – Martin Esslin, André Helbo, David Hornbrook, Patrice Pavis, Val Taylor, Anne Ubersfeld – and these are interwoven, with some changes, into the text. The novelty, perhaps, lies in the attempt to advance beyond partial and disparate endeavours and to present a complete critical model.[14] While every attempt has been made to keep the language simple and straightforward (in a field not noted for the accessibility of its texts), I have employed six key concepts – 'field', 'horizon of expectations', 'gathering', 'narrative', 'dramatic conventions' and 'ideology' – which, in the cause of clarity, may be helpfully explained before embarking on the guide itself.

Field

Field encompasses many social, economic and cultural components external to the play but of importance to its critical interpretation.[15] Bourdieu's concept, *champ*, can be characterised as a collection of common factors and strategies with a particular connection. He includes in the *champ théâtral* all those connecting factors relating to the theatre experience that most other theories still hesitate to incorporate, such as the actors' social biography, the historical and economic circumstances under which the play was created, the audience and its social characteristics, the means of materialising the written text, marketing, public relations, advertising, and so on. According to Bourdieu, all these play an important, possibly decisive, part in the creation of 'cultural products' (artistic works and theatrical performances).[16]

Horizon of expectations

Marvin Carlson defines the horizon of expectations as the framework created by the spectator within which the play will be understood as one particular form of performance and not another.[17] It is immediately possible to discern the horizon of expectations for a play staged out of doors, for example, or for mime, or for a classical tragedy in a proscenium theatre. Carlson also includes the horizon of expectations that develops due to prior familiarity with the *genre* of a play as an important element in its reception.

Gathering

To understand the theatre process fully, Richard Schechner believes it is necessary to examine how a group of spectators gathers together for the play and how they disperse when it is over.[18] There is no single item of a production, he argues, that does not have its effect on the spectator. Schechner therefore wants to expand the scope of theatre study to include such matters as the indifference of the participants, the money invested in the production, the social characteristics of the audience, the means by which the spectators purchased their tickets, their expectations of the event (whether they are there for entertainment, to improve their status, for charity), and so on.

Narrative

Aristotle's claim for the importance of plot, or narrative, is still valid. Although postmodernism has 'disrupted' familiar plot structures and embraced dramatic texts which Aristotle would have found flawed, it is likely that the majority of those who go to the theatre still expect a 'good story'. Broadly speaking, narrative structures may be closed or open. Often deterministic towards human fate, the closed structure tends towards intensive action building up to a climax and invites the audience to join the story at a point close to its unavoidable end (*Oedipus Rex*, *Hedda Gabler*, *Death of a Salesman*). The open structure, by contrast, is likely to emphasise free will as it accompanies the protagonist in various exploits. It may support several sub-plots and the end is not necessarily known from the outset (*King Lear*, *Peer Gynt*, *Mother Courage*). Feminist theory has identified the closed structure with 'masculine' and finds the open structure a characteristic of the feminine narrative.[19]

Dramatic conventions

Elizabeth Burns distinguishes between two types of dramatic convention, 'rhetorical' and 'authenticating'.[20] Rhetorical conventions are those which delineate the framework of the piece – place, set, exposition, and so on. Key elements of the performance itself, they also extend to the gathering and dispersing of the audience. By shaping the spectator–stage relations and signalling the audience's role in the theatrical event, rhetorical conventions programme a spectator's expectations and horizon of expectations. Authenticating conventions are the social conventions which inform the representation of reality on stage. Mimetic in nature, it is they which provide authenticity to the onstage world.

Ideology

The image of an iceberg is employed by Patrice Pavis (1985) to illustrate the connection between the theatrical text and the social reality upon which it draws and to which it relates.[21] The tip of the iceberg that is revealed above the water represents the text itself, while beneath it lies the layer of ideology whose source is 'the iceberg base', the social context. In studying the social significance of theatre texts, Pavis assumes that ideology exists in a text as a collection of truths, stereotypes and prejudices. Familiarity with these is essential for reading and understanding the circumstances of the text's performance and its reception by an audience.

The Spectator's Guide

The guide which follows makes the assumption that the performance of a play can be analysed, that it can be broken down into components and considered as a complete system in which each component contributes to the meaning of the whole. The 'ideological' group of questions, which examine reception of the notional extent of the play's meanings, have been placed at the end of the questionnaire in order to prevent the spectator from evading the need to create a dramatic vocabulary as a precondition for discussion of the social significances of the play. Research has shown that understanding the semiotics of the text – reading the text according to the system of signs that compose it – is fundamental to a discussion of the text in its social context.[22]

The questions in the guide reflect a diachronic progression, following the student from the moment he or she first hears about the production, to the gathering at the place of performance, to the performance itself, and finally to a period of one week afterwards, when the student answers the questions using the information stored in notes and memory. It is assumed that the experience of the play begins from the point when the production is first mentioned and expectations are raised prior to the actual performance, and that it ends with the spectator's memories of the event.[23]

The guide should be presented to students before they see the play in performance and explained thoroughly. A discussion of the process might be expanded with video excerpts from the play, slides, or talks with theatre artists. I realise that some of the questions demand additional knowledge and that some semiotic terms and concepts may require explanation. Others assume knowledge of the written text. But it is important to remember that, like the travel guide, not all roads need to be taken. Teacher and student chart their own route through the questions. Afterwards, of course, students should be given free rein in their answers. It helps, however, if they commit their comments to writing within a few hours or days of the performance.

Before the performance

- How was the production advertised? Did you become aware of it through posters, subscription, newspapers, television, leaflets distributed by the theatre? Or from conversations with people who had seen it? Or some other source?
- Are any of the play's creators (playwright, director, actors, etc.) familiar to you? How did this familiarity affect your choice? Will you continue to choose plays according to such familiarity?
- Do you read the theatre critics before choosing a play? To what extent does their criticism affect your choice? Is the fact that a play is advertised as a 'hit' a sufficient recommendation for you to see it?
- Does the geographical location of the production in a particular area (town centre or suburb, conventional theatre building or experimental space) affect your choice?
- How is the theatrical location where you will watch the play designed? What is its outer covering? A palatial building? Some other special building? Or a more mundane place, such as a street or market-place?[24]
- Is the place suitable for the play from the point of view of geographical location, outer covering, auditorium–stage proportions?
- What is the 'horizon of expectations' (see above) created by the information you have accumulated prior to watching the performance? What expectations do you consider are raised by the physical and geographical location of the production?
- When does the play take place (matinée, evening, weekday, weekend)? How does this affect your choice?
- At what type of audience do you think the play is aimed?
- Do you have any preconceptions about the play? Have you seen it previously in any other version? Have you read the play previously?
- Do you have any special feelings about the kind of style you prefer (professional, artistic, alternative)? How will your personal taste affect the way you review this production?
- How did you come by the tickets? Were they expensive or a financial problem?

The gathering (see above)

- What is the function of the foyer and other gathering spaces in the theatre?
- Describe the gathering.
- What did the spectators do before the performance began (outside the theatre, in the foyer, in the auditorium, in other areas)?

Structure of the performance

- Does the structure of the written text as a whole hold together sufficiently? Is it deliberately loose-structured? To what extent does the structure contribute to the play?
- Are the transitions from scene to scene effective?
- How would you characterise the narrative structure of the text? Is it open, closed, climatic, episodic, masculine, feminine (see above)?

Set design[25]

- The playwright's stage directions can be both directly and indirectly indicated in the written text or found in accompanying material (for example, in an introduction or in the playwright's correspondence). How important are these instructions to the production?
- Did the set accurately reflect expressions in the written text, such as metaphors and other linguistic images?
- What were the spatial characteristics of the set which connected it to the fictional world of the dramatic text which served as its source?
- What were the onstage/offstage relations?
- What were the auditorium/stage spatial relations?
- Did the designer make effective use of the given space? Were the auditorium/stage proportions taken into account?
- To what extent did the set in general fit the spatial characteristics of the chosen stage? Was the seating in the auditorium suitably arranged? To what extent was the spectators' field of vision accommodated?
- Did the set evoke or create a particular atmosphere?
- Did the set serve the genre (for example, by the use of light, cheerful colours for a comedy)?
- What was the nature of the set design? Was it a set designed to imitate reality (mimetic), or a design that attempted a new vocabulary of visual conventions?
- What were the spatial characteristics? Were they open or closed, wide or restricted, empty or full?
- What were the aesthetic components (materials, colours, shapes, style, cultural indicators) of the set?
- Was there more than one set? How did the different sets coordinate? Did they conform to the overall rhythm of the production?
- Did the set enhance the actors' possibilities or restrict them?
- Which particular components of the set engaged your attention, positively or negatively?

Lighting methods[26]

- What are the playwright's direct and indirect directions for lighting the play? Do you believe these should be carried out?
- Did the lighting design express the textual images (metaphors, symbols, metonymies) of the play?
- Do you think that the lighting designer exploited the space in interesting ways?
- What part did the lighting designer play in creating audience/ stage relations?
- To what extent was significant use made of light and shadow in the production?
- How did the designer exploit colour, tone, and lighting angles to achieve atmosphere?
- Did the lighting serve the genre of the play?
- Did the lighting design fulfil the demands of the set?
- Did the play relate to a season, or to a particular time of day? To what extent did the lighting succeed in reflecting this?
- To what extent did the lighting help or hinder the actors?
- How did the lighting fit into the rhythm of the play?
- Which elements of the lighting engaged your attention, positively or negatively?

Acting

- What are the playwright's direct and indirect stage directions regarding acting (for example, in relation to style, characterisation, movement, facial or vocal expression)? To what extent are these directions important for your conception of the play?
- Was the chosen style sufficiently clear? Did the actors keep to it throughout the performance?
- Did the acting tend towards psychological individualism or to the creation of 'stock characters'?
- What were the relations between actor and role? Was the intention 'identification' (Stanislavski) or 'alienation' (Brecht).[27]
- Describe the components of each actor's stage presence (age, sex, gestic presentation, voice).
- What part might the actors' professional experience (life history, roles played, affiliation with certain theatres) have played in their interpretations?
- If appropriate, what was the contribution of an actor's celebrity status to creating interest in the play and raising audience expectations?[28]
- How effectively did the actors exploit the space and possibilities offered by the stage?

- To what extent did the actors activate your imagination through their body movements, gestures and facial expressions?
- Did the actors' movements appear suitable or unsuitable to the action, correct or incorrect for the demands of the written text? Did they match or deviate from the style of the production?
- Did the production require the actors to dance or display any other physical skills? To what extent were such demands fulfilled in an interesting manner? Did they contribute to realising the play on stage?
- How significant was the actors' use of costume, masks or stage properties?
- What did the actors achieve vocally by the use of accent, tone, rhythm, sung speech or vocal characterisation?
- To what extent did the actors appear to be involved with and understand the narrative structure of the play?
- Did the actors understand the technical demands of the genre (tragedy, comedy, melodrama, farce) of the play?
- Did the actors display a sense of timing?
- Were the actors' stage entrances and exits successful?
- To what extent did each actor cooperate with the others?
- How sensitive were the actors to audience response?
- What did you particularly like about the acting, and what do you consider deserved negative criticism?

Costume, make-up, hair and mask [29]

- What are the playwright's direct and indirect stage directions for costume, make-up, hair and mask, and how important were they in the production?
- Did the performance reflect symbolic and metaphoric expressions in the written text by means of costumes, masks, hairstyles?
- How important to the production were the stage directions which related to the period, the sex of the characters, their social or financial status, their interrelations?
- Did the costumes contribute to creating a particular atmosphere? [30]
- How significant was the use the designer made of cut, style, colour, tone, or types of fabric?
- Did the costumes coordinate? Or were they deliberately designed to clash?
- To what extent did the costumes appear to help the actor portray the role?
- To what extent did the costumes and lighting plan coordinate?
- When costume changes were necessary, were they carried out to accommodate the rhythm of the play?
- Do you consider the hairstyles and make-up to have been successful?

- Were masks used? Did they add to the significance of the play?
- Do you consider there to have been coordination between the costume designer (including hair and masks), the actors, and the set and lighting designers?
- Which components of costume, make-up, hair, masks were interesting and which of them appeared to you to be unnecessary or mistaken?

Stage properties [31]

- Does the written text provide directions for the use of stage properties? Does the production use them?
- Does the play provide directions for stage properties to be used in a metaphoric or symbolic way (like the stuffed seagull in Chekhov's *The Seagull*, for example)?
- What was the source of the properties? From what materials were they made?
- How many stage properties were there and was this significant? (During the course of events in Ionesco's *The Chairs*, for example, empty chairs gradually fill up the entire stage and heighten the isolation of the characters.)
- Were there stage properties with a practical purpose (swords for a duel, for example)?
- Were there properties which also functioned as part of the set and complemented the historical or social background of the play?
- Was there repeated use of a particular property during the production, turning it into a motif of some kind?
- Did the play feature a stage property with functional importance to the plot, directing the spectators' expectations (such as Yorick's skull in Shakespeare's *Hamlet*)?
- Did the play feature a property that helped to express a psychological process?
- Did the production make interesting use of stage properties? Did you find anything superfluous?

Music, sound effects

- What are the playwright's direct and indirect stage directions for music and sound? Do you consider them to be important? Could some of them have been omitted or changed?
- Did the music and sound components of the production help to clarify the play's images, metaphors or symbols, and did they assist audience reception of these images?
- Were the music and sound effects, and their volume, suited to the theatrical space in which they were performed?

- To what extent did music and sound effects help the actors to portray their roles?
- How significant was the use of silence, sound and music in creating a relevant atmosphere and understanding of the genre?
- Did the music and sound help to signify the time of day, the historical period or the location of a scene?
- Did the use of sound help in the transitions from scene to scene?
- How did the sound effects blend into the overall rhythm of the performance?
- Did the performance feature a repeated musical line which developed into a motif?
- Did the performance feature an ironic use of music?
- To what extent did the sound and music components integrate with the other components of the production – set, lighting, acting?
- Which components of music and sound did you find most and least successful?

The rhythm of the play [32]

- Does the written text feature directions governing the rhythm of the play?
- What was the general rhythm of the performance (consistent pace, fragmented pace, important changes in pace)?
- Were there noticeable contrasts in rhythm through the use of silence and speech, fast and slow pace, emphasis and lack of emphasis?
- Were there instances of deliberate disruption of rhythm?
- Did the rhythm help to maintain tension and interest in the play?
- Would you have altered the rhythm, entirely or in part?

The role of the dramatic text in the director's work [33]

- What characteristics of the dramatic text served the director? Was the written text in its original form or a translation? Was the script used a free adaptation or version of the original?
- What place did the director's conception give to the playwright's text? Was it a faithful reproduction, an 'archaeological' adaptation (from a Classical Greek play, for example) or a concept which simply used the written text as a starting point for developments using another sign language, such as movement and dance?
- What are the playwright's direct and indirect stage directions and to what extent do you consider the director should have adhered to them?

The director's work

- To what extent did the director understand the demands of the genre, particular problems in the written text and the narrative structure of the play?

- What rhetorical dramatic conventions served the director? (see above)
- What were the functions of the authenticating conventions in the director's work?
- What historical, contemporary or imaginary signs did the director choose in order to construct the fictional world?
- How were cuts or separation into scenes made? Did the director favour continuity or fragmentation?
- Did the director establish the right actors/audience relationship?
- Did the work of the director show preference for the visual or the aural?
- Did the director make effective use of the spatial characteristics of the theatrical place?
- How effectively did the director use rhythm and pacing? How well did he or she succeed in creating an atmosphere? How successful were the special effects?
- Did the director show control of exits and entrances, grouping on the stage, reference to offstage, transitions from scene to scene and technical changes (lighting, or set between acts, for example)?
- Was it possible to discern the director's ability to integrate effectively all the components of the play – or only some?
- What did you consider to have been the positive and negative aspects of the director's work?

The spectator[34]

Some of the following questions also appear at the beginning of the guide.

- Do you think the performance appealed to the entire audience?
- What particular groups of spectators could be easily distinguished at the performance?
- What expectations did you have of the play?
- What do you know about the audience's expectations (from conversations during the interval and after the performance)? Did the audience have prior knowledge of the play? Was it a familiar text or about familiar figures or events? Do you think that information provided in the programme, or from other sources (newspapers, radio, television), contributed to raising expectations among the audience?
- Do you consider these expectations to have been fulfilled?
- What do you consider to have been the spectator's role during the performance? Were you an active or passive recipient, or somewhere in-between?
- Do you believe that the performance held the audience's interest? Were spectators excited, amused, repulsed or angered? Add your own assessment of the play's reception by the audience.

Afterwards

- What linked together the various components of the play?
- Did the production have an identifiable style?
- To what extent did the director's intentions accord with the style of the written text?
- Do you consider that the stylistic choice contributed to the audience's enjoyment and understanding of the play?
- Did you think the sign systems were well coordinated or lacked coordination? If you discerned a lack of coordination, could this have been deliberate?
- What did you particularly like about the performance? What fascinated you? What excited you? What amused you?
- What was disturbing in the production? What were its strong moments, its weak moments, its boring moments?
- Did the last part of the play attempt to create a climactic reaction (of laughter, emotion, ideological awareness, or combinations of these)?
- Was the performance applauded and cheered, and to what extent? Do you consider the applause to have been justified?
- Was the performance followed by a planned or spontaneous discussion? Was there a discussion among the group with whom you watched the play, or with your family or friends?
- Did you read any critical reports or other articles about the production after you had seen it? Did these add to or detract from your experience? Did you learn anything new from these critical commentaries that you had not been aware of during the performance?
- What was left most prominently in your memory after the performance, and why?
- Did the production remind you of other plays, or television dramas, or movies? In what way were they similar or different?

Innovations

- To what extent did the work revitalise familiar theatrical conventions and demolish clichés?
- Were there striking examples of innovation in the production?
- What was banal, or restricting or clichéd?
- Did the striving for originality appear to be more important than performing the written text in a refreshing and interesting way?

The theatrical text as an ideological contention (see above)

- What was the production's 'contract' with the audience? Did the production set out to amuse, to expound a social message, to evoke emotions, to create tension, or a combination of these?

- How did the production relate to historical or social truths?
- Was the performed text convincing and interesting in its ideological contentions?
- Was the 'solution' presented by the play convincing? Or could you perhaps have provided a different solution?

Postscript: an evaluation

In 1994, this guide was piloted in the Education Department of Haifa University. The student group, from all subject areas, was homogeneous and showed no significant differences in their theatre-going habits. Most seldom attended the theatre and were still too young to have accumulated much 'cultural capital'. Only a tiny minority had studied drama before. Before being introduced to the guide, the students completed a questionnaire to determine their demographic characteristics, theatre-going habits and any prior knowledge they might have of theatrical sign systems, the evaluation of performances, theatrical genres and styles of production and the decoding of ideological messages. The guide was then presented to the students over several sessions, during which each element was explained. In these sessions I attempted to exploit as far as possible the knowledge of television that most of them already possessed. After familiarisation with the guide, the students went together to the theatre.

On their return they were given another questionnaire. They were asked to explain, using examples from the play they had seen, some of the concepts which they had confronted in the 'knowledge' section of the earlier questionnaire. Putting the two questionnaires together, it was possible to discern a significant improvement in the students' understanding of drama. A marked improvement was found in their ability to identify elements of a theatrical sign system, for example, and to discern a play's meanings and identify genre and style. The students' evaluation of the actors' craft also improved.

Notes

1 Pierre Bourdieu developed a model of 'hierarchy of legitimacies' with respect to cultural goods and tastes. At the top he places the 'sphere of legitimacy', occupied by music, painting, sculpture, literature and the theatre. P. Bourdieu *et al.* (1990) *Photography: A Middle-Brow Art*, trans. S. Whiteside, Cambridge: Polity, pp.95–8.
2 J. Duvignaud (1976) 'Le théâtre', in J. Duvignaud and A. Veinstein, *Le Théâtre*, Paris: Encyclopoche Larousse, pp.31–2.
3 M. Esslin (1982) *The Age of Television*, San Francisco, CA: W.H. Freeman, pp.1–15.
4 According to unpublished research based on interviews with a sample of eighty theatre teachers in Israel.
5 M. Esslin (1982), pp.1–2.

6 J.-M. Guy and L. Mironer (1988) *Les Publics du Théâtre*, Paris, La Documentation Française, p.10.

7 R. Ingarden (1973) *The Literary Work of Art*, 2nd edn, trans. G.G. Grabowicz, Evanston, IL: Northwestern University Press, p.208.

8 A.-M. Gourdon (1982) *Théâtre, Public Perception*, Paris: CNRS, pp.25–48.

9 M. Esslin (1987) (1987) *The Field of Drama: How the Signs of Drama Create Meanings on Stage and Screen*, London and New York: Methuen, pp.92–3.

10 M. Esslin (1976) *The Anatomy of Drama*, New York: Hill & Wang, pp.75–85.

11 It is worth noting that in recent years commercial links between the two forms of production (writers, directors and actors move from television to theatre and back) have led to theatre showing a tendency to become 'televisionised'. This can be recognised in the increased use of lights and music, the segmenting of the text into many short scenes and the shortening of playing times.

12 J. Fiske (1987) *Television Culture*, London and New York: Routledge, pp.62–83.

13 Notably, T. Kowzan (1975) *Littérature et Spectacle*, Warszawa: PWN, Paris: Mouton, pp.160–221; Helbo, A., Johansen, D., Pavis, P. and Ubersfeld, A. (1987) 'La notation: questionnaires de lecture', in *Theatre Modes D'approche*, Brussels: Labor, pp.203–12 (English translation in A. Helbo *et al.* (1991) *Approaching Theatre*, Bloomington and Indianapolis, IN: Indiana University Press, pp.165–73); D. Hornbrook (1991) *Education in Drama: Casting the Dramatic Curriculum*, London: Falmer Press, pp.95–124; V. Taylor (1992) 'The tutor as audience: approaches to examining student performance', *New Theatre Quarterly* 30, pp.140–5; P. Pavis (1996) *L'Analyse des Spectacles*, Paris: Nathan, pp.34–8.

14 A similar programme which I developed in Israel was well received. See D. Urian (1995) 'A guide to theatre spectatorship', *Drama in Education: Writing, Acting and Spectatorship*, Tel Aviv: Mofet Institute, Ministry of Education, Culture and Sport, pp.91–144.

15 P. Bourdieu (1993) *The Field of Cultural Production*, ed. and int. by R. Johnson, Cambridge: Polity Press, pp.29–73.

16 P. Bourdieu (1992) *Les Règles de l'Art*, Paris: Éditions de Seuil, pp.201–45, 249–92.

17 In M. Carlson (1990) 'Theatre audiences and the reading of performance', *Theatre Semiotics: Signs of Life*, Bloomington and Indianapolis, IN: Indiana University Press, pp.11–12. For a discussion of the hermeneutics of our cultural and historical 'horizons' and the way they frame our understanding of our world and its texts, see H.G. Gadamer (1975) *Truth and Method*, trans. W. Glyn-Doepel, London: Sheed & Ward.

18 See R. Schechner (1997) *Essays on Performance Theory 1970–1976*, New York: Drama Book Specialists, p.122.

19 E. Aston (1995) *An Introduction to Feminism and Theatre*, London and New York: Routledge, pp.38–56.

20 In E. Burns (1972) *Theatricality: A Study of Convention in the Theatre and in Social Life*, New York: Harper & Row, pp.40–121.

21 P. Pavis (1985) 'Production et réception au théâtre: la concrétisation du texte dramatique et spectaculaire', *Voix et Images de la Scène*, Lille: Presses Universitaires de Lille, p.288.

22 See M. Shevtsova (1989) 'The sociology of the theatre', *New Theatre Quarterly* 19, pp.282–300.

23 For a detailed study of audience recollection, see R. Deldime and J. Pigeon (1988) *La Mémoire du Jeune Spectateur*, Brussels and Paris: De Boeck.

24 See D. Bablet (1972) 'Pour une méthode d'analyse du lieu théâtral', *Travail Théâtral* 6, pp.108–19.

25 See D. Bablet (1975) *Les Révolutions Scéniques au xxè Siècle*, Paris: Société Internationale d'art xxè Siècle.
26 See D. Bablet (1973) 'L'éclairage et le son dans l'espace théâtral', *Travail Théâtral* 13, pp.47–56.
27 See C. Counsell (1996) *Signs of Performance: An Introduction to Twentieth-century Theatre*, London and New York: Routledge, pp.24–111.
28 See M. Carlson (1994) 'Invisible presences – performance intertextuality', *Theatre Research International* 19 (2), pp.111–17.
29 See E. Fischer-Lichte (1992), *The Semiotics of Theatre*, trans. J. Gaines and D.L. Jones, Bloomington and Indianapolis, IN: Indiana University Press, pp.64–92.
30 See D. Urian (1984) *The Meaning of Costume*, Oakland, CA: Personabooks.
31 There is a close relationship between the three sign systems, costumes, properties and set. An item of costume can become a property and vice versa. A walking stick can be a clothing accessory for a foppish young man, but when the same item is left behind in a married lady's wardrobe, it becomes a stage property with multiple meanings. Similarly, the border between properties and parts of the set is not always clear. In the plays of Eugene Ionesco and Samuel Beckett, for example, parts of the set, various props, and even the actors' bodies frequently change their functions. See A. Ubersfeld (1981) *L'école du Spectateur*, Paris: Éditions Sociales, pp.125–86.
32 See E. Barba and N. Savarese (1991) *A Dictionary of Theatre Anthropology: The Secret Art of the Performer*, London and New York: Routledge, pp.211–17.
33 See J.-J. Roubine (1980) *Théâtre et Mise en Scène 1880–1980*, Paris: Presses Universitaires de France, pp.45–83; P. Pavis (1992) 'From page to stage: a difficult birth', *Theatre at the Crossroads of Culture*, trans. J. Daugherty, London and New York: Routledge, pp.24–47.
34 See M. de Marinis (1995), *The Semiotics of Performance*, trans. A. O'Healy, Bloomington and Indianapolis, IN: Indiana University Press, pp.158–88.

9

MAKING SENSE OF DRAMA IN AN ELECTRONIC AGE

Jane M. Gangi

> An old tradition leads people to treat a critical attitude as a
> predominantly negative one. . . . People cannot conceive of
> contradiction and detachment as being part of artistic appreci-
> ation. . . . To introduce this critical attitude into art, the
> negative element which it doubtless includes must be shown
> from its positive side: this criticism of the world is active, prac-
> tical, positive. Criticizing the course of a river means
> improving it, correcting it.
>
> Bertolt Brecht[1]

From speaking, writing and printing, to the flickering screen

Constant and increasing exposure to drama of one sort or another is an
extraordinary development in the history of the human race. Long before
they enter our classroom doors, the students we teach will have witnessed
innumerable dramatisations. They come to us saturated, awash in images
emitted from electronic screens. With the rapid expansion of electronically
transmitted commodities available through television, hand-held video games
and personal computers, their and our exposure to electronic media can
only increase.

Teachers of drama practise their art within the context of this highly technologised and dramatised society. Although theatrical events have been a part
of human culture since antiquity, prior to the twentieth century, drama was
confined to sporadic and occasional bacchanals, festivals, rituals, celebrations
and theatre performances. Now, most of us witness, via television, what
would have amounted to several lifetimes of drama for previous generations.
In the West there is little poverty that is so destitute that television with all its
manifestations of dramatic enactments is not available; in some urban areas,
the conditions of poverty mean that children watch considerably *more* television than their middle-class peers. And this phenomenon is not exclusive to
Western society; access to television is global.

How are we to account for this pervasive media environment in the way we teach? What is the significance of this ubiquity of drama encased in electronic forms? Are the theories and practices that have guided the teaching of drama in the past sufficient for the present, and more importantly, for the future? What are the educational implications of this age of mass media? How can both the content of our lessons and the pedagogical approaches we use be responsive to our students' media milieu?

Questions of this magnitude suggest that we should look for answers in domains outside drama. The work of medium theorists, whose task is to study forms of communication and how these forms affect the quality of a culture, may be a good place to start. Originating in the pioneering work of Marshall McLuhan's teacher and mentor, Harold Innis, in 1950s Toronto, and drawing from sociology, anthropology, psychology, history and philosophy, medium theorists seek to gain insight into the nature of the contemporary communications environment. They begin by taking the long look back at previous cultures and communication forms, believing that an examination of the transitions from one form of communication to another can heighten sensibilities when considering contemporary communications shifts. For drama teachers, an awareness of these historical changes can be similarly informative. Although drama teachers may have an interest in the history of theatre, fewer may have considered how the development of their craft has been entwined with the wider history of communication forms. The fact is, all of us share cultural traditions and all of us are influenced by both these traditions and by dominating media forms; reflecting on the relationship between culture and communication may help us resolve some of the dilemmas of teaching drama in an electronic age.

Changes in forms of communication radically alter culture – so argue medium theorists – and historically there have been four major revolutions in communications technologies. The first was the appearance of language itself, the origins of which are both conjectural and debatable. The second was the appearance of the phonetic alphabet sometime around the eighth century BC when primary orality (cultures with no writing) gave way to limited literacy. This shift from orality to literacy was momentous, for although for centuries literacy was attainable only by the élite few who had access to manuscripts, even those who could not read or write still felt the effects of living in a literate culture. Widespread literacy was made possible by the third communications revolution: the invention of the printing press in the fifteenth century. The fourth was the invention of electronically mediated forms of communication, beginning with the telegraph in the nineteenth century.

Examination of the contrasts between oral, manuscript, literate, and finally, electronic cultures can generate insights into the biases and proclivities of a culture dominated by one form of communication or another. Interestingly, these moments of transition coincide with pre-eminent periods in theatre history. When examining these periods several assumptions are

152

made by medium theorists. One is that those living within a culture are rarely aware of its biases. 'Culture hides more than it reveals', says Edward Hall, 'and what it hides, it hides most effectively from its own participants'.[2] In other words, the effects of communications revolutions tend to be invisible to the very people who are most affected. Our forms of communication are part of our culture – some would say the mass media *is* our culture – and yet we may be ignorant of its influence.

Another assumption is that shifts in communication eventually take on a mythological status. Myth transforms history into nature.[3] Actual, historical, recorded technological inventions become no longer recognised as such; no-one can remember when the technology did not exist and so it is taken to have always existed. Many of our students may even be unaware that there was a time when there was no alphabet, or a time when printed material was not widely available. For them, television – a product of the fourth communications revolution – also seems *natural*. The beginnings and continuance of technological forms of communication are rarely recognised or questioned. It is this mythology, this seemingly organic, natural state, identified in Hall's theory of culture, that tends to make the consequences of technology imperceptible to most of us. By looking at some of the shifts in communication changes, my intention is to explore the effects of electronically-mediated technology on contemporary society in general and on the teaching of drama in particular.

Broadly summarised, primary oral cultures are characterised by a communal, externalised way of life. Contemporary concepts of individuality would have been virtually unknown to those who had never experienced the internalising powers of literacy. As a literate person, I take a book off by myself, apart and away from the group. As an oral person, I receive my traditions and my definition of self only from the group, thus experiencing a sense of belonging beyond the comprehension of my literate self. 'Sight isolates', says Walter Ong, 'sound incorporates'.[4] Primary oral cultures tend to be more conservative, more aggregative and therefore more static than literary ones; however, people are united within the group. Ways of being in oral worlds are existentially different from ways of being in literate worlds. 'Moving into the exciting world of literacy', Ong argues, 'means leaving behind much that is exciting and deeply loved in the earlier oral world'.[5] But moving on is what humans did, for literacy offers more intense, complex and meaningful forms of civilisation.

The advent of literacy brings to the individual the possibility of attaining a distance from transmitted culture. Literacy allows a kind of thinking that is reflective, interpretive and abstract, one which promotes questioning. The poetic genre of the oral epic, which for centuries had been the most suitable means of storing cultural and mythological memory, acceded to a new, prosaic genre made possible through private reflection and attained by separation from the group. The exterior orientation of the oral person gave way to the interior orientation of the literate person. Ong contrasts the oral epics recited by the *aidoi*, or travelling bands, of the twelfth to the eighth century BC (eventually transcribed by Homer), with the dramatic form of tragedy which emerged several centuries later after the advent of writing. The *dramatis personae* of Euripides and Sophocles, he concludes, are 'incomparably more complex and interiorly anguished' than are the characters of Homer.[6]

What we now call 'drama' is the offspring of the union between orality and literacy. In Greece, in the fifth and fourth centuries BC, the collision of two forms of communication – speech and writing – created a fertile cultural milieu, and the sophistication of Greek plays from this period is evidence of the fullness that resulted from that union. A vitality arose from the enmeshment of multiple forms, the biases of one keeping the biases of the other in check.

For centuries, however, literacy remained a commodity belonging only to a privileged, scribal culture. The oral tradition continued to thrive as the expression of the illiterate majority. The difference was that this tradition now existed in the *framework* of literacy and all the cultural, economic, and social changes it had brought.

The next major communications shift came with the invention of movable type by Gutenberg in 1450. Exploding the quiet fortresses of European monk-scribes, the printing press led to what has been called the 'gunpowder of the mind' – books.[7] For the first time in history, opposing viewpoints fixed in print gradually became widely available, generating multilayered meanings and perspectives. Elizabeth Eisenstein's analysis of this era infers that the effects of the printing press included deepening introspection, heightened individuality, and a growing nationalism which eventually led to the conception of democracy itself.[8] One of her conclusions is that during the age of the manuscripts and before mass literacy, individuality, as we know it, did not exist. Explaining that prior to the 1400s, artists circulated the same generic wood-cut as the representative self-portrait of them all, content to let the same visual image stand for every member of the group, Eisenstein marvels at the lack of egotism this act reflects: 'The conditions of scribal culture', she deduces, 'held narcissism in check'.[9]

Over the next one hundred years, a new practice – that of strewing words on paper to a wide and unknown audience – gained momentum. In the theatre, the result eventually was a dramatic form which, again, carried the intensity and vividness of both orality and literacy. The fecundity of dramatic writing in Elizabethan England came at the end of a century in which literacy had increasingly become part of the fabric of a society which still carried the imprint of the oral tradition. This in turn led to the rise of a multiplicity of dramatic forms, all immersed in both orality and literacy, including Jacobean, Restoration, Georgian and Romantic drama. However, it was not until the middle of the nineteenth century that mediated forms of communication took another major turn, ushering in the fourth communications revolution. Samuel Morse could not have foreseen the unprecedented exposure to drama through electronic media initiated by his invention of the telegraph: silent films, talking pictures, and now, of course, television. With this new technology came new biases, new ideologies; the image, naturalistic and immediate, rather than the word, took dominance.

As we move inexorably into this high-tech world of images and instancy, are there elements of oral and literate worlds that we have lost? Have we left behind qualities worth recovering? One of the biases of electronic forms is a tendency to disconnect from the past, so the value of history is not easily perceived by young people. Should we be providing in schools what our students will not find elsewhere in their mass media dominated world?

Mediated visions

Unlike the oral world, our present electronic world offers fewer and fewer opportunities to engage in face-to-face, interactive human dialogue and thus undermines our sense of belonging to a group. Additionally, because media production is in the hands of a small minority and aimed towards the multitude, few have a voice. In a more oral culture, including those in the framework of literacy, the opportunity to participate is qualitatively different from those offered by media culture. The oral tradition fosters creative forms which invite participation; this participation, in turn, inculcates a sense of belonging to the group. The various categories of folklore – fables, folk tales, fairy tales, myths, legends, epics and tall tales – are available to all, adults and children alike, as are other art forms of the folk tradition. The many expressions of folk dance are often either a theatrical event or part of a theatrical event; so too from the folk song literature are sea shanties, ballads, spirituals and lullabies. The quality of life of the child who spends endless hours in front of a screen seems meagre indeed in comparison to that of one who can participate unself-consciously in art forms like these. As Daniel Boorstin (1961) has observed, in stark contrast to the 'mass', the 'folk' of history had a voice:

> the mass ... is the target and not the arrow. It is the ear and not the voice. The mass is what others aim to reach – by print, photograph, image, and sound. While the folk created heroes, the mass can only look for them. ... The mass live in the very different fantasy of pseudo-events.[10]

The existence of opportunities to engage actively in multiple forms of symbol-making (drama, music, dance, literature and the visual arts) as well as to experience artistic events creates a more balanced communication environment. As it is, a decidedly non-egalitarian communication imbalance exists as the media products of a small group of producers are consumed by a massive audience. At the same time, an increasing reliance on technology leads to inaction. We are consumers who passively watch rather than create, dance, sing, tell, or enact. We listen to the radio or compact disc player rather than compose or express our own thoughts and feelings through artistic production. Ours is the first generation to substitute a 'secondary, mediated version of experience for direct experience of the world'.[11] In addition to the censorship imposed by producers and broadcasters, we are further silenced by the passivity with which we receive – and trust – our electronic media. Viewing consumes time which could be spent pursuing artistic endeavours of all kinds and fewer and fewer of us have the direct experience of being able to fashion our thoughts and feelings through the symbols of art.

As machines appropriate the lion's share of our functional lives, the danger exists that machines will be allowed to make decisions that only humans should make, a proclivity that did not pass unnoticed by early experimenters in cybernetics. The rapid growth of computers, for example, and our increasing dependence upon them raise difficult moral questions. Some scientists have gone so far as to suggest that there are certain tasks which computers simply ought not to be allowed to do; mechanistic calculation imperils human judgement. And, the computer carries other predilections. Its demand for exactness leads away from complexity and ambiguity. Computer influenced language becomes increasingly utilitarian, insulating us from multiple and intricate meanings. The vast possibilities of language are reduced and our ability to name and understand our experience is diminished as our vocabularies grow smaller. When considering the presence of computers in contemporary classrooms, Neil Postman notes that schools, which have traditionally been the province of oral and literate traditions, are now expected also to provide a space for electronically mediated forms of teaching and learning. In doing so, according to Postman, we are 'breaking a four hundred year old truce between the gregariousness and openness fostered by orality and the introspection and isolation fostered by the printed word':

> Orality stresses group learning, cooperation, and a sense of social responsibility.. . . Print stresses individualised learning, competition, and personal autonomy. Over four centuries, teachers, while emphasizing print, have allowed orality its place in the classroom, and therefore have achieved a kind of pedagogical peace between these two forms of learning.. . .Now comes the computer, carrying anew the banner of private learning and individual problem-solving. Will the widespread use of computers in the classroom defeat once and for all the claims of communal speech? Will the computer raise egocentrism to the status of a virtue?[12]

Yet a Luddite argument is surely senseless. The value of computers to specific groups, the disabled, for example, is well documented. Exploring how we can shape the *use* of computers, however, and what biases of the form we must counterbalance, is both responsible and necessary. There are those who go so far as to argue that electronic forms of media, with their emphasis on the visual and non-verbal, have created a new epistemology. 'Moving to a predominantly visual rather than print medium', says Michael Manley-Casimir, 'fundamentally alters the educational task.... The challenge is nothing less than engaging children and youth in a process of radical criticism'.[13]

A critical inheritance

Because of their dramaturgical training – or supposed dramaturgical training – drama teachers are, in theory, well qualified to foster this process of radical criticism. However, at precisely the moment our students most need it, two thousand years of dramatic criticism lie fallow. Very few of our students will leave their secondary schools with a critical vocabulary which could help them distance themselves from and criticise their media environment. If we are to facilitate a sense of agency in our students so that they can transcend their media-dominated present, then we need to reflect deeply on current drama education practice.

What would a drama curriculum that is responsive to the implications of media shifts look like? First of all, it seems incumbent upon drama educators to accept a definition of their subject which includes television, film, radio, and audio and videotapes.[14] To disregard manifestations of drama in electronic forms smacks of an élitism we can ill-afford; for Martin Esslin, a dramatic theory which ignores the mass media is 'pretentious and irrelevant'.[15] If we are to serve our students well (especially our poorer students), delimiting our vision to exclude mass media is no longer an option. In addition to accepting a more inclusive definition of dramatic art, a reception component must be firmly ensconced in the dramatic curriculum. In the space created for audience response, interpretive discourse – the process by which teachers help students gain a critical vocabulary – can occur. Drama teachers will then be able to do what technology cannot do, by fostering those skills and experiences that, according to Joshua Meyrowitz, 'no communication technology from writing to computers can teach, including interpretation, criticism, and the "methodologies" of learning and thinking'. Another key example of such a skill, he argues, 'is the ability to interact with other people – to speak, listen, argue, and discuss'.[16]

Unfortunately, drama in schools has not made the developing of a critical vocabulary a priority. Peter Slade, one of the most influential early writers on drama education, adamantly opposed the concept of audience,[17] and this prejudice towards criticism continues. Clar Doyle argues that educational drama 'remains flagrantly acritical',[18] and, in her dissertation on dramatic interpretation in the secondary school, Paula Salvio notes that drama programmes 'often lack a critical dimension'.[19] Given today's media milieu, this state of affairs seems more than remiss; surely, the time has come to re-examine the Sladian legacy. In the 1950s, when Slade was at the height of his career, television was in its infancy. Little did he or anyone else suspect that children growing up in the 1950s would eventually spend audacious amounts of time as spectators, and that *their* children would spend even more. As argued earlier in this chapter, culture hides more than it reveals; it is unlikely that in the 1950s Slade, or anyone else, connected audience response in the drama classroom with the rapidly changing media environment.

Not surprisingly, this lack of emphasis on criticism is reflected in the preparation of future drama teachers. In the analysis of his research into preservice theatre teacher education programmes in the USA, Dave Dynak expresses concern that few, if any, of the students he interviewed had access to models for critique. At all the universities investigated, students described difficulties in engaging in 'constructive criticism'.[20] The implications of Dynak's research are that much work awaits in not only generating models for critique, but also in learning how to guide, humanely, the 'responding' component of David Hornbrook's model of making, performing, and responding. Such engagements in constructive criticism have the possibility of becoming improvisational creations in which thought, feeling, intuition and imagination are united. A spirit of goodwill should be the goal; the art of disagreeing agreeably must be taught. Because it is difficult to attain does not mean that it should not be tried. A warm human approach to audience response may temper drama education's long-standing reticence towards criticism.

Drama teachers are uniquely positioned to engage students in this task, given the theatre's rich and controversial history of dramatic criticism. Aristotle, Diderot, Brecht, Boal, the critical languages of semiotics and reader response – access to this heritage, much underused at present, will help students develop a critical vocabulary and distance themselves from their forms of communication. If we do not teach it, students will not learn it; critical vocabularies do not simply transpire.

Towards an analytical methodology

For decades, Martin Esslin has urged the education establishment to wake up to students' media environment and to give them the 'analytical tools of dramatic criticism'.[21] In this 'training ground', according to Esslin, dramaturgs would become 'working models', not for the purpose of encouraging students to adopt their opinions but for their 'methods and attitudes'.[22] Brecht, for example, knew a critical attitude did not have to mean a negative attitude. Building on the work of the Russian Formalists, his epic theatre and its poetics seek active audience response. It must be remembered that Brecht created his theatre in reaction to the dominant naturalistic style which characterised most theatre of his time. The parallels to our own day are striking indeed; the difference is that the delivery of drama through multiple modes of media means that naturalism is now more pervasive than even Brecht could have imagined. In fact, television is so well calibrated to naturalism that the form presents the ideal breeding ground for *more* naturalism, as Raymond Williams observes:

> It could be argued that the television play was the ultimate realisation of the original naturalist convention: the drama of the small enclosed room, in which a few characters lived out their private experience of an unseen public world. Since a major structure of feeling, in the art of the period, was in any case of this kind, it is not surprising that many television plays reproduced this assumption of the nature of representative reality. This was a drama of the box in the same fundamental sense as the naturalist drama had been the drama of the framed stage.[23]

Naturalism has made its way into the rhythms of our lives to such an extent that 'the slice of life', once associated with naturalistic theatre has, according to Williams, 'been raised to a new convention, that of a basic need'.[24] Nor has the ascendancy of naturalism gone unnoticed by medium theorists; Julian Jaynes writes of 'the grinding tides of irreversible naturalism' that have swept away both 'literary languages and archaic speech'.[25]

As drama teachers, it may be that we have unwittingly assimilated too much of the prevailing culture into our drama practices, thus upholding, instead of challenging, the status quo. Hornbrook has forcefully criticised the naturalism that characterises much of the practice in drama in education and part of the grounds of his criticism is that such practice invites into the classroom the very thing of which students already have a steady diet:

> It is ... a mistrust of the critical or analytic, that binds drama-in-education to that same pervasive naturalism which so decisively frames television drama. The reluctance to make the step from describing the world through the eyes of individuals to any interpretation of those descriptions, draws classroom drama irresistibly back to that ideology of non-ideology.[26]

Gavin Bolton and Dorothy Heathcote, prominent and influential figures in drama education, have both advocated the use of drama as a learning tool for a multiplicity of purposes rather than seeing it as an art form with its own intrinsic purpose. Bolton acknowledges the naturalistic emphasis of their practices but believes that Heathcote 'did not intend to bring such a strong flavor of naturalism to children's work'. On the contrary, he argues, she preferred the alienation effect of Brecht.[27] Whatever is asserted, their theory often translates into practice as naturalism, as here in one of Heathcote's own 'conventions': 'The role actually present, naturalistic, yet significantly behaving, giving and accepting responses'.[28]

Marxist critic Terry Eagleton points out that Brecht rebelled against the aesthetic of naturalism because he believed 'that reality is a changing discontinuous process, produced by men and so transformable by them'.[29] In contrast, naturalism asks that its participants suspend disbelief. 'The power of persuasion', built into the style of naturalism, is 'not in dispute', writes theatre scholar Robert Taylor.[30] In contrast, Brechtian theatre asks the audience *and the actors* continually to think, judge, and criticise. Naturalism also underestimates the audience's creative and intellectual capacities. Minimalist, symbolist, and expressionist theatre, for example, all invite spectators to imagine, to co-create, to engage in artistic transactions. Antithetically, naturalistic drama, in the theatre and on television, denies inventive experience to its spectators, ensuring that they are further silenced in an age in which participation and active engagement are not easily come by.

If, as Sita Brahmachari suggests in Chapter 2, drama teachers accept that they have a responsibility to induct students into intracultural dramatic forms, these will help to counteract the overwhelming diet of naturalism students presently encounter in their homes and, too often, in their drama classes at school. Such a curriculum, covering all kinds of dramatic styles, will in turn, lead to all kinds of post-performance discussions. Brecht, of course, knew this and was a multiculturalist before any of us knew the word. Ethnic diversity lies at the very core of Brecht's theory of drama, and, in formulating his own poetics, he drew heavily from other cultures:

> A representation that alienates is one which allows us to recognize its subject, but at the same time makes it seem unfamiliar. The classical and medieval theatre alienated its characters by making them wear human or animal masks; the Asiatic theatre even today uses musical and pantomimic A-effects.[31]

The 'alienation' of this multicultural approach – Brecht's well-known *Verfremdungseffekt* – frees an audience to make choices and does not ask it to suspend judgement. Styles that would invoke this kind of response include classical, medieval, African, Indian, Elizabethan, *commedia dell'arte*, and other forms of presentational (rather than representational) drama. The introduction of dramatic texts of this sort into the drama class will serve to counter the naturalistic bias of much of students' culture and open up replete qualities of interpretive discourse.

Students' critical vocabularies must also be informed by Aristotelian conventions. Already, in many countries, six year olds in whole language classrooms routinely use 'story-mapping', a technique which includes Aristotelian elements like 'setting', 'characters', 'problem', 'events', and 'resolution'. If six year olds can understand and use this kind of vocabulary, and they can, then the Aristotelian terms of plot, character, thought, dialogue, melody and spectacle are also attainable. If medium theorists have urged educators to protect their students by giving them access to Aristotelian concepts and vocabulary, and they have, then drama teachers have an unparalleled opportunity to bring these concepts into the subject of drama.

It is true that Brecht's *Verfremdungseffekt* is not usually associated with Aristotelian poetics. However, in the 1970s, Esslin applied Aristotelian principles to the television commercial in such a way so as to achieve a Brechtian effect. Through analysis, Esslin identifies the three constituent parts of the traditional commercial. The first is the exposition of a potentially disastrous problem. For example, bad breath could destroy romance or drinking the wrong kind of cola could label one as dull instead of young and alive. In the second part, *anagnorisis*, a moment of insight, occurs: a solution to the problem is suggested, usually by a friend or an elder, thus propelling the plot to *peripeteia*, or the turning point of the action. Finally, in the third part (just thirty seconds from when potential troubles began), impending tragedy is staved off by the consumer's happy conclusion to accept the advertiser's product.[32] Applying Esslin's Aristotelian analysis of the television commercial has possibilities for developing critical vocabularies as well as simply being fun. Students' critical vocabularies may be further developed by exploring parallels between television voice-overs and the Greek chorus, or between the *deus ex machina* and the product's logo. They could even create their own three-part commercials (as described above), then, using the Aristotelian elements, analyse each other's work.

Augusto Boal, radical South American politician and theatre director, has criticised Aristotelian poetics in his book, *Theatre of the Oppressed*. Boal believes that Aristotelian catharsis serves to oppress further already marginalised groups. Aristotle, he asserts, has constructed an 'extremely powerful poetic-political system for intimidation of the spectator, for elimination of the "bad" or illegal tendencies of the audience':

> This system is, to this day, fully utilized not only in conventional theater, but in the TV soap operas and in Western films as well: movies, theater, and television united, through a common basis in Aristotelian poetics, for repression of the people.[33]

Like medium theorists, Boal believes that viewers tend to give over the power of decision-making to the image. For him, consumerism is inherent in viewing. Mass-mediated popular culture is little more, says Boal, than 'a vast market in which we sell our goods and our souls'.[34] Exposure to Boal's poetics of the oppressed will certainly cause students to view television in a critical way and could even help them find less reductive ways of living by giving them an increased awareness of the advertisers' agenda. But, even to begin to understand Boal's poetics of the oppressed, students must be familiar with Aristotelian terms. The vocabulary must be there.

Although they have been with us for well over half a century, semiotics and reader response are critical languages which are just beginning to receive attention in drama education. In the previous chapter, Dan Urian offers a model of audience reception based on semiotics, and in the early 1990s Hornbrook modified semiotician Patrice Pavis' framework of questions to stimulate interpretive discourse for classroom use.[35] While not wishing to belittle the possibilities of semiotics in helping students develop critical vocabularies, I think some examination of its limits is called for. To be forceful, any critical perspective must be narrow and, as teachers, we must continually make students aware of the limitations of any one way of understanding. The world is wide and cannot all be explained from one vantage point; students should be helped to see that. It could be argued that semiotics is itself an extension of computer technology, as David Bolter (1984) observes:

> Using treelike designs to describe the creation of sentences came into fashion with Chomsky and his followers, in close connection . . . with the development of high-level programming languages. Today, anthropologists and even literary critics are diagramming everything from social relationships in aboriginal tribes and primitive myths to urbane modern poetry.[36]

If Bolter is right, and the semiotic approach reflects computer programming, then we surrender once again to the monopoly of technology. For Jacques Ellul, the rise of semiotics is further proof of his prediction that, in a technological society, all the arts and sciences will eventually be dominated by *technique*.[37] The scientific, digitised language used by computers has a purpose quite dissimilar to the language employed in humanities. Likewise, semiotic interpretation can simply be too reductive and can deny the possibility of the ineffable. While recognising that we currently lack and currently need analytical tools to help us understand audience response, theatre scholar John Styan expresses concern that semiotics may make a science of art by emphasising the empirical to the exclusion of sensory engagement and, in the process, aesthetic elements may be ignored. Inherent in theatre is a two-way act of communication; inherent in semiotics, fears Styan, is a one-way act of communication: 'Theatre becomes a passageway for a cargo of meanings being carried back to society (after artistic refinement) via the

162

language of signs'. Ultimately the theatre remains mysterious, and 'not all things are knowable – even to semioticians'.[38]

To redress the balance, the watching and understanding of drama must include more than one approach to interpretive discourse. Like a pair of binoculars, semiotics combined with other critical languages, such as reader response, can help us to see the performer–audience transaction in richer ways. Bert States illuminates this simile:

> One eye enables us to see the world phenomenally; the other eye enables us to see it significantly. . . . Lose the sight of your phenomenal eye and you become a Don Quixote (everything is something else); lose the sight of your significative eye and you become Sartre's Roquentin (everything is nothing but itself).[39]

Phenomenology provides the philosophical base for reader response. As developed by Wolfgang Iser in the 1970s, reader response asks us to understand our response to what we read (including theatre performances) as a process of 'concretization'. Iser defines 'concretization' as 'the process by which . . . a reader serves as coproducer of the meaning of a text by creatively filling gaps'.[40] Lest this be taken as a free fall into radical relativism, Louise Rosenblatt reassures us that although the 'import of any work will remain thoroughly personal', and although no one interpretation is definitive, students 'should be led to discover that some interpretations are more defensible than others'.[41] For Rosenblatt, the atmosphere which should prevail during the articulation of students' response is important:

> An atmosphere of informal, friendly exchange should be created. The student should feel free to reveal emotions and to make judgements. . . . Frank expression of boredom or even vigorous rejection is a more valid starting point for learning than are docile attempts to feel 'what the teacher wants'.[42]

Using reader response, properly trained leaders of post-performance discussions have the opportunity to stimulate a positive collective experience in which students will also have the opportunity to play with verbal symbols. It is not my intention, however, to promote one poetics of response over another. All contributors to this book are clear about the need for drama education to move beyond the one-dimensional Eurocentric naturalism which characterises much current practice; likewise, models for response cannot be one-dimensional. It is to the benefit of our students to introduce them to a number of interpretive strategies, help them understand the limitations of each perspective and to show them how the same dramatic text can be interpreted in widely differing ways.

Interpretive strategies

Paula Salvio has demonstrated how this process of interpretation can be accomplished in school with older students. Through her use of dramatic *scoring* – which she defines as 'an interpretive strategy built upon the theories and methods of the modern stage' – she is able to explore the approaches that Brecht, Artaud, Stanislavski and Stanislavski's pupil, Michael Chekhov, might have taken to Sophocles' *Oedipus Rex.* [43] Central to this strategy is her use of the *Modellbuch* (the director's notebook) in which students develop their own questions.[44] Although Salvio does not relate her project to the implications of living in the electronic age, her work has exciting implications for the subject of dramatic criticism; the contrasts and comparisons she educes from her students can lead to critical thinking.

Building on Salvio's approach, students could easily progress to a consideration of other plays, not only through the lens of the theatre director, but also through that of film and television. What is the difference between Brecht's plays, for example, in live performance and when viewed on the screen? When students analyse live and mediated performance they will become aware of a number of differences. Live performance is more spontaneous, more vital, more communal. The give and take that exists between actor and audience in live performance cannot exist in television, nor can television generate the excitement of the ephemeral, unrepeatable performance. Live performance can be more complex, and grants more freedom to the spectator. Film and television may overwhelm viewers with images; the live performance in the theatre engages spectators more holistically. Thus the power of the director is greater and the freedom of the spectator is less in mediated dramatic performances than in live performance.

Engagement with the process of production can narrow the wide gap that exists between producer and consumer and the production of dramatisations electronically is already common practice in some drama classrooms. By experimenting with a variety of styles and then videotaping the product, students have the opportunity to take on the roles of producers, directors, camera technicians, as well as actors. In this kind of 'hands-on' activity, the language of television production is demystified, helping students to see television in new ways.[45]

As well as comparing and contrasting live and mediated theatre, students may also be encouraged to consider the differences between art and entertainment. It has been claimed that the arts, contrasted to entertainment, take on greater importance in an extremely technologised society. Joseph Weizenbaum suggests that an overemphasis on the empirical has 'delegitimatized all other ways of understanding':

People (historically) viewed the arts . . . as sources of intellectual nourishment and understanding, but today the arts are perceived largely as entertainments. The ancient Greek and Oriental theaters, the Shakespearean stage, the stages peopled by the Ibsens and Chekhovs nearer to our day – these were schools. The curricula they taught were vehicles for understanding the societies they represented. Today ... people hunger only for what is represented to them to be scientifically validated knowledge. ... We can count, but we are rapidly forgetting how to say what is worth counting and why.[46]

In his book *Amusing Ourselves to Death*, Neil Postman argues that, because of mass media, we now demand entertainment from *every* field of endeavour. Our students may not even know that a distinction can be made between art and entertainment (although, of course, the two are not mutually exclusive, as Horace knew in the first century BC and as Brecht has more recently reminded us – art can both teach and delight). The relentless demand for entertainment identified by Postman is very apparent when we look at the extent to which some live drama has now itself taken on the characteristics of television. Jonathan Levy disparages the way in which contemporary children's playwrights, modelling their plays after television and cinema, pack episodic scenes full of peak events, thus appealing, 'not to imaginations ... but to nervous systems'.[47] Instead of experimenting with a dramatic form that has its own rhythms, as teachers and artists we feel the pressure to compete with technological spectacle; our rhythms become faster and faster and louder and louder. 'As it affects the meaning of the symbols used by the artist', observed Lewis Mumford, this escalation of sensationalism 'means Emptier and Emptier'.[48]

Whatever form it takes, the subject of drama must include space to explore modes of response. I have argued that this key element is especially important in today's mass media world, best achieved by engaging students in a wide repertoire of dramatic forms, styles and multicultural traditions while making sure they have access to several models for critique. Criticism, understood in its positive connotations, can then work for our students, helping them to distance themselves from the media, so that they can question what they see and hear. This critical attitude can create a detachment that is not only integral to aesthetic appreciation, but also increasingly important as we venture ever more deeply into an electronic future.

Notes

1 B. Brecht (1940) 'Short description of a new technique of acting', in J. Willett (1964) (ed. and trans.) *Brecht on Theatre*, New York: Hill & Wang, p.146.
2 E. Hall (1966) *The Silent Language*, Greenwich, CT: Fawcett Publications, p.30.
3 R. Barthes (1973) *Mythologies*, trans. A. Lavers, London and New York:

Granada, pp.137, 143, and N. Postman (1985) *Amusing Ourselves to Death: Public Discourse in the Age of Show Business*, New York: Penguin Books, p.162.

4 W. Ong (1983) *Orality and Literacy: The Technologizing of the Word*, London: 'Routledge, p.72.

5 Ibid., p15. For accounts of modern primary oral cultures, see J. Goody (1987) *The Interface Between the Oral and the Written*, Cambridge: Cambridge University Press and A. Luria (1976) *Cognitive Development: Its Cultural and Social Foundations*, ed. M. Cole, trans. M. Lopez-Morillas and L. Solotaroff, Cambridge, MA: Harvard University Press.

6 W. Ong (1983), p.152.

7 In D. Riesman (1960) 'The oral and written traditions', in E. Carpenter and M. McLuhan (eds) *Explorations in Communication*, Boston, MA: Beacon Press, p.10.

8 E. Eisenstein (1979) *The Printing Press as an Agent of Change: Communications and Cultural Transformations in Early-Modern Europe*, 2 vols, Cambridge: Cambridge University Press. See also, H. Perkinson (1995) *How Things Got Better: Speech, Writing, Printing, and Cultural Change*, Westport, CT: Bergin & Garvey.

9 E. Eisenstein (1979), p.66.

10 D. Boorstin (1961) *The Image: A Guide to Pseudo-Events in America*, New York: Atheneum, p.56.

11 J. Mander (1978) *Four Arguments for the Elimination of Television*, New York, William & Morrow, p.24.

12 N. Postman (1992) *Technoploy: The Surrender of Culture to Technology*, New York: Alfred A. Knopf, p.17.

13 M.E. Manley-Casimir (1987) 'Children, culture, and the curriculum of television: a challenge for education', in M. E. Manley-Casimir and C. Luke (eds) *Children and Television: A Challenge for Education*, New York: Praeger, p.245.

14 This has been argued elsewhere. See M. Esslin (1987) *The Field of Drama: How the Signs of Drama Create Meanings on Stage and Screen*, London and New York: Methuen; L. Wright and L. Garcia (1992) 'Dramatic literacy: the place of theatre education in schools', *Design for Arts in Education* 93(4), pp.25–9.

15 M. Esslin (1962) *Meditations: Essays on Brecht, Beckett, and the Media*, London: Eyre Methuen, p.242.

16 J. Meyrowitz (1985) *No Sense of Place: The Impact of Electronic Media on Social Behavior*, New York: Oxford University Press, p.257.

17 'In real child drama, the audience has no place at all', P. Slade (1954) *Child Drama*, London: University of London Press, p.350.

18 C. Doyle (1993) *Raising Curtains on Education: Drama as a Site for Critical Pedagogy*, Westport, CT: Bergin & Garvey, p.63.

19 P. Salvio (1989) 'Transforming Rituals of Commemoration: Theatre and Textual Interpretation in the Secondary Classroom', unpublished PhD thesis, New York: University of Rochester, p.49.

20 D. Dynak (1994) 'Profiles of Preservice Theatre Teacher Education Programs at Three American Universities', unpublished PhD thesis, Lansing, MI: Michigan State University, p.366.

21 M. Esslin (1982) *The Age of Television*, San Francisco, CA: W.H. Freeman, pp.6–7.

22 M. Esslin (1961) *Reflections: Essays on the Modern Theatre*, Garden City, NY: Doubleday, Introduction.

23 R. Williams (1974) *Television: Technology and Cultural Form*, London: Fontana, p.56.

24 R. Williams, (1975) *Drama in a Dramatised Society*, Cambridge: Cambridge University Press, p.7.

25 J. Jaynes (1976) *The Origin of Consciousness in the Breakdown of the Bicameral Mind*, Boston, MA: Houghton Mifflin, p.378.

26 D. Hornbrook (1989 [1998]) *Education and Dramatic Art*, 2nd edn, London: Routledge, pp.76–7.

27 G. Bolton (1985) 'Changes in thinking about drama in education', *Theory into Practice* 24(3), p.155.

28 In L. Johnson and C. O'Neill (eds) (1984) *Dorothy Heathcote: Collected Writings on Education and Drama*, London: Hutchinson, p.166.

29 T. Eagleton (1976) *Marxism and Literary Criticism*, Berkeley, CA: University of California Press, p.5.

30 R. Taylor (1988) *The Theatre Underground: A Classical Revolutionary Organization*, unpublished PhD thesis, Lawrence, KS: University of Kansas, p.73.

31 B. Brecht (1948) 'A short organum for the theatre', in J. Willett (1964), p.192.

32 M. Esslin (1979) 'Aristotle and the advertisers: the television commercial considered as a form of drama', in H. Newcomb (ed.) *Television: The Critical View*, 4th edn, New York: Oxford University Press, pp.306–7.

33 A. Boal (1979) *Theatre of the Oppressed*, trans. C. McBride and M. McBride, London: Pluto Press, p.xiv.

34 A. Boal (1992) *Games for Actors and Non-Actors*, London: Routledge, p.247.

35 See D. Hornbrook (1991) *Education in Drama: Casting the Dramatic Curriculum*, London: Falmer Press and D. Hornbrook (1989 [1998]) *Education and Dramatic Art*, 2nd edn, London: Routledge, Appendix II.

36 D. Bolter (1984) *Turing's Man: Western Culture in the Computer Age*, Chapel Hill, NC: University of North Carolina Press, pp.98–9.

37 See J. Ellul (1964) *The Technological Society*, trans. J. Wilkinson, New York: Vintage Press and J. Ellul (1985) *The Humiliation of the Word*, Grand Rapids, MI: William B. Eerdmans.

38 J. Styan (1988) 'The mystery of the play experience: Quince's questions', in M. Issacharoff and R. Jones (eds) *Performing Texts*, Philadelphia, PA: University of Pennsylvania Press, pp.9–26.

39 B. States (1985) *Great Reckonings in Little Rooms: On the Phenomenology of Theater*, Berkeley, CA: University of California Press, p.8.

40 M. Carlson (1989) 'Theatre audiences and the reading of performance', in T. Postlewait and B. McConachie (eds) *Interpreting the Theatrical Past: Essays in the Historiography of Performance*, Iowa City, IA: University of Iowa Press, p.82.

41 L. Rosenblatt (1983) *Literature as Exploration*, 4th edn, New York: Modern Language Association, pp.114–15. In relation to drama education, see also, Hornbrook's discussion of the use of Habermas's *ideologiekritik* in the classroom, in D. Hornbrook (1989 [1998]) *Education and Dramatic Art*, 2nd edn, London: Routledge, pp.126–8.

42 Ibid., p.70.

43 P. Salvio, p.2.

44 Christopher McCullough gives an extended example of the use of Brecht's *Modellbuch* in Chapter 10.

45 A word of caution. Involvement in television production can actually *inhibit* critical thought. Students may become so involved in the technical aspects that content is neglected. See J. Johnsen (1990) 'Study of Television in a Ninth Grade Classroom: Inhibiting a Critical Orientation', unpublished PhD thesis, Columbus, OH: Ohio State University.

46 J. Weizenbaum (1976) *Computer Power and Human Reason: From Judgment to Calculation*, San Francisco, CA: W.H. Freeman, p.16.
47 J. Levy (1987) *A Theatre of the Imagination: Reflections on Children and Theatre*, Charlottesville, VA: New Plays Incorporated, p.6.
48 L. Mumford (1952) *Art and Technics*, New York: Columbia University Press, p.99.

10

BUILDING A DRAMATIC VOCABULARY

Christopher McCullough

> we need to develop the historical sense ... into real sensual delight. When theatres perform plays of other periods they like to annihilate distance, fill in the gap, gloss over differences. But what comes then of our delight in comparisons, in distance, in dissimilarity – which is at the same time a delight in what is close and proper to ourselves?
>
> Bertolt Brecht[1]

Music, art and drama

Historically, theatre has been a marginalised activity within our culture – the order in which the above subheading has been set out is not an accident – and the history of the ways by which we have approached the education of students in these three disciplines reflects this inequality. Whereas music and visual art have been part of the state education system at all levels since at least the beginning of the twentieth century, drama remained confined to the private sector and to exclusive conservatoires concentrating on the training (as opposed to the educating) of actors until the emergence of school and university drama departments in the years following the Second World War.

This unequal relationship between the sister arts poses a number of pertinent questions for a relatively unfledged discipline (in the context of pedagogy) seeking to establish for itself a legitimating vocabulary. Pre-eminent among these is the concern to locate what we may term the 'art object' in drama. In music and visual art there seems to be little difficulty in establishing the relationship of the artist to the object. In the former, the artist conceives and produces the object; in the latter, while there is a division of labour between composer, conductor and performer, it would be difficult to conceive of a composer who could not also conduct an orchestra and play an instrument. My point here is to observe how intrinsic are the links between the activities of making and understanding music. Reading a musical score is not only a highly specialised skill, but one that is essential to the development of musical craft.

In the case of drama, however, there has always been a greater cultural distance between the perceived *artist* (the playwright) and the *interpreter* of the art (the performer). How many actors have either a clear understanding of dramatic structure or are able to write plays? Of course there are some who bridge that gap – playwrights John Osborne and Harold Pinter being obvious examples – but they are few in number. What I am suggesting is that the literary form and its creator have been afforded a position superior to that of the artisan who is employed to give action to the word. The irony and the problem lie, on the one hand, in the seeming familiarity of the play as text – unlike the musical score it appears to be written in the language we speak – and, on the other, in the cultural distance that separates the role of the writer as artist from the actor as interpretive craftsperson.

What music also possesses, apart from the symbiotic relationship between composer, score and performer, is a generally accepted body of knowledge and craft. Not only is music the purest of the arts (according to Western culture, poetry is the only one that comes near to it), but it also has clear disciplinary conventions that may be grouped under the general heading of musicology. I am not saying that drama cannot make a similar claim (it can in terms of dramatic literary criticism); I am questioning whether those of us who teach drama, let alone those who wish to be taught, have yet reached the level of articulation enjoyed by our music colleagues.

Paradoxically, it may be in the cultural relationship, or tension, that exists between writers, directors and actors that we should begin our search for a dramatic vocabulary. In an important sense the cultural history of twentieth-century theatre in Europe has been delineated by the ways in which the figures of writer, director, designer and actor have all fought for pre-eminence. In Edward Gordon Craig, we observe an early example of the phenomenon of the director as *auteur*. The mid-century dominance of the director – Reinhardt, Brook, Stein, *et al.* – seeking authorship of a performance produced a reaction from actors who, after their central role in the nineteenth century, sought a new kind of actor-centred theatre dependent on neither the writer nor the director. If we observe the work of the *Théâtre du Soleil* we may perceive an empowerment of the actor as a creative force through the *création collective* in direct retaliation to the autocratic power assumed by many directors.

The ascendancy of the performer, in its turn, produced a sense of disenfranchisement for the playwright. In December 1980, the Budapest playwrights' conference met to discuss a number of issues relating to the position of playwrights in contemporary European theatre; the main issue on the agenda was the relationship between the playwright and the director. A manifesto was produced that made clear the degree of helplessness felt by writers. English playwright, David Edgar reported on the controversy in *Théâtre International*:

I think the argument over the *Playwrights' Manifesto* was particularly significant for the British and American delegations, because it brought home the depths of feeling that exist among European playwrights about how their work is mangled by directors, and, indeed, their resentment at the way in which directors have become cinema-style 'superstars' over recent years.[2]

Edgar concludes by saying that he, and other playwrights, write for the theatre because they believe that the collaboration between the arts of the writer, director, actor and designer can 'create a unique emotional and intellectual experience for an audience. But they are convinced that the living word and the living writer of that word is and will remain the primary mainspring of the theatre'.[3]

Perhaps, in the articulation of this struggle for recognition and status lie important clues in our search for a 'musicology' of drama which recognises the complex interrelationship of word (written and spoken), action and image. Certainly, we would be foolish not to take serious account of Edgar's final sentence. How should we read it? Should we accept the implication, still present, that the word, and therefore the art of the poet, is pre-eminent over the aural, oral, gestic and visual elements of theatrical performance? Should the drama teacher leave the analysis of the written word to the teacher of English and be content with the role of interpretive craftsperson?

If we are to avoid a ghetto mentality that confines the cognitive encounter with the play on the page to the English department and 'practical' work with the play on the stage to the drama department, we must explore further the complex nature of the theatrical experience. If we are to build a vocabulary for drama, then quite clearly our task is to examine *all* the possible languages of theatre and to articulate the means by which we may bring them together as a coherent and stimulating cultural subject. No serious discourse on the subject of drama can afford to privilege the language of literature above all the other potential theatrical languages. What those theatrical languages are, and how we may attempt to understand them, must at the same time acknowledge that a theory of drama is simultaneously a theory of culture and ideology.

One way to begin this task is to note some of the elements that comprise the intrinsic building blocks of drama's sister arts by referring back briefly to the models of music and visual art. In music, the concepts of mathematical patterns, rhythm, chord structure, melody and harmony are all essential elements of our understanding (as opposed to simply our reception) of music. Likewise, in visual art the elements of texture, shape, pattern, form and colour are necessary concepts in order to be able to understand a painting or a sculpture. And if we move beyond learning how to appreciate the visual and plastic arts or music and progress towards the *making* of art, a grasp of these elements becomes an absolute necessity. Before I am accused of prosecuting an élitist attitude towards education, I do have to say that the methodologies by which these skills may be gained are many and varied, and are in themselves also the subject of ideology. The understanding of art, both as receiver and creator, involves an understanding and experience of the material context of the past and a delight in and understanding of the conditions that 'make us' in the here and now. As Bertolt Brecht points out in the quotation at the beginning of this chapter, a part of understanding past history is also understanding our present histories.

What, then, may we consider to be the main elements of our vocabulary of drama and theatre,[4] the epistemological cornerstones of the subject of drama? The word, both written and spoken, springs most obviously to mind. However, we know that the actor's intonation becomes a significant factor as soon as the written word is spoken, so the audience's aural experience has to be added to our list. Further, if we consider that human action is central to our experience of drama, then our vocabulary cannot do without its visual component. As an audience, we see both action and the environment in which the action takes place. We may re-describe the elements I have identified as: writing or devising, acting/performing, light, sound and scenography.

Teaching these aspects of drama in isolation from one another would not, in my view, be productive. Treating them separately reinforces the idea that drama is a disparate activity and indeed not a cohesive discipline at all; it takes writing back into the English department, scenography into art and design, and lighting into physics. What is needed instead is a pedagogic method that keeps the activity located in the discipline of theatre in its broadest sense, one which allows responding to be intrinsic to making. Whereas acting or theatre technology, for example, may be more appropriately taught separately in higher education, in schools they should be approached as parts of a whole through a project-based approach. Of course, such projects, combining all the elements of theatre-making, will require a clear focus. This focus may take the form of a theatrical production, but it may also be manifest in other, less technically demanding forms of criticism and celebration.

Making drama

The idea of a project-based approach to learning is not new, as every primary teacher knows, but it is one that still suggests the possibility of empowerment and engagement for the learner, both as an individual and collectively. The pleasure of a project structure in drama is that it enables students to observe and experience the interrelation of meaning and craft that has been articulated throughout this book. In a recognisable way, it is craft that binds the elements of the project together and enables what has been understood to be celebrated in theatrical form.[5]

On the assumption that we encourage students to make drama because we believe that the *process* of making must be as important (if not more so, in some instances) as the outcome, is 'learning by doing' to be the basic principle of a project-based pedagogy? Although I have few problems with the idea of 'learning by doing' I do not think that it is enough; we can no longer be content with the idea that simply to 'do' drama is in itself radical. Many of the assumptions that seemed intrinsic to drama in the 1950s and 1960s do not fit easily into an ever-changing consciousness, and in Britain we do not inhabit the same material or ideological world that we did in the decades of educational expansion which followed the 1944 Education Act.[6] Exercises common to both educational drama and to theatre practice, for example, often ignore the difference between the male and female body, and how we read those bodies. Many of the exercises and games that were intended to 'liberate' the participants in the drama workshops of the 1970s were essentially male-orientated and tended, at the very least, to restrict female participants. Similarly, if the *form* of what we do cannot be assumed to be invariably appropriate, neither can the *subject matter* of our drama classes be taken to be constant for all time. If we accept the argument that we must always be conscious of the provisionality of form and content, we must also recognise our need to be aware of states of cultural flux. The challenge facing the heuristic and experiential education offered by 'learning by doing', in other words, is to develop the means to contextualise what is done. In order to know *what* we are learning by doing, we need to develop what we might call 'critical learning by doing'. Such a critical approach to experiential learning will allow drama, both educational and professional (I do not like to draw hard distinctions between them), to become a theory and experience of culture.

If we wish to mount a challenge to the idea that drama transcends the material conditions of production, that drama is to do with universal truths or phenomenological essences which it is the business of the teacher to uncover, the obvious starting point would seem to be the material conditions of history. This approach allows us to observe the making of art as a *product* of culture, rather than in itself 'culture', aloof from daily realities. In taking this conceptual approach, however, we cannot assume that a student (of whatever age) will automatically enthuse about the economic conditions of a late sixteenth-century public playhouse! If the subject matter of drama is to be treated in a certain way, consideration must also be given to how we teach it. There is little point in deconstructing ourselves as cultural entities if the teacher is attempting to pontificate from a position of assumed status and superior knowledge.

So, what are the learning structures that might be offered by a project of the kind I am proposing? To focus on history as a text to be read and interpreted; to understand drama as a part of a culture that simultaneously means and challenges meaning; to craft research that relates objective analysis to a personal relationship with the material (what does this knowledge mean to you?); to work towards a reading (we may alternatively write 'performance') of the material in some kind of public articulation of ideas through enactment. A collective focus supported by this kind of guided approach will also require the development of skills, but skills that are determined by the broader concept of craft.[7] Where an aspect of a project reveals a certain way of writing plays, for example, we may ask the question, why does a play from one context look and sound different from a play from another context? Equally, in relation to acting, certain literary formulations demand that words and actions must be spoken and carried out in certain ways, thus giving rise to a need to understand the conventions of performance. In this way, the skill of acting is not taught in a vacuum, but arises from the ideological determinants of historically contextualised craft. For the students themselves, if what is being learned through research raises the need for a skill, then surely the will to acquire the skill will be more intense.

How, then, does one set about constructing such a pedagogic project? I propose to attempt to answer this question by using the example of an existing text in order to show how a dramatic vocabulary is built into the writing. In doing this, my aim is to tease out the dramatic vocabulary by applying critical analysis and at the same time to explore the proposition that *critical reading* is intrinsically part of the creative process of making, performing and responding to drama.

The death of dumb Kattrin: the drama project in action

Brecht's plays have always presented British students of theatre with something of a problem. Nearly everyone has heard of Brecht and his work, to such an extent that he is almost as ubiquitous a presence on drama examination syllabuses as Shakespeare. However, the relationship between Brecht and his British audience (spectators, critics, directors) has not been an easy or straightforward one and Brecht's plays have never sat easily within the curriculum of English-speaking theatre.[8] The mainstream critical approach to Brecht by English critics has been to appropriate the man and his plays away from the offensive political ideology, with the intention of rescuing the art from the politics. What follows is a critical reading of Scene 11 from *Mother Courage and her Children* which explores the relationship between the dramatic language on the page, the dramatic vocabulary signalled by the script (silences, action, visual imagery, and so on) and the potential meaning of the scene as a whole. This particular scene has suffered much from the depoliticisation project and, as we shall see, one of the problems in performance is how to avoid pathos.

Brecht kept comprehensive records of his productions in the form of annotated photographs and a key accessory in this analysis will be Brecht's own *Modellbuch* for the scene.[9] In utilising this supplementary text, I am fully aware of the inherent instructional dangers in the concept of a *Modellbuch*. But, when claiming that a scene has the potential for a plurality of meanings, the very recognition of these problems is important if our aim is to introduce students to the means of articulating a critical response to a theatrical text. While the concept of iterability is important – the meaning of a text is located in the reading of that text at the historical moment of its reception – it is also important to be informed by a historical reading of the context of the original production. To deny history as an informing text is also to contradict the historical processes by which our own individual contexts (race, gender, social class, and so on) influence what things mean to us.

The title to Scene 11 of *Mother Courage* reads as follows:

JANUARY, 1636. CATHOLIC TROOPS THREATEN THE PROTESTANT TOWN OF HALLE. THE STONE BEGINS TO SPEAK. MOTHER COURAGE LOSES HER DAUGHTER AND JOURNEYS ONWARDS ALONE, THE WAR IS NOT YET NEAR ITS END.[10]

The method of presenting us with a synopsis of the scene before we embark upon it is intrinsic to the play's dramatic methodology, and from this device we learn something about the nature of the play's episodic structure. The spectators, informed of the events before they occur, are released from the tension of suspense in order that their focus may be directed elsewhere. Awareness of this form of dramatic structure raises two points, one relating to how we read the play's dramatic narrative, and the other to the practical question of how this information is imparted to an audience in performance. Both questions are important to the play's methodology of constructing meaning. The *Modellbuch* describes the events of the scene thus:

> Dumb Kattrin saves the city of Halle. The city of Halle is to be taken by surprise. Soldiers force a young peasant to show them the way. A peasant and his wife ask Kattrin to pray with them for the city of Halle. The dumb girl climbs onto the roof of the stable and beats the drum in order to awaken the city of Halle. Neither the offer to spare her mother in the city, nor the threat to smash the wagon, keep Kattrin from going on drumming. Dumb Kattrin's death.[11]

This is the scene in its essence. Kattrin's mother (Mother Courage) is away conducting business in the city, as she always tends be when one of her children is most threatened. This is not because she is a careless mother. It is because the only means she has at her disposal to protect her children from the war is that of the black-marketeer. Ironically, the very means of survival open to her and her children are also instrumental in the destruction of her three children.

How does this scene work and what is the material language of theatre that will give it flesh in performance? And how is it possible that a scene depicting a young woman who cannot speak, who sacrifices her life for the population (in particular the children) of the city of Halle, can be understood in any term *but* pathos? One clue may be found in the *Modellbuch* under the sub-heading, 'Bad comedians always laugh, bad tragedians always cry'. The point is that there is much humour in the scene, but it is 'serious' humour based on the observed social oppression of all the characters: the soldiers who kill Kattrin, the peasants whose son is forced to lead the soldiers to the city, and Kattrin herself. I will take headings from the *Modellbuch* as the structure by which to analyse the scene and discuss the dramatic vocabulary used in each section.

The city of Halle is to be taken by surprise. Soldiers force a young peasant to show them the way.

The soldiers enter. Two points to note. Everything in the play points to the fact that the ordinary soldiers in the war are peasants also, as powerless to control events as those they harass or people like Mother Courage and her three children. Further, the intention of their action – the surprise attack on the city – demands silence. This silence and the simultaneous noise of the scene provide both the scene's tension and the first hint of its dark humour. The stage direction describes the soldiers thus:

Out of the wood come a lieutenant and three soldiers in full armour.

THE LIEUTENANT: And there mustn't be a sound. If anyone yells, cut him down.
THE FIRST SOLDIER: But we'll have to knock – if we want a guide.
THE LIEUTENANT: Knocking's a natural noise, it's all right, could be a cow hitting the wall of the cowshed.[12]

In the Royal National Theatre's 1995 production, with Diana Rigg in the title role, the soldiers looked more like refugees from a light opera than peasant soldiers of the Thirty Years War. They were smart in their blue uniforms and far too efficient in their disposal of Kattrin. What we may gather from these first three lines is more resonant of Laurel and Hardy than it is of efficient soldiery. The contradiction between the officer's opening instruction and the first soldier's response, leading to the officer's resolution, sets the tone for the characterisation and narrative thrust of the scene. We may envisage the soldiers creeping on stage in full (noisy) armour, debating the best way to balance the need for silence against the requirement to knock on the peasants' door.

By threatening to sabre the cattle, the soldiers force the son of the house to show them the pathway to the town. The peasant mother and father are left with Kattrin and seemingly with no option but to pray for the inhabitants of the city. In the *Modellbuch*, Brecht, uses his well-known *Verfremdungseffekt* to offer a way for the actors to avoid a general confusion of stage action in response to the peasants' fears for the people of Halle. His point is that if there is a general excitement on the stage there is a danger that the audience may sympathise with the peasants' lack of action. Instead, he wants the scene to show that their justification for not wanting to endanger their own lives is that their actions are far too insignificant to make any difference to the fate of the city and its inhabitants; the only 'action' left open to them is prayer. His instruction to the actors in rehearsal was to add 'said the man' or 'said the woman' after each line:

THE PEASANT WOMAN: The watchman'll give warning (said the woman).
THE PEASANT MAN: They must have killed the watchman . . . (said the man).[13]

By employing this technique in rehearsal the actors slow down what they do and their delivery of the words with the result that the characters are clearly seen to be trying to justify their inactivity and recourse to prayer.[14]

> *A peasant and his wife ask Kattrin to pray with them for the city of Halle.*

Brecht raises further points of interest regarding the question of acting, in particular portraying old age. We have already gathered from this scene that the actions of the actors on stage need to say much more about the social context of behaviour than the mere personalising of a fictive identity. Under the heading 'To Act Old Age', he offers advice that relates closely to the fact that self-interest leads the peasants to see prayer as their only possible form of intervention in events.[15] Age, in this context, is not a question of stooping and changing a young actor's voice into that of an old peasant woman. Brecht argues that the age of the woman was created through 'the disfiguring and rapes that she was exposed to, the miscarriages and processions behind coffins of little children, hard labour during childhood, physical abuse from parents and husband, psychic abuse from clergy, the necessity of bootlicking and snivelling etc.'.[16] To this woman, begging, whining, or indeed praying are not emotional states, but are well practised actions, as necessary for survival as the haggling over a price is for Mother Courage. The action becomes a *social mode of conduct*. When the peasant woman prays, she will find the most comfortable way to kneel down. For the actor it must also be an objective action.

177

A further example of this relationship between the fictional action of the text and the actor is to be found in Brecht's *The Caucasian Chalk Circle*. Azdak, the village clerk, is feeding an upper-class fugitive who is on the run and starving. Azdak gives the fugitive cheese, which he eats greedily and quickly.

AZDAK: Finish your cheese, but eat it like a poor man, or else they'll catch you. Do I even have to tell you how a poor man behaves? *He makes him sit down, and then gives him back the cheese.* The box is the table. Put your elbows on the table, and now surround the plate with your arms as though you expected the cheese to be snatched from you at any moment.... Now hold the knife as if it were a small sickle; and don't look so greedily at the cheese, look at it mournfully – because it's already disappearing – like all good things.[17]

Once again, the action of the poor man is not 'natural' but has its root in his material condition. The action, or *gestus*, informs us of two factors: it tells us how a poor man may eat and it gives an instruction to the actor not to try to pretend to be poor in some 'natural' way but to observe the material conditions that determine the *gest*.

For the peasants in *Mother Courage*, it is necessary to be exonerated from blame, for blame usually means a beating. Brecht suggests that when the actress playing the old peasant woman about to pray approaches Kattrin, she should shuffle up to her reproachfully: 'She is accusing the stranger (Kattrin) of an unforgivable omission'.[18]

The dumb girl climbs onto the roof of the stable and beats the drum in order to awaken the city of Halle.

This section of the scene is the turning point dramatically. Kattrin kneels to pray behind the peasants, hears the reference to the children of the city perishing in the attack and reacts. The two salient stage directions are: '*To Kattrin, who groans*', and '*Kattrin rises troubled*'. Whereas the peasants have assured themselves that non-intervention in the fate of the people of the city is their only option, Kattrin, prompted by the reference to what might befall the children, takes action. Behind the peasants' backs she creeps to the wagon and takes out a drum (the same one that she brought back to camp on the day she was disfigured), climbs onto the stable roof and starts drumming to warn the citizens of Halle.

The dramatic turning point for this scene's narrative is provided by Kattrin's decision, but it is simultaneously a turning point in the sound pattern of the scene. Whereas, before, silence was the pre-eminent element (even the peasants' prayers were muted) now a pattern of sound is building. Again, the sounds have a specific development and are far from being

178

haphazard. In the same way that the earlier reaction of the peasants to the problem was restrained so that we could see their calculated passivity, so now, the sound patterns are central to the meaning of the scene. Kattrin's drumming is relentless; it needs to be if it is to be effective. The peasants' reaction is less deliberate because they are now only reactive, both to the plight of the city and to Kattrin's gesture. The old man attempts to climb the ladder, but Kattrin deftly pulls it up behind her (which must be difficult when drumming). They look for stones to throw at Kattrin in order to dislodge her. Their prayers left behind, they now seek their own survival by demonstrably aiding the enemy soldiers. Meanwhile, Kattrin has moved from cognition into action with neat efficiency.

Neither the offer to spare her mother in the city, nor the threat to smash the wagon, keep Kattrin from going on drumming.

This section of the scene is crucial to an understanding of its performative language and the way potential meaning is embedded within the script. The officer and the soldiers come running back to the peasants' house threatening Kattrin and ordering her to stop drumming. So, we now have added to the rhythm of Kattrin's drumming, the cacophony of the soldiers' threats. This marks the start of a double-edged play of action that the performers need to observe in its subtle complexity if the scene is going to avoid pathos. The soldiers have a problem. They need silence in order to carry out their surprise attack, but they add to the noise of the drumming in their attempt to silence Kattrin. Their first attempt is to cajole her with the promise that her mother will be saved. The officer promises her that his word, as an officer, is his bond:

THE FIRST SOLDIER: Show us your mother and we'll spare her.
THE LIEUTENANT *pushing him away*: She doesn't trust you, no wonder with your face. *He calls up to Kattrin*: Hey, you! Suppose I give you my word? I'm an officer, my word's my bond!

Kattrin drums harder.[19]

Kattrin's response underlines the irony of the officer's position. The pattern of action is established and the dialogue indicates an accelerating level of ineptitude and confusion on the part of the soldiers. In contrast, Kattrin, the dumb girl, displays an ever-increasing strength, and significantly, we see that she has now found her 'voice'. Through her determination this voice grows in power, while the soldiers descend into near farce. Their next answer to Kattrin's drumming is to make more noise in order to drown out the drumming. They think of smoking her out, but of course that would also attract the attention of the town. In the end they decide to shoot her, which may well be a final answer, but of course, it adds to the general noise.

Analysing the dialogue describing the three attempts to dislodge Kattrin, we are able to discern the language of dramatic action growing from the literary text. Making a louder noise in order to drown the sound of Kattrin's drumming sets the level of the soldiers' incompetence. The first plan is to make a 'peacetime noise' by chopping wood. When this plan fails, the idea of smoking her out is suggested alongside the threat to smash the wagon. Each of these actions briefly interrupts Kattrin's drumming. The stage directions tell us that Kattrin watches and listens to the soldiers' plans; she is keeping an eye on the events beneath her. The interruptions come in, as Brecht points out in the *Modellbuch*, after: 'Heavens, what is she doing?' (Kattrin pulls the ladder up after her); 'I'll cut you all to bits' (Kattrin notes the threat to the peasants, but keeps on drumming); 'Listen you! We have an idea – for your own good' (Kattrin hears, but not even the plight of her mother can stop her drumming now); 'No wonder with your face!' (Kattrin hears and as a consequence drums even harder); 'We must set fire to the farm' (Kattrin has been listening and laughs, and drums even harder); 'We'll smash your wagon' (Kattrin stares at the wagon and pauses. Noises of distress, but she goes on drumming).

The point of the scene is the empowerment of Kattrin through her decision to alert the city. Pathos comes if onstage confusion is allowed to hide the significance of the characters' action and inaction – the dumb girl Kattrin is so distraught at the potential plight of the children that she rushes to the drum and makes a frantic bid to raise the alarm. To interpret what Kattrin does in this manner is to ignore the structure for action laid down in the writing. The constant interruptions allow us to see how *deliberate* Kattrin is. She is not in a wild state of despair. She has made a deliberate decision that highlights the peasants' acquiescence into cowardly self-interest, while exposing the farcical blustering of the soldiers. While drumming, the actress playing Kattrin must look down at the peasants and the soldiers, and take up their challenge. The resulting action should be portrayed as a very clear pattern of cause and effect so that we avoid heroic cliché.

Dumb Kattrin's death.

The point has already been made that these soldiers are not efficient professionals. When the officer orders one of his men to go and fetch a musket to shoot Kattrin, it is a final desperate act, not the considered decision of the regular soldier. The *Modellbuch* informs us that at one of the later productions the soldiers displayed complete apathy, grinning at the frustration of their officer's ineffective dealing with Kattrin.[20] The notes show that the soldiers trot off with 'the well-known kind of tardiness that cannot be proven'. The text gives us clues as to the appropriateness of this approach.

The soldiers arrive with the musket.

THE SECOND SOLDIER: The Colonel's foaming at the mouth. We'll be court-martialled.

THE LIEUTENANT: Set it up! Set it up! *Calling while the musket is set up on forks*: Once and for all: stop that drumming![21]

These few lines are most instructive in the clues they give about the range of possible stage actions. Just noting the exclamation marks and the repetition of the words 'Set it up!' indicates that this is not a situation that the officer has under control. However, the soldiers do eventually fire at and kill Kattrin. The Lieutenant says, 'That's an end to the noise'. These words are followed by the stage direction:

> *But the last beats of the drum are lost in the din of cannon from the town. Mingled with the thunder of cannon, alarm-bells are heard in the distance.*[22]

In his book on the stage history of *Mother Courage*, Peter Thomson points out that the scene 'is a symphony of sound effects, to which the cannon of the awakened city provides the final chords'.[23] At this climactic point, the final mingling of many different sounds needs to be carefully orchestrated. It is a climax which cannot afford to appear haphazard for it is the result of Kattrin's 'orchestration' of the noises leading up to it.

Dramaturgy in the classroom

My example of a project-based approach to *Mother Courage* illustrates one way of approaching the task of identifying the dramatic vocabulary that lies dormant within the written text. It is not a complete strategy in itself but if, by identifying the main elements of a performance vocabulary, we enable students to experiment with the language of stage action, we will have established a working principle.

The short analysis has concentrated largely on a performance reading of the *sound* of the text. Although I have made some reference to the business of the *gestus* of action, particularly in the case of the old woman, there are other elements of the dramatic vocabulary used here that might be highlighted and addressed. This is not the place to pursue these matters at length. However, my suggestion is that understanding the way different theatre practitioners go about translating a literary text into a performance can give students valuable insights not only into what at the beginning of this chapter I tentatively called the 'musicology' of theatre and what we might now have the confidence to call *dramaturgy*, but also into the possibilities which might inform their own creative work.

The Swiss theatre designer, Adolphe Appia, for example, teaches us to think about the mood and emotion of a drama, not in terms of sound, but in terms of light and space. When creating the space for performance, we have a range of possibilities before us that relates directly to what an audience will perceive the play to be about. For certain plays, pictorial realism is as inappropriate as emblematic or symbolic images are for others. Objects on the stage, whether abstract shapes, or concrete emblems, have to relate to each other and form an intrinsic whole with what is being said and done. Older students might like to be reminded of Vsevolod Meyerhold's critically informed theatricality, a reaction to the search for a psychological verisimilitude inherent both in the nineteenth-century naturalism of Constantin Stanislavski and in much of contemporary television drama. Among many others, André Antoine, Jacques Copeau and Jean-Louis Barrault instigate the debate that surrounds the function and purpose of the director, matters of some immediacy to any group of students involved in group devising. While the direct study of some practitioners may be appropriate only for certain age groups, it does not mean that the general principles behind their work cannot inform the work of others. If students in schools can observe and experience the working of texture, shape and pattern in the visual arts there is no reason why they should not also learn to understand how light can shape the mood of what is said by an actor.

My concern so far has been with two languages – the written and the performed. But in order to develop the potential for performance that lies within a script, we also need to be able to contextualise the histories embedded in the material with which we are working. I would argue that a project-based approach should involve teaching that encompasses aims over and above the business of 'putting on plays'. A broader aim of working on *Mother Courage*, for example, might be to help students understand how Brecht's particular way of creating theatre deals with the subject of war. We have seen how the play is structured dramaturgically, and how that structure determines certain conventions of performance. This comprehension may lead students to a wider investigation, involving other plays that promote different attitudes towards war. They may, for example, look at Shakespeare's *The Life of Henry the Fifth* and wonder how its meaning would have been changed if Brecht had adapted it.

The underlying educational principle remains. Theatre exists within the broad context of cultural meaning and does not, as is sometimes proposed, transcend a specific context, or exist by immutable and universal aesthetic laws. It follows that if, rather than setting out a syllabus of items to be learned in drama, we were to identify a number of ideas that were worth interrogating, we may arrive at a more interesting mode of pedagogy. In one sense, I mean that investigating the processes by which culture is made at a specific point in history is, potentially, a more engaging activity than the pursuit of a linear chronology of items to be remembered. A project-based approach offers a theme within which the practice of learning moves between the drama studio and the classroom as required by the subject matter. At the same time, it is important to remember that as much cognitive activity may occur on the floor of the drama studio as practical experience may be gained through textual study in the classroom.

I hope I have made it clear that the kind of open-ended learning that is offered by a project-based approach does not have to be limited by the strict adherence to given forms. By way of example and conclusion, I would draw attention to a project conducted by two colleagues in my own university department.[24] A group of second year undergraduate students was divided in half with the intention that one group would work on *Mother Courage* and the other group would work on Chekhov's *The Cherry Orchard*. The project lasted six weeks and involved movement between studio sessions, seminar discussions and independent research with the aim of articulating their work (through performance) to an invited audience. The twist (and the real learning experience) came when the groups were told that they had to treat the Brecht play as if it had been written by Chekhov, and the Chekhov play as if it had been written by Brecht.

Notes

1 B. Brecht (1940) 'Appendices to the short organum', in J. Willett (ed. and trans.) *Brecht on Theatre*, New York, Hill & Wang, 1964, p.276.
2 D. Edgar (1981) 'The playwright's manifesto', *Théâtre International* 1, Paris: International Theatre Institute, p.9.
3 Ibid.
4 Some words of explanation regarding my use of these terms will be of use at this point. My fellow contributors refer to drama as both a composition in which the story is related by means of dialogue and action and dramatic art. Theatre may refer to a place or to dramatic performances. However, we may also consider drama as an action taken in art and theatre (etymologically) as more to do with watching and seeing performances. I tend to slip between references according to the particular context of the sentence in a way that I hope does not contradict any of the other forms of usage.
5 See David Hornbrook's model for a project-based approach to drama in Chapter 4.
6 For a detailed account of these changes and educational drama's response to them, see D. Hornbrook (1989 [1998]) *Education and Dramatic Art*, 2nd edn, London: Routledge, especially Chapter 3.
7 For more on the centrality of skills to drama, see Chapter 3, and on the relationship between skill and craft, see Chapter 4.
8 This issue is discussed in C.J. McCullough (1992) 'From Brecht to Brechtian: estrangement and appropriation', in G. Holderness (ed.) *The Politics of Theatre and Drama*, London: Macmillan.
9 Brecht's *Modellbuch* for *Mother Courage and Her Children* contains an extensive record of the production at the Deutsches Theater in Berlin in 1949, directed by Brecht and Erich Engel. Excerpts from the *Modellbuch* are available in J. Willett (ed. and trans.) (1964) *Brecht on Theatre*, New York: Hill & Wang and in T. Cole and H.K. Chinoy (1964) (eds.) *Directors on Directing*, London: Peter Owen.

10 B. Brecht (1962) *Mother Courage and her Children*, trans. E. Bentley, London: Methuen. Other translations consulted: B. Brecht (1984) literal translation by Sue Davies (adaptation Hanif Kureishi) *Mother Courage and Her Children*, London: Methuen/Royal Shakespeare Company; B. Brecht (1949) *Mutter Courage Und Ihre Kinder*, eds. H.F. Brooks and C.E. Frankel, London: Heinemann.
11 T. Cole and H.K. Chinoy (eds) (1964) *Directors on Directing*, London: Peter Owen, p.333.
12 B. Brecht (1962).
13 Ibid.
14 In T. Cole and H.K. Chinoy (eds) (1964) *Directors on Directing*, London: Peter Owen, p.336.
15 Ibid., pp.337–40.
16 Ibid., p.338.
17 B. Brecht (1960) *The Caucasian Chalk Circle*, trans. J. Stern and T. Stern with W.H. Auden, London: Methuen, sc.5.
18 T. Cole and H.K. Chinoy (1964) (eds) *Directors on Directing*, London: Peter Owen, p.338.
19 B. Brecht (1962).
20 T. Cole and H.K. Chinoy (1964) (eds) *Directors on Directing*, London: Peter Owen, p.340. The production in question was at the Deutsches Theater, Berlin, 11 September, 1951.
21 B. Brecht (1962).
22 Ibid.
23 P.W. Thomson (1997) *Brecht: Mother Courage and Her Children*, Cambridge, Cambridge University Press.
24 Peter Thomson and Martin Harvey.

BIBLIOGRAPHY

Abbs, P. (1989) *The Symbolic Order*, London: Falmer Press.
—— (1994) *The Educational Imperative*, London: Falmer Press.
Arts Council of Great Britain (ACGB) (1992) *Drama in Schools: Arts Council Guidance on Drama Education*, London: ACGB.
Aston, E. (1995) *An Introduction to Feminism and Theatre*, London and New York: Routledge.
Aston, E. and Savona, G. (1991) *Theatre as a Sign System*, London: Routledge.
Auslander, P. (1995) '"Just be yourself"; logocentrism and difference in performance theory', in P.B. Zarrilli (1995) *Acting (Re)Considered*, London: Routledge, pp.59–67.
Bablet, D. (1972) 'Pour une méthod d'analyse du lieu théâtral', *Travail Théâtral* 6, pp. 108–19.
—— (1973) 'L'éclairage et le son dans l'espace théâtral', *Travail Théâtral* 13, pp.47–56.
—— (1975) *Les Révolutions Scéniques au xxè Siècle*, Paris: Société Internationale d'art xxè Siècle.
Bailin, S. (1994) *Achieving Extraordinary Ends: An Essay on Creativity*, Norwood, NJ: Ablex.
Banerjee, U. (1992) *Indian Performing Arts*, London: Sangam Books.
Banes, S. (1994) *Writing Dance in the Age of Postmodernism*, Hanover and London: University Press of New England.
Barba, E. and Savarese, N. (1991) *A Dictionary of Theatre Anthropology: The Secret Art of the Performer*, London and New York, Routledge.
Barrie J.M. (1928) *The Plays of J.M. Barrie*, London: Hodder and Stoughton.
Barthes, R. (1973) *Mythologies*, trans. A. Lavers, London and New York: Granada.
Beckett, S. (1961) *Happy Days*, London: Faber & Faber.
Beer, J. (ed.) (1991) *Samuel Taylor Coleridge: Poems*, London: J.M. Dent.
Bennett, S. (1990) *Theatre Audiences: A Theory of Production and Reception*, London: Routledge.
Berkoff, S. (1994) *One Man's Show*, London: London Weekend Television.
Bharucha, R. (1993) *Theatre and the World*, London: Routledge.
Boal, A. (1979) *Theatre of the Oppressed*, trans. C. McBride and M. McBride, London: Pluto Press.
—— (1992) *Games for Actors and Non-Actors*, London: Routledge.

Bogdanov, M. (1981) *Hiawatha*, London: Heinemann.

Bolter, D. (1984) *Turing's Man: Western Culture in the Computer Age*, Chapel Hill, NC: University of North Carolina Press.

Bolton, G. (1985) 'Changes in thinking about drama in education', *Theory into Practice* 24(3), p.155.

—— (1986) 'Weaving theories is not enough', *New Theatre Quarterly* 2(8), p.370.

Boorstin, D. (1961) *The Image: A Guide to Pseudo-Events in America*, New York: Atheneum.

Bourdieu, P. (1992) *Les Règles de l'Art*, Paris: Seuil; English language edition trans. S. Emanuel (1996) *The Rules of Art*, Cambridge: Polity Press.

—— (1993) *The Field of Cultural Production*, ed. R. Johnson, Cambridge: Polity Press.

Bourdieu, P., Boltanski, L., Castel, R. and Chamboredon, J.C. (1990) *Photography: A Middle-Brow Art*, trans. S. Whiteside, Cambridge: Polity Press.

Brandon, J. (ed.) (1993) *The Cambridge Guide to Asian Theatre*, Cambridge: Cambridge University Press.

Brecht, B. (1940) 'Appendices to the short organum', in J. Willett (ed. and trans.) *Brecht on Theatre*, New York: Hill & Wang, 1964, p.276.

—— (1948) 'A short organum for the theatre', in J. Willett (ed. and trans.) *Brecht on Theatre*, New York: Hill & Wang, 1964, p.192.

—— (1949) *Mutter Courage Und Ihre Kinder*, ed. H.F. Brooks and C.E. Frankel, London: Heinemann; trans. E. Bentley (1962) *Mother Courage and her Children*, London: Methuen; literal trans. S. Davies, adaptation H. Kureishi (1984) *Mother Courage and Her Children*, London: Methuen/Royal Shakespeare Company.

—— (1960) *The Caucasian Chalk Circle*, trans. J. Stern and T. Stern with W.H. Auden, London: Methuen.

Brindley, S. (ed.) (1994) *Teaching English*, London: Routledge.

Britton, J. (1994) 'Vygotsky's contribution to pedagogic theory', in S. Brindley (ed.) (1994) *Teaching English*, London: Routledge.

Bruner, J. (1996) *The Culture of Education*, Cambridge, MA: Harvard University Press.

Burns, E. (1972) *Theatricality: A Study of Convention in the Theatre and in Social Life*, New York: Harper & Row.

Butterfield, H. (1931) *The Whig Interpretation of History*, London: Bell.

Calouste Gulbenkian Foundation (1982) *The Arts in Schools*, London: Calouste Gulbenkian.

Carlson, M. (1989) 'Theatre audiences and the reading of performance', in T. Postlewait and B. McConachie (eds) *Interpreting the Theatrical Past: Essays in the Historiography of Performance*, Iowa City, IA: University of Iowa Press, p.82.

—— (1990) 'Theatre audiences and the reading of performance', *Theatre Semiotics: Signs of Life*, Bloomington and Indianapolis, IN: Indiana University Press.

—— (1994) 'Invisible presences – performance intertextuality', *Theatre Research International* 19 (2), pp.111–17.

Carpenter, E. and McLuhan, M. (eds) (1960) *Explorations in Communication*, Boston, MA: Beacon Press.

Carter, G. (1993) 'Gary Carter talks to Lloyd Newson', *The Dance Theatre Journal* 10(4), p.9.

Chekhov, A. (1951) *The Cherry Orchard*, trans. E. Fen, Harmondsworth: Penguin Books.

Churchill, C. (1982) *Top Girls*, London: Methuen.

—— (1985) 'Light Shining in Buckinghamshire', *Plays: One*, London: Methuen.

Clifford, J. (ed.) (1986) *Writing Culture*, Berkeley, CA: University of California Press.

Coghlan, L. (1994) 'A feeling in my bones', in A. Kempe (1994b) *Dramascripts Extra*, Walton-on-Thames: Thomas Nelson.

Cole, T. and Chinoy, H.K. (1964) (eds) *Directors on Directing*, London: Peter Owen.

Coleridge, S.T. (1817) *Biographia Literaria*, ed. G. Watson, London: J.M. Dent, 1975.

Collingwood, R.G. (1938) *The Principles of Art*, Oxford: Oxford University Press.

Coult, T. and Kershaw, B. (eds) (1983) *Engineers of the Imagination: The Welfare State Handbook*, London: Methuen.

Counsell, C. (1996) *Signs of Performance: An Introduction to Twentieth-century Theatre*, London and New York: Routledge.

Courtney, R. (1980) *The Dramatic Curriculum*, New York: Drama Book Specialists.

Croft, S. (1993) 'Collaboration and exploration in women's theatre', in T.R. Griffiths and M. Llewellyn-Jones (eds) *British and Irish Women Dramatists since 1958*, Milton Keynes: The Open University Press.

Crompton, J. (1976) 'CSE examinations in drama', *Young Drama* 4(2), pp.57–66.

Cross, D. (1990) 'Leicestershire GCSE Drama: a syllabus with a clear direction', in *2D: Journal of Drama and Dance* 9(2), pp.18–24.

Deldime, R. and Pigeon, J. (1988) *La Mémoire du Jeune Spectateur*, Brussels and Paris: De Boeck.

Department for Education (1995) 'Order for Art', 'Order for Music', 'Order for English', *The National Curriculum*, London: HMSO.

Department of Education and Science (1990) *The Teaching and Learning of Drama*, London: HMSO.

Deshpande, V. (1987) *Indian Musical Traditions*, London: Sangam Books.

Dobson, W. (1996) 'Shooting at straw targets or how to construct a postmodern paradigm in drama-in-education', *The NADIE Journal* 20(2), pp.29–39.

Doyle, C. (1993) *Raising Curtains on Education: Drama as a Site for Critical Pedagogy*, Westport, CT: Bergin & Garvey.

Duvignaud, J. (1976) 'Le Theatre', in J. Duvignaud and A. Veinstein (1976) *Le Theatre*, Paris: Encyclopoche Larousse.

Duvignaud, J. and Veinstein, A. (1976) *Le Theatre*, Paris: Encyclopoche Larousse.

Dynak, D. (1994) 'Profiles of Preservice Theatre Teacher Education Programs at Three American Universities', unpublished PhD thesis, Lansing, MI: Michigan State University.

Eagleton, T. (1976) *Marxism and Literary Criticism*, Berkeley, CA: University of California Press.

—— (1983) *Literary Theory*, Oxford: Basil Blackwell.

Edgar, D. (1981) 'The playwright's manifesto', *Théâtre International* 1, Paris: International Theatre Institute, p.9.

Edmiston, B. (1991) 'Planning for flexibility: the phases of a drama structure', in *The Drama/Theatre Teacher* 4(1).

Eisenstein, E. (1979) *The Printing Press as an Agent of Change: Communications and Cultural Transformations in Early-Modern Europe*, 2 vols, Cambridge: Cambridge University Press.

Ellul, J. (1964) *The Technological Society*, trans. J. Wilkinson, New York: Vintage Press.

—— (1985) *The Humiliation of the Word*, Grand Rapids, MI: William B. Eerdmans.

Esslin, M. (1961) *Reflections: Essays on the Modern Theatre*, Garden City, NY: Doubleday.

—— (1962) *Meditations: Essays on Brecht, Beckett, and the Media*, London: Eyre Methuen.

—— (1976) *The Anatomy of Drama*, New York: Hill & Wang.

—— (1979) 'Aristotle and the advertisers: the television commercial considered as a form of drama', in H. Newcomb (ed.) *Television: The Critical View*, 4th edn, New York, Oxford University Press, pp.306–7.

—— (1982) *The Age of Television*, San Francisco, CA: W.H. Freeman.

—— (1987) *The Field of Drama: How the Signs of Drama Create Meanings on Stage and Screen*, London and New York: Methuen.

Finlay-Johnson, H. (1911) *The Dramatic Method of Teaching*, London: James Nisbet.

Fischer-Lichte, E. (1992) *The Semiotics of Theatre*, trans. J. Gaines and D.L. Jones, Bloomington and Indianapolis, IN: Indiana University Press.

Fish, S. (1980) *Is There a Text in This Class?*, Cambridge, MA: Harvard University Press.

Fiske, J. (1987) *Television Culture*, London and New York: Routledge.

Fleming, M. (1997) *The Art of Drama Teaching*, London: David Fulton.

Francis, J. (1990) *Attitudes among Britain's Black Community towards Attendance at Arts, Cultural and Entertainment Events*, London: Arts Council of Great Britain, Networking Public Relations.

Gadamer, H.G. (1975) *Truth and Method*, trans. W. Glyn-Doepel, London: Sheed & Ward.

Gargi, B. (1991) *Folk Theatre of India*, Calcutta: Rupa.

Geertz, C. (1973) *The Interpretation of Cultures*, New York: Basic Books.

—— (1983) *Local Knowledge: Further Essays in Interpretive Anthropology*, New York: Basic Books.

Giddens, A. (1996) 'There is radical centre ground', *The New Statesman* (29 November).

Gillham, G. (1991) 'Review: "Education and Dramatic Art" by David Hornbrook', *SCYPT Journal* 21, p.46.

Gilroy, P. (1995a) *Small Acts: Art of Darkness*, London: Trentham Books.

—— (1995b) '"To be real": the dissident forms of black expressive culture', *Let's Get It On*, London: Institute of Contemporary Arts.

Gombrich, E. (1984) *Tributes*, in P. Abbs, *The Symbolic Order*, London: Falmer Press, 1989, p.89.

Goodman, L. (1996) *Feminist Stages*, Amsterdam: Harwood Academic Publishers.

Goodwyn, A. (ed.) (1998) *Teaching Literature and Media Texts*, London: Cassell.

Goody, J. (1987) *The Interface Between the Oral and the Written*, Cambridge: Cambridge University Press.

Gosh, M. (trans. and ed.) (1967) *The Nāṭyaśhāstra*, Calcutta: Manisha Granthalaya.

Gourdon, A.-M. (1982) *Theatre, Public Perception*, Paris: CNRS.

Granville-Barker, H. (1987) *The Voysey Inheritance*, ed. D. Kennedy, Cambridge: Cambridge University Press.

Griffiths, T. R. and Llewellyn-Jones, M. (eds) (1993) *British and Irish Women Dramatists since 1958*, Milton Keynes: The Open University Press.

Guy, J.-M. and Mironer, L. (1988) *Les Publics du Theatre*, Paris: La Documentation Française.

Hall, E. (1966) *The Silent Language*, Greenwich, CT: Fawcett Publications.

Halliday, M.A.K. (1985) *Spoken and Written Language*, Geelong: Deakin University Press.

Hargreaves, D. (1982) *The Challenge for the Comprehensive School*, London: Routledge & Kegan Paul.

Heathcote, D. (1980) 'From the particular to the universal', in K. Robinson (ed.) *Exploring Theatre and Education*, London: Heinemann.

Helbo, A., Johansen, D., Pavis, P. and Ubersfeld, A. (1991) *Approaching Theatre*, Bloomington and Indianapolis, IN: Indiana University Press; first published as 'La notation: questionnaires de lecture', in *Theatre Modes D'approche*, Brussels: Labor, 1987.

Holderness, G. (ed.) (1992) *The Politics of Theatre and Drama*, London: Macmillan.

Holman, D. (1989) *Whale*, London: Methuen.

Hornbrook, D. (1989[1998]) *Education and Dramatic Art*, 2nd edn, London: Routledge.

—— (1991) *Education in Drama: Casting the Dramatic Curriculum*, London: Falmer Press.

—— (1992) 'Can we do ours, miss? Towards a dramatic curriculum', *The Drama/Theatre Teacher* 4(2), p.18.

Hughes, L. (ed.) (1970) *Poems from Black Africa*, Bloomington and Indianapolis, IN: Indianapolis University Press.

Ingarden, R. (1973) *The Literary Work of Art*, 3rd edn, trans. G.G. Grabowicz, Evanston, IL: Northwestern University Press.

Iser, W. (1974) *The Implied Reader: Patterns of Communication in Prose Fiction from Bunyan to Beckett*, Baltimore, MD: Johns Hopkins University Press.

Issacharoff, M. and Jones, R. (eds) (1988) *Performing Texts*, Philadelphia, PA: University of Pennsylvania Press.

Jackson, T. (ed.) (1993) *Learning Through Theatre*, London: Routledge.

Jain, N. (1992) *Indian Theatre: Tradition, Continuity and Change*, Delhi: Vikash Publishing House.

Jaynes, J. (1976) *The Origin of Consciousness in the Breakdown of the Bicameral Mind*, Boston, MA: Houghton Mifflin.

Jellicoe, A. (1987) *Community Plays – How to put them on*, London: Methuen.

Johnsen, J. (1990) 'Study of Television in a Ninth Grade Classroom: Inhibiting a Critical Orientation', unpublished PhD thesis, Columbus, OH: Ohio State University.

Johnson, L. and O'Neill, C. (eds) (1984) *Dorothy Heathcote: Collected Writings on Education and Drama*, London: Hutchinson.

Jones, T. (1992) *In Search of Dragon's Mountain*, Walton-on-Thames: Thomas Nelson.

Kempe, A. (1989) 'Towards a common syllabus', *2D Journal of Drama and Dance* 9(1).

—— (1994a) 'Dramatic literature in the classroom: time for an inspector to call?', *Drama* 3(1), pp.9–15.

—— (ed.) (1994b) *Dramascripts Extra*, Walton-on-Thames: Thomas Nelson.

—— (1996a) *Drama Education and Special Needs: A Handbook for Teachers in Mainstream and Special Schools*, Cheltenham: Stanley Thornes.

—— (1996b) 'The whole text and nothing but the text', *Australian Drama Education Magazine* 2, Brisbane: National Association of Drama in Education, pp.8–13.

—— (1998) 'Reading plays', in A. Goodwyn (ed.) *Teaching Literature and Media Texts*, London: Cassell.

Kempe, A. and Warner, L. (1997) *Starting with Scripts*, Cheltenham: Stanley Thornes.

Kershaw, B. (1992) *The Politics of Performance: Radical Theatre as Cultural Intervention*, London: Routledge.

Kitson, N. and I. Spiby (1997) *Drama 7–11: Developing Primary Teaching Skills*, London: Routledge.

Kowzan, T. (1975) *Littérature et Spectacle*, Warszawa: PWN, Paris: Mouton.

Kress, G. (1982) *Learning to Write*, London: Routledge & Kegan Paul.

Kris, E. (1952) *Psychoanalytic Explorations*, New York: International Universities Press.

Krishna Rao, U. (1990) *A Dictionary of Bharata Natyam*, London: Sangam Books.

Leigh Foster, S. (ed.) (1996) *Corporealities: Dancing Knowledge, Culture and Power*, London: Routledge.

Lesschave, J. (1985) *The Dancer and the Dance: Merce Cunningham in Conversation with Jacqueline Lesschave*, London: Marion Boyars Publishers.

Levy, D. (ed.) (1992) 'The B File', *Walks on Water*, London: Methuen.

Levy, J. (1987) *A Theatre of the Imagination: Reflections on Children and Theatre*, Charlottesville, VA: New Plays Incorporated.

Lorca, Gabriel Garcia (1941) *Yerma: A Tragic Poem in Three Acts and Six Scenes*, New York: Scribner's.

Luckham, C. (1992) *Moll Flanders*, Walton-on-Thames: Thomas Nelson.

Luria, A. (1976) *Cognitive Development: Its Cultural and Social Foundations*, ed. M. Cole, trans. M. Lopez-Morillas and L. Solotaroff, Cambridge, MA: Harvard University Press.

McCullough, C.J. (1992) 'From Brecht to Brechtian: estrangement and appropriation', in G. Holderness (ed.) *The Politics of Theatre and Drama*, London: Macmillan.

—— (1996) *Theatre in Europe*, Exeter: Intellect.

Mander, J. (1978) *Four Arguments for the Elimination of Television*, New York: William & Morrow.

Manley-Casimir, M.E. and Luke, C. (eds) (1987) *Children and Television: A Challenge for Education*, New York: Praeger.

Marinis, M. de (1995) *The Semiotics of Performance*, trans. A. O'Healy, Bloomington and Indianapolis, IN: Indiana University Press.

Martin, R. (1996) 'Overreading the promised land: towards a narrative of context in dance', in S. Foster (ed.) *Corporealities: Dancing Knowledge, Culture and Power* , London: Routledge, pp.177–98.

Maybin, J. (1994) 'Teaching writing: process or genre?', in S. Brindley (ed.) (1994) *Teaching English*, London: Routledge.

Menon, K. (1991) *A Dictionary of Kaṭhakaḷi*, London: Sangam Books.

Merleau-Ponty, M. (1973) *The Prose of the World*, Evanston, IL: Northwestern University Press.

—— (1974) *Phenomenology, Language and Sociology*, trans. J. O'Neill, London: Heinemann.

Meyrowitz, J. (1985) *No Sense of Place: The Impact of Electronic Media on Social Behavior*, New York: Oxford University Press.

Michaels, W. (1993) 'Plots have I laid: Shakespeare in the classroom', *NADIE Journal* 17(2), pp.23–9.

Midland Examining Group (1986) *GCSE Leicestershire Mode III Drama*, Cambridge: Midland Examining Group.

Miller, J. (1986) *Subsequent Performances*, London: Faber & Faber.

Morris, G. (ed.) (1996) *Moving Worlds*, London: Routledge.

Mumford, L. (1952) *Art and Technics*, New York: Columbia University Press.

National Curriculum Council Arts in Schools Project (1989) *The Arts 5–16: Practice and Innovation*, London: Oliver & Boyd.

Neelands, J. (1984) *Making Sense of Drama*, London: Heinemann.

—— (1994) 'Writing in imagined contexts', in S. Brindley (ed.) (1994) *Teaching English*, London: Routledge.

Newcomb, H. (ed.) (1979) *Television: The Critical View*, 4th edn, New York: Oxford University Press.

Nichols, P. (1967) *A Day in the Death of Joe Egg*, London: Faber & Faber.

Nicholson, H. (1996a) 'Voices on stage', in M. Styles, E. Bearne, V. Watson (eds) *Voices Off: Texts, Contexts and Readers*, London: Cassell, pp.248–63.

—— (1996b) 'Drama, identity and gender', *Drama and Theatre in Education: Contemporary Research*, ed. J. Somers, New York: Captus Press, pp.75–85.

O'Brien, J. (1996) *Secondary School Pupils and the Arts: Report of a MORI Research Study*, London: Arts Council of Great Britain.

Oddey, A. (1994) *Devising Theatre*, London: Routledge.

Office for Standards in Education (OFSTED) (1994) *Improving Schools*, London: HMSO.

—— (1996) *The Annual Report of her Majesty's Chief Inspector of Schools: Standards and Quality in Education, 1994/95*, London: HMSO.

O'Hear, P. and White, J. (eds) (1993) *Assessing the National Curriculum*, London: Paul Chapman.

Ong, W. (1983) *Orality and Literacy: The Technologizing of the Word*, London: Routledge.

O'Toole, J. (1992) *The Process of Drama*, London: Routledge.

Pateman, T. (1991) *Key Concepts: A Guide to Aesthetics, Criticism and the Arts in Education*, London: Falmer Press.

Pavis, P. (1985) 'Production et réception au théâtre: la concrétisation du texte dramatique et spectaculaire', *Voix et Images de la Scène*, Lille: Presses Universitaires de Lille, p.288.

—— (1992) *Theatre at the Crossroads of Culture*, trans. J. Daugherty, London and New York: Routledge.

—— (1996) *L'Analyse des Spectacles*, Paris: Nathan.

Perkins, D. (1981) *The Mind's Best Work*, Cambridge, MA: Harvard University Press.

Perkinson, H. (1995) *How Things Got Better: Speech, Writing, Printing, and Cultural Change*, Westport, CT: Bergin & Garvey.

Peters, R. S. (ed.) (1967) *The Concept of Education*, London: Routledge & Kegan Paul.

Pirandello, L. (1954) *Six Characters in Search of an Author*, trans. F. May, London: Heinemann.

Postlewait, T. and McConachie, B. (eds) (1989) *Interpreting the Theatrical Past: Essays in the Historiography of Performance*, Iowa City, IA: University of Iowa Press.

Postman, N. (1985) *Amusing Ourselves to Death: Public Discourse in the Age of Show Business*, New York: Penguin Books.

—— (1992) *Technoploy: The Surrender of Culture to Technology*, New York: Alfred A. Knopf.

Priestley, J. B. (1947) *An Inspector Calls*, London: Heinemann.

Rapi, N. (1996) 'Interview', in L. Goodman (1996) *Feminist Stages*, Amsterdam: Harwood Academic Publishers.

Read, H. (1943) *Education through Art*, London: Faber & Faber.

Readman, D. (1993) 'Drama out of a crisis', in *The Times Educational Supplement* (23 April).

Richmond, F., Swann, D. and Zarrilli, P. (eds) (1990) *Indian Theatre: Traditions and Performance*, Honolulu, HI: University of Hawaii Press.

Riesman, D. (1960) 'The oral and written traditions', in E. Carpenter and M. McLuhan (eds) *Explorations in Communication*, Boston, MA: Beacon Press, p.10.

Robinson, K. (ed.) (1980) *Exploring Theatre and Education*, London: Heinemann.

—— (1993) 'The arts: which way now?', in P. O'Hear and J. White (eds) *Assessing the National Curriculum*, London: Paul Chapman.

—— (1995) *Education inland Culture*, Strasbourg: Council of Europe Cultural Policy and Action Division.

Rosenblatt, L. (1983) *Literature as Exploration*, 4th edn, New York: Modern Language Association.

Rosenthal, R. (1985) 'Rachel Rosenthal creating her selves', in P.B. Zarrilli (ed.) (1995) *Acting (Re)Considered*, London: Routledge, p.304.

Ross, M. and Kamba, M. (1997) *State of the Arts in Five English Secondary Schools*, Exeter: University of Exeter.

Roubine, J.-J. (1980) *Théâtre et Mise en Scène 1880-1980*, Paris: Presses Universitaires de France.

Salvio, P. (1989) 'Transforming Rituals of Commemoration: Theatre and Textual Interpretation in the Secondary Classroom', unpublished PhD thesis, New York: University of Rochester.

Schechner, R. (1997) *Essays on Performance Theory 1970–1976*, New York: Drama Book Specialists.

Scheffler, I. (1967) 'Philosophical models of teaching', in R.S. Peters (ed.) *The Concept of Education*, London: Routledge & Kegan Paul.

School Curriculum and Assessment Authority (1996) *Monitoring the School Curriculum: Reporting to Schools*, Hayes: SCAA Publications.

—— (1997) *Expectations in Art at Key Stages 1 and 2*, Hayes: SCAA Publications.

Schools Council English Committee (1974) *Examinations in Drama*, London: Schools Council.

Selden, R. (1985) *A Reader's Guide to Contemporary Literary Theory*, Brighton: Harvester Press.

Shevtsova, M. (1989) 'The sociology of the theatre', *New Theatre Quarterly* 19, pp.282–300.

Slade, P. (1954) *Child Drama*, London: University of London Press.

—— (1958) *An Introduction to Child Drama*, London: Hodder & Stoughton.

Soper, K. (1993) 'Postmodernism, subjectivity and value', in J. Squires (ed.) *Principled Positions*, London: Lawrence & Wishart, p.24.

Squires, J. (ed.) (1993) *Principled Positions*, London: Lawrence & Wishart.

States, B. (1985) *Great Reckonings in Little Rooms: On the Phenomenology of Theater*, Berkeley, CA: University of California Press.

Storey, D. (1970) *Home*, London: Samuel French.

Stravinsky, I. (1947) *Poetics of Music*, New York: Vintage Books.

Styan, J.L. (1984) *The State of Drama Study*, Sydney: Sydney University Press.

—— (1988) 'The mystery of the play experience: Quince's questions', in M. Issacharoff and R. Jones (eds) *Performing Texts*, Philadelphia, PA: University of Pennsylvania Press, pp.9–26.

Styles, M., Bearne, E. and Watson, V. (eds) (1996) *Voices Off: Texts, Contexts and Readers*, London: Cassell.

Taylor, C. (1995) *Philosophical Arguments*, Cambridge, MA: Harvard University Press.

Taylor, L. (1993) 'Early stages: women dramatists 1958–68', in T.R. Griffiths and M. Llewellyn-Jones (eds) *British and Irish Women Dramatists since 1958*, Milton Keynes: The Open University Press.

Taylor, P. (ed.) (1996) 'Introduction: rebellion, reflective turning in arts education research', *Researching Drama and Arts Education*, London: Falmer Press.

Taylor, Robert (1988) *The Theatre Underground: A Classical Revolutionary Organization*, unpublished PhD thesis, Lawrence, KS: University of Kansas.

Taylor, Rod (1992) *The Visual Arts in Education: Completing the Circle*, London: Falmer Press.

Taylor, V. (1992) 'The tutor as audience: approaches to examining student performance', *New Theatre Quarterly* 30, pp.140–5.

Thiong'o, N. (1981) *Decolonising the Mind*, London: Heinemann Educational.

—— (1993) *Moving the Centre*, London: Heinemann Educational.

Thomson, P.W. (1997) *Brecht: Mother Courage and Her Children*, Cambridge: Cambridge University Press.

Ubersfeld, A. (1981) *L'école du Spectateur*, Paris: Éditions Sociales.

Urian, D. (1984) *The Meaning of Costume*, Oakland, CA: Personabooks.

—— (ed.) (1995) *Drama in Education: Writing, Acting and Spectatorship*, Tel Aviv: Mofet Institute, Ministry of Education, Culture and Sport.

Verma, J. (1996) 'Towards a black aesthetic', in *Performing Arts International* 1, p.10.

Watkins, B. (1981) *Drama and Education*, London: Batsford.

Way, B. (1967) *Development through Drama*, London: Longman.

Weisberg, R. (1986) *Creativity: Genius and Other Myths*, New York: W.H. Freeman.

Weizenbaum, J. (1976) *Computer Power and Human Reason: From Judgment to Calculation*, San Francisco, CA: W.H. Freeman.

Willett, J. (ed. and trans.) (1964) *Brecht on Theatre*, New York: Hill & Wang.

Williams, E. (1982) *Night Must Fall*, London: Heinemann.

Williams, R. (1974) *Television: Technology and Cultural Form*, London: Fontana.

—— (1975) *Drama in a Dramatised Society*, Cambridge: Cambridge University Press.

—— (1977) *Marxism and Literature*, Oxford: Oxford University Press.

Winston, J. (1996) 'Emotion, reason and moral engagement in drama', *Research in Drama Education* 1(2), p.197.

Witkin, R. (1974) *The Intelligence of Feeling*, London: Heinemann.

Wittgenstein, L. (1963) *Philosophical Investigations*, trans. G.E.M. Anscombe, Oxford: Basil Blackwell.

Wollheim, R. (1987) *Painting as an Art*, Princeton, NJ: Princeton University Press.

Wright, L. and Garcia, L. (1992) 'Dramatic literacy: the place of theatre education in schools', *Design for Arts in Education* 93(4), pp.25–9.

Zarrilli, P. (ed.) (1995) 'Introduction: theories and meditations on acting', *Acting (Re)Considered*, London: Routledge.

INDEX

195

Printed in the United Kingdom
by Lightning Source UK Ltd.
105940UKS00001B/218